Frontier Passages

Frontier Passages

Ethnopolitics and the Rise of

Chinese Communism, 1921–1945

XIAOYUAN LIU

WOODROW WILSON CENTER PRESS
Washington, D.C.

STANFORD UNIVERSITY PRESS
Stanford, California

EDITORIAL OFFICES

Woodrow Wilson Center Press
One Woodrow Wilson Plaza
1300 Pennsylvania Avenue, N.W.
Washington, DC 20004-3027
Telephone: 202-691-4010
www.wilsoncenter.org

Order from:

Stanford University Press
Chicago Distribution Center
11030 South Langley Avenue
Chicago, IL 60628
Telephone: 1-800-621-2736

2 4 6 8 9 7 5 3 1

Library of Congress Cataloging-in-Publication Data

Liu, Xiaoyuan, 1952–
Frontier passages : ethnopolitics and the rise of Chinese communism,
1921–1945 / Xiaoyuan Liu.—1st ed.
p. cm.
Includes bibliographical references and index.
ISBN 0-8047-4960-4 (hardcover : alk. paper)
1. Minorities—Government policy—China—History—20th century. 2.
Zhongguo gong chan dang—History—20th century. 3. Nationalism and
communism—China—History—20th century. 4. China—Politics and
government—1912–1949. I. Title: Ethnopolitics and the rise of Chinese
communism, 1921–1945. II. Title.
JQ1506.M5L58 2003
323.151′09′041—dc22   2003016314

ABOUT THE CENTER

The Center is the living memorial of the United States of America to the nation's twenty-eighth president, Woodrow Wilson. Congress established the Woodrow Wilson Center in 1968 as an international institute for advanced study, "symbolizing and strengthening the fruitful relationship between the world of learning and the world of public affairs." The Center opened in 1970 under its own board of trustees.

In all its activities the Woodrow Wilson Center is a nonprofit, nonpartisan organization, supported financially by annual appropriations from the Congress, and by the contributions of foundations, corporations, and individuals. Conclusions or opinions expressed in Center publications and programs are those of the authors and speakers and do not necessarily reflect the views of the Center staff, fellows, trustees, advisory groups, or any individuals or organizations that provide financial support to the Center.

Contents

Maps

Acronyms and Abbreviations

CCP   Chinese Communist Party

DFZZ   *Zhongguo Gongnong Hongjun Disi Fangmianjun Zhanshi Ziliao Xuanbian, Changzheng Shiqi* (Selected materials on the combat history of the fourth front army of the Chinese workers' and peasants' red army, the long march period)

GLZGWZ   *Gongchanguoji, Liangong (Bu) yu Zhongguo Geming Wenxian Ziliao Xuanji* (Selected documentary materials on the Comintern, Soviet Communist Party and the Chinese revolution)

IMPRP   Inner Mongolian People's Revolutionary Party

KMT   Kuomintang (National People's Party)

MPR   Mongolian People's Republic

MWWH   *Minzu Wenti Wenxian Huibian* (Collection of documents on the national question)

PRC   People's Republic of China

ZSGG   *Zhong Su Guojia Guanxi Shi Ziliao Huibian* (Collected documents on the history of the Chinese–Soviet state relationship)

XMGW   *Xinshiqi Minzu Gongzuo Wenxian Xuanbian* (Selected documents on the nationality work during the new era)

ZZWX   *Zhonggong Zhongyang Wenjian Xuanji* (Selected documents of the CCP Central Committee)

Preface

This book is as much a personal quest for understanding as a scholarly endeavor. More than three decades ago, when Mao Zedong's "Cultural Revolution" in China turned countless middle-school youths into "volunteers" to go to the countryside, I got an "opportunity" to go to Inner Mongolia. Some elder people offered their kind advice to me: "Don't go! That is a place where yellow sand buries white bones!" Some others said to me: "Oh, Inner Mongolia is such a nice place! You can see thriving herds of sheep and cattle everywhere and listen to camel bells singing all the time." Of course, at the time I did not have much of a choice. I went to Inner Mongolia and found out that neither of the descriptions of the place was accurate. But the stark contrast between these images has stuck in my memory ever since.

Many years later, I realized that those people who counseled me, just like most of the people living in China proper, did not have any direct experience of China's borderlands. The images of Inner Mongolia that they passed on to me were no more than two typical stereotypes about China's ethnic frontiers created and repeated in ancient Chinese poems.

It is remarkable that these opposing stereotypes are similar in only depicting the *place* and ignoring the *people,* and their devotees over the centuries have remained blind to ethnicity. In my own case, I have no reason to believe that somehow I would have become interested in China's borderlands and ethnic affairs without my sojourn in Inner Mongolia during the "Cultural Revolution." And what a tumultuous time it was for anyone to become ethnicity conscious! I have to admit from the outset that writing this book was not a completely objective process.

One of the main arguments presented here—that the Chinese Communist Party (CCP) gained a practical ethnopolitical strategy only after its leading body migrated from southern China to a border region in the remote northwest—is partially conceived from my own experience. In those years, my co–"intellectual youths" and I had to learn how to live in a nomadic Mongolian community after we were temporarily separated from the Han Chinese ethnographic zone. At first glance, my approach may seem to have violated the canon about the objectivity of the discipline of history. Yet because history cannot be relived, a historian's parallel experience to a historical event or process may help generate some relevant insight.

As a scholarly endeavor, this is a volume leading to a broader inquiry into the historical position of ethnicity in the formation of the modern Chinese national state. I began to research the question several years ago, because my earlier scholarly activities in the field of diplomatic history had led me to believe that compartmentalized approaches to studying "foreign" and "domestic" affairs cannot reveal the complexity of modern China's course. China's ethnic frontiers appear to constitute a "gray region" between the two categories and therefore can be investigated as seams in the historical fabric of China.

My focus in this inquiry is on the events leading up to 1949, a year when communist power, territorial and political reunification, ethnopolitical reconfiguration, and realignment in foreign affairs converged in China and started a new phase, which this study names "China's historical renewal." The current volume ends with 1945 and clarifies the CCP's ethnopolitical preparations for making its final dash for power between 1945 and 1949. China's ethnopolitics in the civil war period, especially the issues of autonomy or independence for Inner Mongolia, Xinjiang, and Tibet, will be treated in separate studies.

In pursuing this line of historical inquiry, I am not only seeking to join the dialogue within a small group of scholars specialized in China's ethnic subjects or in the CCP's policies toward ethnic minorities. I am also attempting to reconnect ethnicity and frontiers with the so-called mainstream, actually Han-centric, developments in China's post-Qing history. The CCP's ethnopolitics is indeed about the party's policies toward ethnic minorities. But it is also much more; it involves a set of "solutions" to such fundamental issues as the ethnic composition of the "Chinese nation" or *zhonghuan minzu,* the territoriality of China, and China's relations with its immediate neighboring areas in particular and with the international community in general. In China, where the Han people account for 92 percent of the total population, ethnicity and ethnic frontiers can be easily marginalized. The ethnographic reality of China has affected scholarly disciplines.

Indeed, China's minorities have fascinated social and political scientists for some time. Especially in the past decade, several significant studies have been done by Chinese and Western scholars that constitute a small boom in the field. Yet these highly specialized studies of certain selected ethnic groups remain at the margin of the general knowledge. As far as historians are concerned, except for a few exceptions (e.g., works by Christopher P. Atwood, Linda Benson, Andrew D. W. Forbes, Tom A. Grunfeld, and Jonathan Lipman), most historians of twentieth-century China have studied developments in the country's eastern half. When coming to interpretations of the CCP's ethnopolitics before and after 1949, we usually meet a conventional wisdom that the ethnopolitical facet of Chinese Communism is mainly a variant of the Marxist dogmas on the "national question" and the question's "model solution" in the former Soviet Union.

As a result, in our minds the historical link between China's current multiethnic system and its own polyethnic past remains murky, and the regional link between China proper and frontier China seems more accidental than normal. In this study, I deal with these issues by repositioning the CCP's ethnopolitical stance in the context of China's long history, especially that of the country's modern, nationalizing experience. Though it does not try to discount any of the generic effects of Communism in China, the study nevertheless stresses that Chinese Communist ethnopolitics evolved along a peculiar path determined by several long- and short-term conditions. The former included China's cultural-historical legacies and ethnographic configuration, and the latter the CCP's changing political fortune and related geostrategic movements.

As a diplomatic historian by training, I wrote the book and crossed more than one disciplinary boundary, realizing in the meantime that interethnic encounters were just as complex, delicate, and volatile as international confrontations. I owe an enormous intellectual debt to all the scholarly works cited in this study. In one respect, I feel more fortunate than scholars who worked on the ethnic angle of Chinese Communism before the 1990s. In 1989, the Central Archives of the People's Republic of China issued an eighteen-volume publication, *Zhonggong Zhongyang Wenjian Xuanji* (Selected documents of the Chinese Communist Party Central Committee).

Two years later, the CCP's United Front Department published *Minzu Wenti Wenxian Huibian* (Collection of documents on the national question) for "internal circulation." Together with more recent publications of documents on the relationship between the CCP and the Comintern, on the military-political operations of the Chinese Red Army, and on the activities of the CCP's local apparatus in the border region, these materials have fundamentally changed the prospect of the field for academic researchers. Although archival research on the CCP's history remains unlikely in China, these documents provide a considerable opening through which the CCP leadership's "inner thinking" and policymaking process can be studied empirically, not just theoretically.

In the long process of writing this book and finding a home for it, I was fortunate to have the help of many scholars. The ideas presented here first took shape when I was completing a research residency at the Fairbank Center, Harvard University, between 1997 and 1999. Ezra Vogel and William Kirby were the best hosts possible, always ready to help and facilitate my projects. At the end of my stay, Merle Goldman graciously chaired an East Asian Colloquium that allowed me to test my initial hypotheses. Some of my arguments were published in an article in a volume George Wei and I co-edited, *Chinese Nationalism in Perspective* (Greenwood Press, 2001). I am grateful to the publisher for permitting me to elaborate these arguments in this book. As the project progressed, Christopher Atwood, Uradyn Bulag, Tom Grunfeld, Robert Hathaway, and Steven Levine were most generous in taking the time to read part of or the whole manuscript. I benefited immensely from their insights and constructive criticisms. I am indebted to Chen Jian for calling my attention to the publication of *Minzu Wenti Wenxian Huibian,* and to Uljeyt and Nong Weixiong for helping me locate important sources. For thoughtful comments and suggestions, my gratitude goes to Yu Minling, Wang Jianmin, Wang Chaoguang, George Wei, Andrejs Plakans, Joseph Taylor, Christine Pope, and John Paden. Any remaining problems in the book, of course, are mine.

The research and writing of the book began when I was holding an SSRC–MacArthur Fellowship and a research grant from the Smith Richardson Foundation. The final stage of the work was completed with the support of a Woodrow Wilson Center–George Washington University Asian Policy Fellowship. During the last fellowship, the Department of History, Iowa State University, generously granted me leave time and provided indispensable support. Robert Hathaway, director of the Asia Program of the Woodrow Wilson Center, and Joseph Brinley, director of the Woodrow Wilson Center Press, enthusiastically endorsed the book project once they learned about it. Yamile Kahn and Muriel Bell, editors at the Woodrow Wilson Center Press and the Stanford University Press, respectively, welcomed the book project with open arms and helped improve the book's quality in various ways. I also wish to thank Bill Nelson for producing the maps in the book. The book could never have materialized without the constant encouragement and kind advice of Lawrence Gelfand, Warren Cohen, and Akira Iriye.

Finally, Hongxing, Ying Ying, Tanya, Xiaoxi, Xiaohong, and Erlao were with me at every stage of the project and their support enabled me to continue. This book is for them.

Note on Transliteration

In this study, most of the Chinese names are transliterated with the pinyin system. But there are instances in which the Wade-Giles forms are maintained due to their wide acceptance in the field, such as Sun Yat-sen and Kuomintang. All the titles of the Chinese books cited in this study are spelled out in pinyin followed by an English translation. To save space in the notes, the titles of Chinese journal articles are cited only with their English translations; however, the pinyin transliterations of the article titles are provided in the bibliography. The transliterations of names of non-Han Chinese origin rely heavily on scholarly practices in the relevant fields, such as Mongolian and Tibetan studies. As the discussion unfolds, special efforts are made to make certain peculiar and important Chinese terms, such as *zhonghua minzu* (Chinese nation), more accessible to readers who do not read Chinese.

Frontier Passages

1

Prologue: From the World of China to China of the World

Since the disintegration of the Soviet Union and Yugoslavia, the continual ethnic conflicts among the former members of these bygone systems have proved that the famed Marxist-Leninist solution of the "national question" only managed to seal temporarily the craters of these potentially volcanic bodies.[1] To many observers, these conflicts have an ominous implication for China, whose multinationality system has so far been understood as a variation of the Soviet model.

An intriguing question has been posed as to how long the multinationality system in China will be able to last. Even within China, an alarm has been sounded to stress that more than ever the country needs to foster the "conscience of national unity" among its more than fifty ethnic groups because its "socialist nationality relationship" is by no means immune to the current international trends.[2] This concern about outside influence is balanced by an ongoing debate among China scholars in the West over the inner vigor of the Chinese state. Will the erosion of the totalitarian system in China, as in the former Soviet Union, unleash a long-suppressed despondency of its "hidden nations"?[3] Although some studies have predicted a relatively stable future for China's polyethnic system, others have forecasted a marked uncertainty or even an inevitable, if not imminent, collapse of that system.[4]

What is in question here is not the daily interethnic relations within the populace of China but the official mode of these relations sanctioned and promoted by the central authorities in Beijing. Without question, official interethnic relationships in China have to reflect the long process of intergroup negotiations mainly between the predominant Han, who account for about 92 percent of China's 1.2 billion population, and the non-Han peoples who

1

reside mostly in China's vast ethnic borderlands.[5] Yet it is also obvious that the current interethnic system in China conveys primarily the policy intention of China's ruling party, the Chinese Communist Party (CCP). Thus, accurate knowledge about the origins and evolution of the CCP's ethnic policies and politics in the past is essential to our understanding of China's interethnic situation today and instructive for any serious forecast for the future.

As of today, in the English-speaking West, the study of the CCP's historical ethnopolitical experience has been represented by a couple of classic studies that examine the subject within the framework of the Marxist-Leninist-Stalinist theories on the "national question." This approach continues to influence recent scholarship on current ethnic affairs in the People's Republic of China (PRC).[6] For at least three reasons, however, this ideological paradigm has only limited usefulness in explaining the CCP's historical and current ethnic practices. First, although the CCP has used the Marxist-Leninist terminology to articulate its stand on China's "national question," the dogmatic appearance of the party's official literature tends to conceal, not reveal, the pragmatic reasons behind the CCP's changing policies in different periods. In her pioneer work, June Dreyer suggests that because the "socialist scriptures" are themselves ambiguous and open to interpretation, "the Chinese [Communists] could formulate minorities policy in a wide variety of ways and still remain ideologically orthodox."[7] If this is the case, how, then, can the Marxist classics really help us understand the CCP's assorted policy behaviors?

Second, the ideological paradigm tends to exaggerate the difference between the CCP and the other nationalist groups in China. For instance, Dreyer stresses the difference between the CCP and the Kuomintang (KMT, or National People's Party) to such an extent that she cannot be certain "whether the Chinese Communists were reacting positively to the Soviet model or negatively to the Nationalist practice" in deciding their own policies toward the minorities.[8] Although the nationalist character of Asian communists caused a constant bewilderment in the West during the Cold War, the West's own post–Cold War era provides a conducive environment in which the paradox of Asian communist nationalism may be better understood. The reality is that the CCP and the KMT had much to share in their nation-building programs, and, by the end of World War II the two parties had reached a consensus on the basic aspects of China's "national question."

Third, the ideological paradigm tends to derive conclusions on the CCP's practices from a general reading of classic Marxist-Leninist treatises but not from a grasp of the empirical evidence about the CCP's particular history. This shortcoming originated in the information segregation between the two sides of the Cold War and, especially, in the self-imposed information censorship on the "Communist" side. During the information-muffling age, reliable information about contemporary China and its recent past was scarce, and the CCP's behaviors were easily understood in the West according to the established patterns applied to their Soviet predecessors. For instance, this is the case for the "commandments" that Walker Connor has attributed to Lenin's revolutionary strategy on the "national question."

These "commandments," according to Connor, prescribed different policies for mobilizing the minority nationalities and incorporating them into the revolution. The key element of the strategy was that the Communist Party endorse the minorities' right to national self-determination before it took power and deny that right afterward.[9] A major factual error occurs, however, when Connor applies this behavior pattern to the CCP: The CCP stopped endorsing the minorities' right to self-determination long before it seized power in China. Therefore, reasons other than the Leninist strategy are needed to explain the CCP's practices.

An alternative view is to stress the CCP's connection with China's ancient and better studied past and to assert that the "present high culture [of the People's Republic of China] is in its essentials the continuation of the high culture—the civilization—of imperial China."[10] Interestingly, like the Marxist-ideology paradigm, this traditional-culture approach also stresses the anachronism of the current system of the PRC. Resting their perceptions respectively on China's recent and remote past, these threads of inquiry cannot detect a dynamism that bridges China's past and future. Yet the CCP's act in history is characterized neither by a fantastic leap into the future nor by a fanatic holding on to the past. The late China scholar Benjamin I. Schwartz once pointed out that in the CCP's worldview Communism constituted only a "third category" following Confucianism and the nation-state outlook borrowed from the West. The CCP's worldview is therefore a potpourri of these three convictions and propensities that "supplemented and complicated" one another.[11] The tensions among these elements indicate that, like any other revolutionary force in history, the CCP has acted as both a vehicle of tradition and an agent of change.

In focusing on the making of the CCP's ethnopolitical stance between 1921 and 1945, this study considers the product of the process neither as a replica of the Soviet model nor as a relic of China's long history. Instead, it shows how contingencies and circumstances dictated the relationship between the CCP's policymaking and the three convictions identified by Schwartz. In the process, historical inheritance and historic innovations took place. Because the historical settings of China's modern ethnopolitics are vital to our understanding of the making of the CCP's ethnopolitical stance, it is necessary to clarify those relevant historical conceptions and precedents before our subject can be examined in detail. After all, no matter how the CCP's ethnopolitical orientation is defined, it is but a part of China's historical renewal.

Historical Renewal

Historical renewal is commonplace in the development of human societies. In his study of the ethnic origins of nations, Anthony D. Smith points out the resilience of all ethnic communities, which he names *ethnie:*

> *Ethnie,* once formed, tend to be exceptionally durable under "normal" vicissitudes and to persist over many generations, even centuries, forming "moulds" within which all kinds of social and cultural processes can unfold and upon which all kinds of circumstances and pressures can exert an impact.[12]

Survival through resistance, change, and adaptation is the instinct of any human community. The passage above denotes two fundamental qualities of any distinct ethnic community: tenacity and flexibility—or, in Smith's words, "mutability in persistence" and "persistence through change."[13] In this sense, the significance of a historical process lies in its connection with the past as much as in its projection into the future.

In history, such occurrences as revolution, conquest, war, massive demographic change, technological and scientific breakthroughs, and the like may look drastic. But this is so only according to the observer's own ephemeral perception. In the view of history, these can have only a limited impact on their social environment. These occurrences, even when they appear to have a positive outcome, are inevitably counterbalanced by the force of historical inertia consisting of traditional values, cultures, and systems. Hu Shi, a pioneer reformist intellectual in early twentieth-century China, was particularly perspicacious about the relationship between the force of change and the magnitude of historical inertia in a society:

Once becoming national, a culture naturally achieves an enormous conservativeness that can resist both the rise of any novelty from within and
the inroad by any foreign form from the outside. This is the inertia commonly shared by all cultures, and it does not require any intentional cultivation and protection. . . . Those radical changes affecting the various
aspects of a culture ultimately have their limitations; they cannot exter-
minate the fundamental conservativeness of the original culture.

Therefore, although Hu Shi fiercely advocated implementing "complete
Westernization" in China, his pragmatic goal was to achieve only the "crys-
tallization of a cultural upheaval" that could combine the valuable components of both the Chinese and Western civilizations.[14]

Yet an actual historical process can hardly be one of cultural "crystal-
lization" according to any prescribed formulas. The process necessarily involves negotiations among forces pulling in different directions. In an
emerging social mould, the conservatives would play a role of bending the
new environment to meet the "original" civilization, and the reformers or
revolutionaries a role of making the old norms workable under the new circumstances. Every so-called historical progress has to be validated by such
a compromise. In other words, in the making of history there are no absolute
"losers" and "winners" but only forces working from the different sides of
the same process. In history, no one and nothing that has been banished to
the "dustpan of history" will not have its successors alive and kicking in the
renewed, "next" stage of human affairs. Similarly, every one and everything
that has entered the annals of history with luster cannot avoid carrying a
certain stigma of a vanquished past. In this manner, a society or culture re-
news itself.

The process of historical change *and* reverence has been played out again
and again in the extended chronology of China, one of the oldest *ethnie* and
youngest nation-states in the world.[15] Anthony Smith finds three types of
ethnic renewal movements (territorial, genealogical or dynastic, and cultural) with "ethnicism," the ideological precedent of modern nationalism,
as the driving force behind them. According to his definition, ethnicism is
fundamentally a "defensive . . . response to outside threats and divisions
within," and it "seeks a return to the *status quo ante,* to an idealized image
of a primitive past."[16] The actual situations found in Chinese history are
richer, though. Traditional ethnicism could be as assertive and grandiose as
modern nationalism. The "idealized image" of the past served to justify ex-
pansions as often as it guided "restorations."

In addition, the renewal of the Chinese state system has not always been accomplished by the same *ethnie*. As China inched into the modern age in the past few centuries, the "idealized image" of China's past also changed significantly. By the turn of the nineteenth and twentieth centuries, when nationalism superseded ethnicism in China, a new idea about "China of the world" had already substituted for the old "world of China" image in the Chinese mind.

The World of China

Having successfully vanquished the "warring states" and unified China, Qin Shi Huang (the first Qin emperor), founder of the first unified dynasty in Chinese history (221–206 B.C.), defined his domain in these words: "All lands within the six-sided universe [*liuhe*] belong to the emperor: Crossing the Running Sand in the west, reaching Beihu in the south, possessing the Eastern Sea in the east, and passing the Great Xia in the north, all loci with human presence are the emperor's subjects."[17] Thus, "grand unity" (*da yi tong*), a key element of China's ethnicism in antiquity, became a political reality.

Recently, when disputing the validity of comparing China with the former Soviet Union, Ezra Vogel contended that "the Soviet Union was unified in the last century; China was unified 2,200 years ago."[18] Yet during the last two millenniums, China has not always been a unified country. The "first emperor," Qin Shi Huang, could not guarantee his empire's continuation. After his unifying dynasty, China would again and again be divided. But a most remarkable fact in Chinese history is the survival of "grand unity" as a perceived normality despite the country's reoccurring divisions. A favored practice among scholars in today's China is to use a 7:3 ratio to depict the unitary and the divisive periods in China's history, indicating that China has been unified most of the time.[19] Although the premise of the practice can be questioned, the so-called longevity of the Chinese state system does reflect the system's phoenixlike ability to survive the numerous division-and-unification cycles in history. The only thing even more tenacious than the system is the "grand unity" ideology, which has continued in both the unified and divisive laps of Chinese history as an ideal.

In a study that compares China and Europe, R. Bin Wong contends that after Europe and China achieved their respective initial unification, the former evolved into a multistate system whereas the latter remained a unitary entity. Although admitting the ideological coherency of China's civilizational unity, Wong mainly attributes the longevity of the Chinese state system to an "administrative infrastructure to sustain the empire as a political reality."[20] Consequently, whereas the European tradition has fostered an international order of equal nation-states, the Chinese tradition has nourished an inclusive world of the Middle Kingdom (*Zhongguo*).

Such a reading of the "Chinese tradition" is valid only if those incongruous facts are treated as exceptions. Some case studies have proved that there were times in Chinese history when the "central dynasty" was just one of the several states in China and "parity" was actually practiced in the interstate relations of the Chinese world.[21] Taking these cases into account, the difference between the European and the Chinese world orders is not one between a nation-state system of equality and an imperial system of stratification. Rather, the tradition of the Chinese world system afforded many options, including ideas and practices that could support either a condescending central dynasty surrounded by tributary states or an interstate relationship based on parity. The "grand unity" ideology, however, held that the central-dynasty mode was normal and desirable and that the parity mode was convenient and expedient. Whenever a state in the world of China became strong enough, it would seek to achieve hegemony over the others by enforcing its rule in the name of grand unity. Otherwise, equal and reciprocal relationships might be conducted by a weak "celestial dynasty," even though it continued to claim spiritual superiority over its counterparts.

The realm in which traditional Chinese statecraft performed was *tianxia* (all under heaven). This is another ambiguous yet enduring conception of Chinese ethnicism. The term carries an overt universalist connotation, but its practical meaning kept shifting in the course of time. When Confucius and his followers contemplated the human cultivation of virtue, they held *tianxia* as the highest and broadest realm, above human self, family, and state, for the exercise of moral excellency.[22] The term was also used to denote the domain of the Middle Kingdom's actual or imaginary influence, or the arena for contenders to contest for the legitimacy to rule the Middle Kingdom and its world. When Qin Shi Huang claimed his universal reign over every corner of the world frequented by the human trace, the ideology of grand unity and the conception of all under heaven meshed perfectly.

It can easily be seen, however, that under these conceptions China's traditional political discourse carried an inner contradiction between a unlimited claim and a limited control. From the Qin Dynasty to the PRC, countless battles and diplomatic maneuvers were waged to contest or to pacify all under heaven (*zheng tianxia* or *ping tianxia*). Despite these events' universalistic themes, their actual significance was no more than repeated redefinition of the Middle Kingdom's territorial limits, its relative position in the imaginable world, and the relationship between the society and the state.

In today's China, *tianxia* remains an incendiary conception. The term's devotees uphold it as the perimeter of grand unity and hastily conclude that it is the conceptual predecessor to the modern "Chinese Nation" (*zhonghua minzu*). Those who oppose using the term point out that its original meaning was too self-centered and responsible for the narrow-mindedness of the Chinese psyche recurring in the past two millenniums.[23] Neither opinion, however, seems to do historical justice to the term.

The original definition of the term was indeed self-centered in depicting the geopolitical and ethnocultural relationship between the Chinese *ethnie* and its neighbors. One of the early versions appeared in the first geographic classic in Chinese history, *Yu Gong* (*Tributary to Yu*).[24] Using the mythological Xia Dynasty (2000–1500 B.C.) as its "idealized primitive past," *Yu Gong* expressed its authors' political aspirations for political unity in the time of the Warring States. It divided all under heaven, which at the time included only the eastern part of today's China, into nine regions (*jiu zhou*) and described "five subject-domains" (*wu fu*) ruled by the center. These were "idealized" domains in a sense that they were orderly arranged around the ruling center, each being a belt of 500 *li* in width. According to their genealogical, cultural, and political relationship to the central kingship, these domains were named as *dian fu* (imperial domain), *hou fu* (marquis domain), *sui fu* (pacified domain), *yao fu* (banished domain), and *huang fu* (uncultivated domain).

The residents of these five domains were subject to different degrees of control, shouldered different tributary and servitude obligations, and enjoyed different privileges. By keeping the similar and loyal in the close quarters and the different and distrusted at distance, the central court thus achieved both control and security by surrounding itself with layers of buffer zones.[25] This may be viewed as the earliest political fiction of the world that idolized a nonexistent Chinese political order in antiquity and ignored the geographic reality of the world. But this was also the embryo of what Prasenjit Duara identifies as the "concentric, radiant concept of universal empire" that would be amplified and enshrined by Confucianists in the centuries to come.[26]

After *Yu Gong*'s time, China—"concentric" and "radiant" but not necessarily "narrow-minded" and "closed" all the time—grew into an empire that participated in world history much more actively and willingly than is presumed by the conventional wisdom. As our own time is being affected profoundly by a suspense-filled drama of gargantuan proportions called the "rise of China," historical precedents for China's current upsurge have been rediscovered by new scholarship. What has been accomplished by this scholarship is not to dispute the existence of historical moments when the Middle Kingdom was parochial and xenophobic but to reject such moments as the normal and permanent state of traditional China.[27]

Again, the long history of China provides numerous variations with regard to China's position in the world. In light of the new scholarship, the question is no longer whether or not the ancient Chinese ever gained knowledge about the rest of the world but rather how they put their knowledge to use at different times. It is still valid to argue that the Chinese rulers were disposed to claim China's centrality in the world, but further exploration is needed to ascertain under what circumstances China chose to become a "passive axis rather than an active center" of the world.[28]

Thus, the meaning of *tianxia* in Chinese history is completely contingent upon the balance of power between China's central dynasty and its principal external counterparts at a give time. As an abstract claim for cultural superiority, the conception could be aloof from the geographic constraints of China; it might be used either by a strong central dynasty to seek active contacts with the outside world or by a weak central court to justify its pragmatic arrangements with powerful neighbors. As a concrete denominator for territorial control, however, the term could not travel far. First and foremost, China itself became an elephantine realm to be controlled and pacified; the magnitude of the task was large enough to be considered as one concerning all under heaven. Indeed, the Middle Kingdom's self-obsessive propensity constituted a sharp contrast to the European state system, whereby states were constantly faced with mutual or "foreign" competition and threats.[29] In constantly discharging its daunting responsibility to administer the vast and diverse Chinese society, the imperial bureaucracy had to give self-preservation the highest priority.

Even though the imperial bureaucracy was introverted by nature, its dealings with external affairs could not be avoided. According to the celestial court's self-serving worldview, it had a verticalized external relationship with neighboring areas. From the Qin to the Qing, China's successive central dynasties maintained two parallel yet distinct agencies separately in charge of the affairs of "subject states" (*shuguo*) and "guest states" (*keguo*). The "subject states" were those that had surrendered themselves to a certain form of administration by the celestial court, and the "guest states" merely "subscribed to the virtue" (*gui yi*) of the court.[30] As long as the Middle Kingdom managed to act as the provider of order for the traditional world of Asia, these categories were incorporated, administratively or ritually, into *tianxia*. But once the Chinese imperial system crumbled, the nature of these states' relations with China would change. The most audacious among them would even attempt to assume the "mandate of heaven" and replace the Chinese court as the lawgiver of the Chinese world.

Therefore, before the rulers of China developed a modern consciousness about "Chinese–foreign" relations some time in the nineteenth century, they conceptualized China's external engagement as a relationship between Hua (Chinese) and Yi (barbarians). Because literacy in traditional China belonged to the privileged social elite, it is difficult to ascertain from the Chinese classics that the ancient ethnic and cultural identities referred to therein actually reflected an "across-the-board sentiment" in traditional Chinese society.[31] The various strains of traditional Chinese ideology, categorized as either ethnicism or culturalism by the scholarship of our own time, are extremely elitist and probably cannot be studied vertically.[32]

Yet the perennial fixation of the Hua–Yi contrast in traditional China's political discourse at least proves that there existed extremely important, chronic contacts between the Han society of China and the non-Han peoples around China, especially those of Inner Asia. Malcolm Anderson's incisive observation about a periphery's significance for an emerging national center can be applied to China's traditional ethnocultural centrism: "In certain circumstances the frontier acquired a mythic significance in building nations and political identities, becoming the *mythomotoeur* of the whole society."[33] The Chinese ruling elite needed the non-Han frontiers to maintain its self-image as a civilized, central celestial court that received "ten thousand states coming for audience" (*wan bang lai chao*).

In ancient Chinese minds, the world was consisted of the Hua at the center and the various Yi peoples in the "four seas" (*si hai*) around the center.[34] Originally, "Yi" might not have been a culturally derogatory conception. According to Owen Lattimore, the initial "Chinese" belonged to a materially more advanced group that grew out of the neolithic "un-Chinese" populace in the area of today's China.[35] This can be verified by the fact that the earliest "Chinese" chose Hua as their collective name. Hua means "fluorescent" or "splendorous," indicating a relatively prosperous and luxurious lifestyle. Although the term Yi has been invariably translated into "barbarian" by Western students of China, it might be used by the early Chinese just to refer to the "ordinary" others.

However, when a nomadic, "non-Chinese" civilization emerged in the Inner Asian steppes and became strong enough to challenge the agrarian Chinese culture, the original, largely economic differentiation between the Chinese and the "not-yet-Chinese" within China was overshadowed and eventually replaced by an ethnocultural "distinction between the Hua and the Yi" (*hua yi zhi bian*).[36] The more elaborate these two civilizations grew, the less surmountable the "barriers" between the two seemed to become, though the flows of people, goods, and ideas between the two sides never stopped.

Despite the Confucianist assertion that the Hua and the Yi were "not the same kind" (*fei wo zu lei*), the separation between what can be termed as "ethnocultural states" in the world of China was not as rigid or ossified as the nation-states in the European world. It is almost an axiom in the field that "China could be conquered but its system remained." It is problematic, however, to assert further that the Chinese state always "domesticated its conquerors."[37] Because the ancient ethnocultural states in the Chinese world were not separated by clearly demarcated and commonly accepted borders, it is difficult to determine where the Chinese system stopped and other systems began. As a matter of fact, it was commonplace for culturally and ethnically mixed systems to function within the ambiguous frontier zones between the Middle Kingdom and its neighbors.

Unlike the European nation-state system, which divided its members with clearly demarcated national borders, the Chinese ethnocultural-state system connected its participants with graduated, culturally mutually penetrating, and ethnically mixed zones. During the Tang Dynasty, a practice used by the central court to control the non-Han groups along the frontiers was to establish "prefectures and superior prefectures of loose rein" (*jimi zhou fu*). The idea was to "keep the [non-Han] tribes intact in order to use them as defensive barriers and not to alienate them from their indigenous customs."[38] China's northern neighbors reciprocated by duplicating the practice. Such non-Han dynasties as the Liao, the Xixia, and the Jin adopted their own dual systems to administer their domains. They used a "state system" (*guozhi*) to administer their own peoples and a "Han system" (*hanzhi*) to control the Han population along the southern fringes of their territories.[39]

Such cultural, populace, and systemic overlap can be confounding to the modern mind. Even scholars of Chinese history cannot avoid falling into

endless debates. They ask questions such as these: Was a state at the periphery of a central dynasty in China part of the Middle Kingdom? Should
a "loose rein" prefecture be viewed as under China's "sovereignty," or was
it an "independent" state? These are indeed "hard" questions in modern
times. But they are hardly relevant to the ancient ethnocultural-state system that fashioned mutual relations with "soft" means and conceptions.
In traditional China's "loose rein" (*jimi*) approach, the ruling families' inter-
marriages, gift presentations, tributes, title bestowals, patronage, and ordinary trade were used to stabilize interstate relations. Once a "peripheral"
state had formed these kinds of ties with China's "central dynasty," it became a loose part of the Chinese dynasty and a separate entity at the same
time. But in a highly politicized modern world, these two halves of the
same walnut have been separately stressed for different agendas.[40]

Only if not infected by such ahistorical enthusiasm can one recognize
that this walnut was an awkward product of the tree of China's traditional
universalism; no matter how strong a central dynasty in China was, its universal claim for overlordship could never be sustained by its limited ability
for territorial control. Loose rein, then, became the only possible device to
maintain the balance between the two. But the advantage came with a drawback. The "soft," ethnically mixed border zone was a double-edged sword
that could cut either outward or inward.[41] In addition, China's imperial claim
that all under heaven shared the same ruler actually opened the door for the
non-Chinese states to share China itself. Thus the seemingly eternal realm,
the world of China or *tianxia,* never achieved the same degree of consis-
tency as the European nation-state system.

Although the "Chinese state system" was initiated by the ruling elites of
the Middle Kingdom, who named themselves Hua (or Han after the Han
Dynasty), during its long evolution the system was really a "shared" one.
Successive powerful dynasties, Han and non-Han, emerged to gain hegemony in the world of China and to continue and modify the Chinese state
system. Thomas J. Barfield identifies an "outer frontier" and an "inner frontier" strategy used again and again by the steppe states in their dealings with
China. The former involved overt raids aimed at obtaining human and material treasures from the Middle Kingdom; the latter necessitated nominal
submission to the central dynasty's superiority in order to get its assistance
with steppe politics.[42] Either by challenging or by pandering to the authority of the celestial court, these steppe strategies helped sharpen the Chinese
elites' ethnicism and "racialize" their worldview.[43] But there were also times
when a third strategy was adopted by powerful steppe states. That was for

they themselves to become the executioners of the "mandate of heaven" from the throne of the celestial court.

Before China had its first unified dynasty, quite usually some "barbarian" states (*manyi*) took a posture of "possessing an armed force to watch over China's governance." Among these, Qin, a "sinicized" frontier state, emerged as the first unifier of China.[44] The powerful and cosmopolitan Tang Dynasty significantly expanded the domain of the Chinese Empire, but its founders also had a "barbarian" background. This partially explains why its founder Li Shimin professed a love of the Hua and the Yi as the same.[45] In the thirteenth century, the Mongols vanquished the Song Dynasty of China and made China part of their pastoral empire encompassing the Eurasian land mass. The Mongols first and foremost based their legitimacy on the logic of military conquest. But in China, the Mongol rulers also claimed legitimacy in the Chinese political tradition. Khubilai Khan named his dynasty "Yuan" to "show the meaning that all under heaven belong to one family" (*tianxia yijia*).

The Yuan court also followed an official Chinese tradition of compiling its predecessor dynasty's history to prove the shift of the "mandate of heaven." The effort resulted in three separate histories for the bygone Song, Liao, and Jin Dynasties, the last two being northern, non-Han dynasties (Kitan and Jurchen).[46] Eventually, the Mongols had to retreat to the grassland, but the provincial system established by them has continued in China ever since.

Thus, so-called Chinese history is really both Chinese and non-Chinese. Although a Chinese cultural theme managed to continue in the history of the Chinese state system, China's historical process and the resultant entity are indisputably multicultural and polyethnic. After China entered the modern world system, ascendant Chinese nationalism would dominate the political realm and rewrite China's history. Such a development is ironic, because it was the Qing, a Manchu dynasty, that presided over China's entry into the modern age.

China of the World

In the wake of the Sino-Japanese war of 1894–95, the reformer Kang Youwei advised Emperor Guangxu in a memorial: "All under heaven [*tianxia*] should be ruled as a situation of coexisting states [*lieguo bingli zhi shi*], but not as a unified entity under the [emperor's] robe [*yitong chuishang zhi shi*]."[47] Although continuing to pay lip service to China's universal over-lordship, Kang was telling the emperor that China was only one of the world's states and that the Qing Empire had to readjust to the world of nation-states.

Among all the "renewal" actions and movements that took place in traditional China, the Qing Dynasty exerted the most direct impact on and had the closest relationship with the modern Chinese state. During the Qing's very eventful life span of more than two and half centuries, three main developments made the Qing Empire the forerunner of the modern Chinese nation-state: the realization of the grand unity of all under heaven, the demarcation of China's national borders, and the separation of domestic and foreign affairs.

Realization of the Grand Unity of All under Heaven

When modern nationalism arose in China, China was not in a divisive lap of its historical cycle. Instead, the Qing Empire extended China's territorial domain to the natural barriers of the eastern Asian land mass and achieved a grand unity of gigantic scale. Although in the nineteenth century China fell into the clutches of the "unequal treaty system" forged by Western powers, the situation did not deprive the Qing court of its nominal authority over China's principal territories. This condition provided a tremendous territorial domain for Chinese nationalists to transform into a Chinese nation-state. In other words, the unified *tianxia* bequeathed from the Qing Empire was translated by the Nationalists into the logical homeland of the "Chinese nation." To accept less would violate the rule of the mandate of heaven and would thereby undermine the legitimacy of the successor regime, the Republic of China.

Had the Chinese Republic been formed in the wake of a divisive period in Chinese history, the question of the "Chinese nation" would have been answered very differently. Ironically, if Chinese history is to be divided into laps of a unification-and-division cycle, it is the Chinese Republic, a period of riotous nationalism, that started a divisive lap. China's Nationalists and Communists had many reasons to fume over China's repeated humiliations in foreign affairs during the Qing period. But it is ahistorical to blame the Qing as the dynasty that lost the "greatest amount of territories" in Chinese history.[48] The founders of the PRC understood history better than many commentators in today's China. Zhou Enlai, the first PRC premier, once praised the Manchus of the Qing Dynasty for making China a country with "such an extensive territory" and unprecedented unity.[49]

Demarcation of China's National Borders

Chinese Nationalists of the twentieth century blamed the Qing for losing state land, because between the seventeenth and the nineteenth centuries the Qing court had indeed signed over territories in its treaties with foreign powers. What is forgotten is that the Qing Empire was the first in Chinese history to establish definite boundaries with its neighboring states. In the modern world, frontier disputes tend to happen between "immature states" that are in the midst of nationalizing and modernizing processes.[50] By the time of the Qing, however, China had already developed an overly mature state system lasting thousands of years. The question of boundaries confronted China at this time simply because there had been no imperative need for a clear border demarcation before. If "frontiers are markers of identity,"[51] the identity of imperial China was marked by its ambiguous frontier zones. These were distinctively "inter-ethnocultural" but not "international." In the traditional world of ethnocultural states, state security was achieved through managing interethnic peripheries as buffer zones and by keeping a safety distance between different ethnic cores.

A traditional state could not completely "fill up" its frontier areas because it lacked means of effective communications and transportation. These circumstances dictated that its frontier policy operate within "zones" but not along "lines." In this regard, China was not unique in world history. This is not to say that ancient Chinese rulers never tried to use lines to demarcate their domains. In Chinese history, a repeated practice involved rulers of a unified dynasty issuing "gazetteers of unification" (*yi tong zhi*).

These official gazetteers were to show the extension of the grand Chinese Empire. Maps in the gazetteers used lines to indicate the separation between the celestial dynasty and the Yi states along its peripheries. What these maps did not show was the borderlines between the Yi states. This kind of map making, of course, was merely a unilateral mental exercise by China's ruling elites. China's borderlines in these maps had nothing in common with the commonly accepted international borders of the modern international system.[52] Moreover, the exercise was not limited to paper; Chinese emperors also built the Great Wall to separate their "civilized" subjects from the groups to the north remaining in "outer darkness."[53]

Following the Mongols' precedent, the Manchus ignored the Great Wall and entered China to assume the mandate of heaven. Pamela Crossley's research has proved that the "Manchus" were not a uni-ethnic group but an amalgamation of Jurchens, Mongols, Chinese, and other ethnic groups. Actually, the Manchus' conquest of China was "primarily a phenomenon of Chinese fighting Chinese" because of the large number of Chinese in the Manchu banner troops.[54] Unquestionably, the "Chinese martials" and Mongol cavalries served as the fodder of the Manchu ruling family's grand design.

Once having taken the throne of the celestial court, the Qing emperors also inherited much of the traditional Chinese outlook. But because they had their ancestral roots in the "outer zone" of the Chinese Empire, the Manchu rulers could never feel comfortable in the "inner" and ethnically Chinese zone. Consequently, the Qing rejected China's linear defense tradition on two grounds: The strategy had proved futile in defending China, and it appeared illogical for the Manchu court's policy to counterbalance the inner Chinese populace with the outer ethnic groups.[55] In the meantime, the founders of the Qing Dynasty consciously resorted to the alternative Chinese tradition: the buffer zone strategy.

In the late seventeenth century, when faced with Russia's southward expansion, Emperor Kangxi stressed to his underlings that "this court does not set up frontier defense but use the Mongol tribes as a barrier." At the time, China's security policy was to "use the Liuchiu [Ryukyu] to defend the southeast, Korea the northeast, Mongolia the northwest, and Vietnam the southwest."[56] The seemingly ageless principle of "using barbarians to control barbarians" (*yi yi zhi yi*), however, suddenly became obsolete when the European nation-state system began to overcome the Chinese ethnocultural order.

In a fascinating recent study, Laura Hostetler positions Kangxi's Qing Empire among those world powers that used cartography to lay claims on their imperial realms and ethnography to ascertain the composition of their subjects.[57] Yet Emperor Kangxi really departed from the Chinese tradition by introducing an *international* practice into the empire's external affairs. In 1689, while the Qing Empire was still expanding, Kangxi's government concluded the Treaty of Nerchinsk with Russia and established China's first northern border sanctioned by an international agreement. Unfortunately, in the next two centuries, although the same practice would be continued, the Qing government gradually lost initiative. The old Chinese world of ambiguous border zones was rapidly replaced by a rearranged Asian continent crowded with Western empires and rotten Asian kingdoms. In Benedict Anderson's words: "Triangulation by triangulation, war by war, treaty by treaty, the alignment of map and power proceeded" in Asia.[58] It was the Asian countries' territories that were triangulated, mapped, fought over by war, and redefined by treaties; the power gained in the process belonged to the West.

As it was coerced by foreign powers' uninvited "assistance," the Qing Empire had to redefine its territorial domain continually. The Qing government was compelled to accept the European norms of international practices even in conducting its relations with China's traditional neighbors. Thus China's modern boundaries were demarcated with Sikkim (1792), Nepal (1793), and Korea (1885, 1887).[59] By changing China from a self-centered empire surrounded by borderlands of ambiguous status into a "bordered land" connected with other nation-states, the Manchu rulers did a historical chore on behalf of the Chinese Nationalists.[60] But the Qing government overlooked one aspect: It left China's maritime frontier largely undefined. To a land-bound empire like China, the waves of the eastern seas seemed to constitute a huge buffer zone, though the arrival of the "ocean people" (*yang ren*) proved otherwise. The territorial disputes in our own time between China and some countries in the South China Sea indicates that the Qing's oversight has not been solved by its Nationalist and Communist successors.

Separation of Domestic and Foreign Affairs

"Barbarians" coming from the ocean were not unheard of in Chinese history. What was new in the eighteenth and nineteenth centuries was that they did not come to "subscribe to the virtue" of the celestial dynasty but to demand to do things in their own ways. Unlike what has been suggested by some China scholars, the arrival of the West in China at this time did not begin China's own "great geographic discovery."[61] The ancient Chinese had known about the existence of other civilized societies all along and their emperor, the "son of heaven," had just waited for the peoples from afar to bring the world to his throne.

Now, these new "ocean people" wanted to drag China out to the world. The world's states not only did not recognize China as the order provider and the land of the highest moral authority but also wanted China to behave as one of them. While the ethnocultural system of the Chinese world was disintegrating, China's ruling elites reluctantly learned that China's best defense against the inroads by Westerners was to adopt their way of separating state

affairs into a domestic and a foreign sector. This insight would revolution-
ize both China's relations with foreign countries and its frontier affairs.

Some scholars in China—defining the "Chinese nation" (*zhongghua
minzu*) as a primordial entity—have read history backward and have argued
that the areas of contemporary China have always been parts of China in
history. Accordingly, the conflicts between China's central dynasties and
those peripheral states in ancient times were "internal contradictions," and
the Middle Kingdom's frontier defense was "internal defense."[62] The purpose of this contention is to lay a historical foundation for the PRC's territorial claims. Yet this view assumes an anachronism in implying that ancient
China already conducted its state affairs in two distinct "domestic" and "foreign" realms.

The actual situation was very different. In the traditional world of China,
its ruling elites defined the relations between the central dynasty and other
states primarily with such conceptions as "distance," "closeness," "intimacy," and "aloofness" (*yuan jin qin shu*). When the distinction between
internal and external was indeed made, it was made first and foremost on the
basis of cultural and ethnic distance. A motto in the Confucian classic *Chun
Qiu* (*The Spring and Autumn Annals*) exhorted rulers of China to "internalize the Xia [Chinese] states and externalize the Yi and Di [non-Chinese]
states" (*nei zhu xia er wai yi di*).[63] Accordingly, depending on its power and
prowess, the central dynasty had to consider the question as to what states
should be internalized or externalized and *to what degree*. It would be a
massive misinterpretation of history to identify traditional China's inner and
outer affairs with the domestic and foreign relations of the modern times.

The Qing government went through a tortuous course in separating its
domestic and foreign affairs. These were traditionally mixed together in
China's "frontier affairs" (*bian shi*). As a "peripheral," non-Han group that
had come to rule China, the Manchus were especially diligent in dealing
with frontier affairs. For the purpose, a Lifan Yuan, or Ministry of Dependencies, was added to China's already unwieldy imperial bureaucracy. The
office's charge was to "control and pacify [the dependencies] in order to
consolidate the state domain." It mainly dealt with the Qing's oscillating
relations with Mongolia, Tibet, the northwestern "Hui sector" (Muslims of
Xinjiang), the southwestern tribes, and Russia.[64] Beginning with the reign
of Emperor Qianlong (1736–99), the court's official gazetteers also began
to include certain Western powers in the category of *si yi* (the four barbarous
kinds).[65]

Thus the Qing's initial response to the increasing contacts between China and the West was, ironically, to "internalize" the latter into all under heaven, or the Hua–Yi equation. Gong Zizhen, a relatively enlightened scholar-official of his time, was then in charge of the "guest department" of the Ritual Ministry. He actually put the "western ocean countries" (*xiyang zhuguo*) and China's traditional tributary states such as Korea and Vietnam into the same "guest state" category. Gong saw only one difference between these Western and Asian states: The former did not pay tributes to China on a regular basis, and the latter did.[66]

By 1861, however, having been frustrated again and again by the armed forces of these irregular guest states, the Qing government belatedly learned the hard way that its "way of barbarian management" (*yu yi zhi fa*) might eventually result in a scenario that would be extremely embarrassing according to Chinese social protocols, *xuan bin duo zhu* (a presumptuous guest usurps the role of the host). Now the European way of treating states as separate but equal entities seemed to make more sense than China's way of dealing with them as members of one family with superior or inferior status. In the year, the court decided to establish the Zongli Yamen (the Office for the Management of the Business of All Foreign Countries), the prototype of China's modern foreign office. Hence, this was the official beginning of China's *foreign* affairs in the modern sense. Yet, privately, Qing officials still preferred to call the office *fu yi ju* (the bureau of barbarian pacification).[67]

Before the Qing Dynasty came to its end in the early twentieth century, Yi, this racially and culturally loaded term, would be used less and less frequently in the official discourse. *Yangren* (oversea people), then *Xiren* (Westerners), and finally *waiguoren* (foreigners) would be adopted. Along the way, the cultural and racial stigmas carried by these names diminished.[68] Reluctantly, the Qing conceded that the "western ocean countries" were not barbarians coming to subscribe to the virtue of the celestial dynasty. They were foreign states that could not be subject to China's authority and had to be respected as China's equals. This concession was made, of course, to safeguard the court's control of its own domain. From now on, the safety of the Middle Kingdom was no longer a matter of the court's exclusive, unilateral "barbarian management"; it would also have to rely on foreign countries' recognition of China as a "sovereign state."

When the celestial dynasty relinquished its authority over the outer realm of all under heaven, it was compelled to change its way of running the inner domain as well. As a sovereign state, the Qing had to eliminate any ambiguity about what was foreign and what was domestic to its authority. When the dealing with guest states became foreign affairs, the management of the "subject states" had to be domesticated. Consequently, the business of the Lifan Yuan became decisively "domestic."[69] The international community's recognition of the Qing sovereignty over the former border zones came amid what has been termed a "frontier crisis" for China after the mid–nineteenth century. In a series of treaties with Russia and the United Kingdom, the Qing government not only signed off territories in the peripheries but also opened China's interior for Westerners' commercial, cultural, and religious activities.[70] With such a high price tag, the Qing was recognized by foreign powers as the sovereign in territorially redefined China. Fearing further loss of land, the Qing government had to replace the loose rein approach of managing the originally "hollow frontier" (*xubian*) with measures to create a "substantiated border" (*shibian*). These measures mainly included establishing new provinces, military and administrative reforms, agricultural migration, and "developmental" policies to promote commerce, communication, and industries in the border areas.[71]

Understood in the traditional framework of the Chinese Empire, these measures were intended to escalate the imperial dependencies (*fanshu*) at the peripheries to the status of the royal territories (*bantu*). This was actually how the official debate was phrased in the final decade of the Qing over the possibility of changing Tibet's dependency status to a provincial status.[72] But because these measures were mainly initiated to respond to the imposing European international order, they assumed a modern significance in transforming China's relationship with the borderlands from *suzerainty* to *sovereignty*.

This of course constituted a radical departure from the traditional loose rein doctrine that "cultivated their [frontier peoples'] beliefs but did not alter their customs, and perfected their governance but did not change their practices" (*xiu qi jiao bu yi qi su, qi qi zheng bu yi qi yi*).[73] The late Qing's effort to centralize territorial control by domesticating the frontier areas constituted nothing less than government-enforced sinicization. This development was a watershed in the Qing domination of China, which lasted 267 years. During the better part of the period, the Manchu rulers tried to keep the Han Chinese and other ethnic groups apart and resisted becoming sinicized themselves.[74] The Qing court's efforts to "nationalize" its empire did not save itself from the Chinese Revolution of 1911. These efforts, however, would become the Qing's most enduring legacies to modern China.

China Nationalized

The overthrow of the Qing in 1911 was followed by a turbulent period of wars and revolutions. The Chinese Nationalists and the Chinese Communists struggled against each other and foreign foes to rehabilitate or to renovate a dysfunctional republic. These two movements were twin phenomena of the same era, and they provided two alternatives for China's way out of its modern predicaments. China of the twentieth century cannot be understood without the two being considered side by side. At different times during the twentieth century, the two parties acted as each other's "inner" or "outer" frontiers. When the KMT was the power holder of the remnant Republic of China, it was challenged by the CCP's rebellious "incipient state" in the countryside of southern and northwestern China.[75] After 1949, the two parties switched positions, and the KMT continued its refugee republic in Taiwan in defiance of the CCP's PRC on the mainland.

Both the KMT and the CCP are direct heirs of the Qing, though their respective predispositions have determined their different relationships with the Qing legacy. To date, there has been no systematic historical study of the KMT's ethnic policies and practices between 1911 and 1949. This will not be attempted in this inquiry. To clarify the context of the CCP's activities, however, it is necessary to highlight the Chinese Nationalists' response to certain important issues that the Qing bequeathed to China's political elites in the twentieth century.

A fundamental change brought to China's political life by the Qing's demise was the decline of ethnicity. The Qing was an ethnopolitical enterprise for three centuries. A key to the "Manchu way" of ruling China, as Mark Elliott contends, was to maintain the Manchus' "ethnic sovereignty" over the Han and non-Han populations. This was achieved by institutionalizing the Manchu identity with the banner system.[76] To continue their rule of China, the Manchu ruling family conducted ethnopolitics skillfully and identified the Manchus, the Mongols, the Tibetans, the Hui, and the Han as its five "imperial constituencies."[77] To the Qing rulers, nothing was more important than diligently maintaining the delicate balance among these constituencies on a daily basis. The high visibility of these ethnic categories in the Qing's time and the "territorial" character of some of the non-Han groups are among the "traditional sources" of modern China's ethnopolitics.[78]

The Chinese Nationalists flirted with these categories only briefly. After the Han again became the "ruling stock" in China, the Nationalists understood the significance of the numerically much smaller frontier peoples mainly in China's relations with those territorially voracious neighboring powers. For this reason, Sun Yat-sen and associates suspended their earlier anti-Manchu program and embraced a "five-race republic" formula. During most of the republican period, however, the KMT's policy was to repress any overt display of ethnic identity by the non-Han peoples. In this regard, they were tapping China's pre-Qing tradition of treating the Yi not as a permanent and equal kind with the Hua but as immature peoples to be sinicized.

The partisans of twentieth-century China treated the Qing's territorial legacy in a similarly ambivalent way. From Sun Yat-sen to Jiang Jieshi, the Nationalist leadership was never in doubt about "grand unity" as China's normality,[79] though they could not give the Qing, the target of their revolution, the credit for fleshing out the ancient ideal. In practice, nevertheless, they just continued the late Qing's effort to "nationalize" the empire. The difference between the Manchu rulers of the late Qing and the KMT is that the former never got the chance to preside over China in the name of a nation-state, and the latter proclaimed a nation-state but never had the fortune to rule all of China. Therefore, during its less than forty-year life span on the mainland, the Republic of China existed as an awkward political-territorial entity not only because its leaders endeavored to stretch the "short, tight, skin" of the "Chinese nation" "over the gigantic body" of the Qing Empire[80] but also because none of the Republic's governments ever amassed the strength to restore China's lost and alienated territories to match its sweeping irredentist claims.

At the time of the Qing's demise, as far as the non-Han borderlands were concerned, the centralization process started by the Manchu court was reversed. During most of the republican period and in different ways, Mongolia, Xinjiang, and Tibet remained beyond the reach of the "central" government of China. But the very contumacy of these territories only made the KMT more impressive as a successor to the Qing Empire. With the exception of Outer Mongolia, which achieved complete independence via a Sino–Soviet treaty of 1945, the Nationalist government managed to convince the international community to accept its territorial definition of China. The KMT succeeded in this regard not because it "nationalized the property of the [Qing] imperial household."[81] The Republic of China never achieved this in reality. The Nationalist government's achievement was entirely modern and foreign to China's tradition; it played the diplomatic game of the nation-states well and used the Western, sovereign-mania system to block both the borderlands' complete separation and foreign powers' total control therein.[82]

To deny the non-Han borderlands their own statehood was one thing, but to enlist them as loyal members of a new China was entirely another. The interethnic power transition from the Manchus to the Han elites in 1911 put the peripheral ethnic groups' loyalty to the center on hold. As an ethnic minority that ruled China, the Manchus had justified their legitimacy either with their alleged connections to the Confucian tradition or with arguments on their own virtues favored by heaven.[83] Yet their actual command of the other ethnic constituencies' loyalty was mainly based on the simple logic of military conquest. The end of the Qing also ended the rally center for all under heaven. To the successor Chinese Republic, Sun Yat-sen assigned a task in his ubiquitous inscription, "all under heaven is for all" (*tian xia wei gong*). With this axiom, Sun probably aimed to prod the autocratic Chinese society into a journey of democratization. Ethnopolitically, however, Sun's message could also be understood as a call for a new polyethnic accord in China based on equality.

Yet later developments proved that this was not the KMT's policy. The KMT substituted the Qing's uni-ethnic imperial center with a single-race republic. In the name of the "Chinese nation" (*zhonghua minzu*), the KMT government demanded that non-Han groups to assimilate themselves into a Han-centric, "newly amalgamated 'race.'"[84] The coinage of *zhonghua minzu* was a good example of combining ethnocultural conservatism with political progressivism. To its Chinese audience, the term literally meant the "central Hua nation." Whereas *minzu* (nation or, literally, people's clan) denoted the instinctively popular and egalitarian connotation of modern nationalism,[85] *zhonghua* carried the full meaning of the ethnocultural stratifications in Chinese history. No single authorship could be claimed for the hybrid. The term was probably coined about the time of the Revolution of 1911 and was perhaps related to the choice of the name for the new Chinese Republic, *zhonghua minguo* (literally, central Hua people's state).[86]

E. J. Hobsbawm takes China as one of the rare examples in world history where ethnicity and popular political loyalty are linked.[87] Such a linkage was probably in the minds of the proponents of *zhonghua minzu* and *zhonghua minguo* who had their eyes on the Han populace as the fodder of China's Revolution. But it soon became clear to the Chinese Nationalists that anti-Manchu Chinese ethnicism was useful only for one political action (the Revolution of 1911). After that, anti-Manchuism became antiquated for China's Nationalist revolution against foreign imperialism. The switch made by the Chinese Nationalists from Chinese ethnicism to Chinese nationalism was abrupt but never complete. Consequently, although the "Chinese nation" theme served China well in its modern anti-imperialist struggle, the conception was unilateral, arbitrary, and repulsive to the Han's non-Han peers in China's interior and borderlands.[88]

In sum, although numerous historical precedents and "traditions" can be used to qualify and characterize the ethnic aspect of modern China's political and social life, it is the Qing that prepared the immediate ethnopolitical hotbed for China's modern nationhood to grow. With this in the backdrop, Chinese leaders throughout the twentieth century could not avoid dealing with the "national question," a modern variation of the infinite Hua–Yi relationship. They had to calculate the intensity of the question in the Chinese state's domestic and foreign affairs. In dealing with the many facets of China's ethnopolitics, the KMT government prioritized "territories" over "people," foreign diplomacy over domestic reforms, political-military suppression over socioeconomic and cultural engagement. The KMT's relentless drive for achieving administrative uniformity and for consolidating national defense rendered the ethnic policies of the Republic of China a barren landscape. As a matter of fact, the KMT government never had an ethnic policy as such. The government pushed for assimilating the non-Han peoples of the borderlands but viewed the process as merely part of its "frontier administration" (*bian zheng*).[89]

Thus, when the CCP entered China's ethnopolitics in the early 1920s, it entered a rather rich and peculiar culture that had a long past and remained dynamic. Since the mid–nineteenth century or even earlier, under the impact of the West, China's ethnopolitics had been transformed from an ethnocultural process to a "nationalizing" enterprise. The separation between foreign and domestic affairs had resulted in both the externalization of China's relations with foreign countries and the internalization of the center–periphery relationship within the now bordered Chinese state. When the Marxist-Leninist subject "national question" was introduced into China, it was principally targeted at this internalized center–periphery relationship. If seen within the ideological paradigm discussed above, the CCP seems to have served largely as a syringe that injected foreign communist dogmas into China's ethnopolitical culture. This approach, intentionally or not, puts the CCP squarely in opposition to China's nationalizing enterprise because, by nature, communism is supranational. Yet history has taught us that communism in its theoretical sense has not been practiced in any place, not even in the artificial Soviet Union. How, then, can the CCP be understood only or mainly as a Chinese vehicle for imported communism?

This study returns the CCP to China's own mainstream state affairs in the twentieth century, which aimed to transform China from a traditional, ethnocultural entity into a modern nation-state. The injection of communism, as suggested by Benjamin Schwarz, did further complicate the process, but it by no means altered the direction of China's nationalizing enterprise. As for the CCP, its historical mission included both serving as a syringe of communism and acting as an agent of Chinese nationalism. If this double identity appears contradictory, this is how the CCP participated in China's historical renewal.

In this study, the evolution of the CCP's ethnopolitics between 1921 and 1945 is highlighted with an ancient conception from China's ethnocultural tradition, *hua,* which means "change" or "transform" and can be best transliterated with the suffix "-ize" in English. When they could afford to be open-minded, Confucianists in Chinese history believed that the barriers between the Han Chinese and the barbarians could be crossed because the latter were "longing for becoming" (*xiang hua*) Chinese. The KMT government's assimilation policy for the non-Han groups was to "change" them "into the same" or "into Han"(*tong hua* or *han hua*). Unlike the Confucianists and the KMT, the CCP did not find its own ethnopolitical axis immediately. The search process was more concerned with what the CCP itself would become than what the CCP would do about the non-Han peoples.

During the period under consideration, the CCP's ethnopolitics was successively "Bolshevized," "sovietized," "northernized," "nationalized," and "borderized." These conceptions are used as the titles of this inquiry's five main chapters. Each of these phases added a certain new element or elements to the CCP's understanding and conduct of ethnopolitics and also modified or deemphasized other previously existing elements. The CCP's Communist ideology was only partially responsible for these changes; its cultural inheritance, political conditions, and physical environments played far more important roles than have usually been understood.

2

Bolshevization: Limitations of Conversion

In the wake of the Revolution of 1911, the greatest disappointment for China's reformers and revolutionaries alike was that the ineffective Qing Empire was replaced only by a dysfunctional republic. During its first few emperorless years, China's intensified external crises and internal chaos made the Chinese Republic a cure even worse than the Manchu imperial disease. The circumstances fostered a wide range of political ideas and movements but appointed none as the definitive design for a new China. In 1916, exasperated by Japan's new scheme (the Twenty-One Demands) to take advantage of China's weakness, the young Mao Zedong wrote to a friend:

> [China] is ten thousand *li* [Chinese miles] in length and breadth but has submitted herself to the three [Japanese] islands; [China] has four hundred million people but has allowed them to be enslaved by the thirty million [Japanese]. Should Manchuria and Mongolia be lost, the northern frontiers would be shaken and the barbarians' cavalries [*hu qi*] would pour into the Central Plains. . . . Within twenty years [China's] survival will have to be settled by war [with Japan].[1]

Mao's prediction of a war between China and Japan would miss by only a year. In 1937, an undeclared Chinese–Japanese war would start. In 1916, however, Mao's words mostly reflected an emotion shared by many of his contemporaries. The emotion showed a bitter anti–foreign imperialism and meanwhile harbored a deep concern about China's own imperial domains such as Manchuria and Mongolia. Not long after the overthrow of the Qing, China's nationalists became accustomed to the idea that the survival of the

27

young Chinese Republic was tied to the integrity and security of the late Qing's territories.

Yet it would have been against Mao's iconoclastic nature for him to care only about keeping China intact. In his thinking, he was one of the least inhibited revolutionaries in history. To him, no establishment was sacred and untouchable, including the very entity of China. Although he might have considered Manchuria and Mongolia important for China's national defense, at the time he did not at all view the "grand unity" of China, either in the form of the Qing Empire or any of the earlier dynasties, as a necessary condition for the new China. As a matter of fact, in 1920, one year before the Chinese Communist Party (CCP) was established, Mao unequivocally voiced his objection to the idea that, to survive, China had to remain a unified "big country" (*daguo*).

In a series of articles for the Hunan edition of the *Da Gong Bao* (Grand Public Daily), Mao contended that all the twenty-four dynasties in Chinese history were "storied buildings set on sand" and that each of them had managed to last for some time only because its rulers had been willing to "kill so many people." He compared China's control of the non-Han frontier regions with the Western powers' scramble for overseas colonies, which had resulted in the "Manchus' disappearance and the near extinction of the Mongols, Hui, and Tibetans." According to him, the basis for a "China in reality" had never existed. For China, "the best solution is not to seek a general reconstruction"; China's "twenty-two provinces, three special districts, and two dependent regions [*fan di*] . . . should better be separated into twenty-seven states."[2] He would soon retreat from his "separatist" stand, which looked extreme even to many of his fellow revolutionaries.[3] Yet his case shows that if left to their own devices, the Chinese revolutionaries would have pursued many different paths to national salvation.

During the twentieth century, the two revolutions in China and Russia crossed their paths. The encounter changed the courses of both and had a maximal impact on the Chinese side. Before the Russian Revolution, Marxism was only one of the few Western radical ideologies that competed with one another for converts in China. After the Bolsheviks took power in Russia, backed by the new Soviet state and preached diligently by agents of the Communist International (Comintern), Marxism soon became an appealing "organizational ideology" for China's most radical revolutionaries.[4] The CCP was born as a result.

In its historical evolution, Chinese Communism is a phenomenon growing from Chinese nationalist roots nurtured by China's peculiar cultural soil and historical conditions. As in many other Asian countries, the rendezvous between Chinese nationalism and Marxism is curious because, theoretically, Marxism is the very antithesis of nationalism. The Russian Bolsheviks, the medium that quickened Marxism in China, distinguished themselves in World War I by their supranational programs.[5]

But the members of the young CCP in the early 1920s were not in a quandary of self-contradiction. They were yet to develop the necessary theoretical sophistication for becoming conscious of the discrepancy between Marxist internationalism and their own nationalist proclivity. Their conversion to Marxism was not based on a thorough intellectual digestion of Marxist theories. When the CCP was established, only a very small Marxist literature was available in Chinese.[6] But this situation did not diminish a bit Chinese revolutionaries' action-oriented urge or prevent them from having their own communist organization.

In this sense, the CCP's adoption of the Bolshevik brand of Marxism was almost inevitable because at the time only Soviet Russia and the Comintern were able to provide the CCP with the necessary organizational guide. What followed the party organization was a period of "very conscious and intense ideological building," a process dubbed in communist literature as "Bolshevization."[7] This was a two-way process in which the Russian Bolsheviks were anxious to indoctrinate their new Chinese comrades and the Chinese Communists were anxious to duplicate the successful Russian model of revolution.

During the CCP's initial years, the Marxist-Leninist dogmas on "class struggles" and the "national question" became two of the most important ideas injected into the Chinese revolution. Yet these did not come to China as universal decrees but, as the term Bolshevization indicated, as precedents produced in Russia's cultural and political conditions. The degree of incompatibility between the Bolshevik models and China's conditions would soon be exposed.

Anti-Imperialism in Two Tones

In the last years of his life, Vladimir Lenin warned his associates that "no single issue was more decisive for the future destiny of the revolutionary state than a national policy leading to the transcending of all nationalism."[8] Setting the "proletarian dictatorship" in Russia as their immediate revolutionary goal, the Bolsheviks nevertheless had to cope with nationalism, which, by their definition, was "bourgeois" in nature and therefore a negative force. The multinational character of the tsarist empire, in which ethnic Russians accounted for less than half of the total population, necessitated both Bolshevik theories and tactics in dealing with the "national question."

In their struggle for power, to achieve a supranational "proletarian unity" in Russia, the Bolsheviks were first compelled to reverse the tsarist policy of national suppression. Lenin's formidable criticism of international imperialism had to be translated into actions first and foremost in Russia. During and after World War I, the Bolsheviks endeavored to gain sympathy from the non-Russian peoples in the former tsarist empire. They adjusted their "national policy" according to the fluctuating military and political conditions in Europe and Russia. At first, they supported the establishment of the non-Russian peoples' own republics, but then they demanded that these new republics join a Soviet federation.

While achieving the upper hand in Russia's civil war, the Bolsheviks' formula gradually changed from a nation-centered theme regarding the "right of peoples to self-determination" to a class-based argument about the "right of the working class to consolidate its power." By 1924, the Bolsheviks completed the reunification of the former Russian empire in the form of the new Soviet state. At this juncture, Lenin's agents to the non-Russian territories and the disheartened "national communists" in these areas remained in agreement on only one thing: The Bolshevik revolution in these territories increasingly took a "colonist character."[9]

Bolshevism was unsuitable for China's communists in both a positive and a negative sense. On one hand, fewer than 10 percent of China's population were non-Han, and therefore the "national question" that was troubling the Bolsheviks in Russia seemed marginal in China. On the other hand, China did not have a sizable industrial working class, and thus there was not much of a basis for beginning a "proletarian revolution" in the first place. Yet the Bolshevization of China's radicals was a very crude form of indoctrination.

The Chinese revolutionaries just picked what they needed from the foreign ideology. Although China had an overwhelming Han populace, its first revolution in the twentieth century did indeed deal with the "national question" in a reversed sense: the Han majority's grievances against the Manchu ruling minority. After the overthrow of the Qing, the Chinese Nationalists decided to shelve their anti-Manchu doctrine to maintain an ethnically and territorially unified China. As a result, their revolution began to lose momentum because it lacked a clearly defined internal adversary. The Chinese Communists avoided this fate by adopting the Marxist doctrine of class struggle, which could be applied to situations other than a proletarian–bourgeois confrontation. In 1927, for instance, when Mao defined the Chinese revolution as a "rebellion, a violent action in which one class overthrows another," he substituted the proletarian–bourgeois confrontation with a peasant–landlord conflict.[10]

Mao was creative in his use of the class struggle doctrine. But in the CCP's early years, his ideas were regarded as unorthodox within the party and were by no means dominant. When the Chinese Communists first learned from the Bolshevik model of revolution, what generally happened was their substituting of "the cliches of Bolshevism . . . for independent analysis" of China's problems.[11] During the CCP's founding conference in the summer of 1921, the delegates were rather dogmatic in focusing their attention on how to organize China's tiny urban working classes.[12] At a time when the Chinese peasants, the vast majority of the Han population, were overlooked, the question of the non-Han peoples, who were habitually viewed as part of the remote borderlands, seemed even less relevant to the young CCP.

If the Chinese Communists were enthused by the Leninist tenet on the "national question," it was because Leninism treated revolutions in Asian colonies and semicolonies as part of the world proletarian revolution. There is no evidence suggesting that at the time of the CCP's inauguration its members had any knowledge about the long and complex debate on the "national question" within the European socialist movement.[13] Neither did the CCP members' own backgrounds give any reason for them to be concerned about China's own "national question." It has been accurately pointed out that at the beginning the CCP was an "intellectual's party" devoid of any laboring elements.[14] Actually, the CCP's early members were overwhelmingly Han intellectuals from eastern and southeastern China. Some of them might be familiar with China's traditional Hua–Yi discourse, but this group did not have any first-hand knowledge about the conditions of the non-Han peoples and China's internal ethnopolitics.[15]

Thus, in the summer of 1922, when the CCP leadership suddenly showed an interest in China's own "national question" during the party's Second National Congress, the interest could only be adventitious. In the background were several events that had happened a few months earlier in Moscow. In January of the year, the Comintern sponsored the First Congress of Toilers of the Far East in Moscow. The Chinese delegation to the occasion included representatives of the Kuomintang (KMT, or National People's Party), the CCP, and some other groups. At a session, the Chinese delegates were unexpectedly exposed to a barrage of criticisms from the Comintern leadership and the Mongolian delegation against China's traditional relationship with Mongolia. While some KMT delegates tried to defend the "Chinese" position, the CCP delegates were put on the spot to take a stand in favor of the Comintern leadership.

Probably having been alerted by this event, Zhang Guotao and Qu Qiubai, two founding members of the CCP present at the Moscow conference, diligently collected documents on the "national question" that had been adopted a year before by the Comintern's Second Congress. According to Zhang Guotao's recollection, before this time, the CCP had learned from Maring (a.k.a. Hendricus Sneevliet), a Comintern agent in China, only fragmentary information about a Comintern resolution on the national and colonial questions. The Moscow conference therefore was the CCP's first opportunity to learn systematically about the Soviet leadership's intentions on these matters. Zhang and Qu obtained these documents in both English and Russian versions. After translating the documents into Chinese, they dispatched the new set of Bolshevik dogmas to the CCP leadership in China.[16]

Despite the marginal significance of China's ethnic minorities to the Chinese Communist movement at the time, the CCP's "waking up" to China's "national question" constituted a vital development in the party's history. This is so not because the development opened a new venue for the CCP's activities in China but because it enhanced the party's relationship with Moscow. The Bolsheviks—directing revolutionary movements in the world from Moscow in a manner comparable to Vatican's presiding over its overseas missions—demanded that fellow communists in foreign countries follow their own organizational and doctrinal models. To complete its Bolshevization, therefore, the CCP had to adopt the whole Soviet package, including the program against one's own country's imperialism. Thus the CCP's previously one-dimensional anti–foreign imperialism, which was "petty bourgeois" by the Bolshevik definition, had to be supplemented and purified by a new, conscientious objection to China's own imperialist suppression of the non-Han peoples.

During its Second National Congress, the CCP resolved to become a formal "Chinese branch" of the Comintern. To qualify, the party was obliged to adopt the Bolshevik formula for a two-dimensional anti-imperialism, which was spelled out in the Comintern's requirements for prospective member parties:

As for the question of colonies and oppressed peoples, there ought to be an especially clear orientation for those parties in countries where the bourgeoisie possesses such colonies or oppresses other nations. Every party desirous of becoming part of the Third International must sternly denounce "his ferocious imperialists' tyrannical suppression of the colonies"; [the party] needs to support the liberation movements in such colonies not only in word but also in deed, demanding the expulsion of the imperialists from the colonies, fostering a genuine friendship between its own nation's laborers and the colonial laborers and the oppressed peoples, and maintaining a continuous movement in the army of the suzerain country against its suppression of the colonial peoples.[17]

Whereas Moscow raised the "national question" to the level of a touchstone, differentiating a "genuine" proletarian party from a bourgeois one, the CCP anxiously embraced the Comintern formula in its entirety. In the Second National Congress's final series of documents, the CCP for the first time attempted to articulate an attitude toward China's own "national question."

The timing of the CCP's adoption of the Comintern formula is ironic. This was a time when the Soviet regime in Russia began increasingly to apply a policy of "colonist character" to its non-Russian fellow republics. Then, in China, if China's ethnic frontiers in the north and west should be viewed as its colonies, the so-called central government of China had lost its ability to carry out the "ferocious imperialists' tyrannical suppression" for some time. The embryonic CCP, of course, had neither the information nor the ability to question the empire building by Soviet Russia. At the time, even the independent-minded Mao admitted that the Chinese comrades, including himself, lacked both theories and experiences and therefore "always believed in the correctness of the leading comrades [in Moscow]."[18]

Therefore, according to the CCP's Second National Congress, the Chinese revolution would necessarily assume two liberation tasks, one for "China proper" (*benbu*) and the other for the "frontier regions" (*jiangbu*). As for the relationship between the two sections, the CCP contended that China proper, *including* Manchuria, was in the early stage of capitalist development and was therefore relatively advanced. But the frontier regions—meaning Mongolia, Tibet, and the northwestern Muslim territories (*Huijiang*)—had historically been inhabited by several "alien races" (*yizhong minzu*) that remained in primitive, nomadic conditions.

The socioeconomic differences between the two sections of China proper and the frontier regions, compounded by the land-grabbing warfare among the Chinese warlords, made their unification not only impossible but also undesirable. Therefore, in China proper the warlord regimes first had to be eliminated and replaced with a unified democratic republic. In the frontier regions, the current task was to establish "democratic and self-governing states (*minzhu zizhibang*)." Only after these tasks were accomplished and only on the basis of a "free federation principle" could a Chinese federation of republics be established and China proper and the frontier regions be reunified.[19]

The CCP program summarized above exhibited both historical residuals and departures. It provided no new insight on the conditions of either the Han or the non-Han societies of China. The alleged socioeconomic dichotomy between China proper and the frontier regions massively distorted the much more complex situations in both. The contention actually continued the old Hua–Yi stratification but replaced the old ethnoculture premise with a superficially deployed Marxist terminology.

Another historical legacy can be seen in the fact that the CCP followed the "frontier administration" tradition of the Qing Empire and gave no recognition to the non-Han ethnic groups living in China proper. The CCP documents' choice to use "alien races" to name the non-Han peoples also betrayed their authors' upbringing with Confucian classics, which contained the often quoted utterance "those who are not our kinds must have alien hearts (*fei wo zu lie qi xin bi yi*)." Conversely, although not explicitly categorizing the borderlands as China's colonies, the CCP program departed from the Sinocentric normality of "grand unity" and was willing to support the separation and reunification between China proper and the non-Han regions on an equal footing. Coming from a nationalist root and brought up within the Chinese cultural tradition, these scholar-party members certainly did not relinquish their conviction in China's "reunification."

In the next year, 1923, Chen Duxiu and Li Dazhao, the two top founding members of the CCP, engaged each other in a debate on the future form of the Chinese state. They respectively argued for a uniform and a federal state organization, but both agreed on China's unification.[20] Unlike the Chinese Nationalists, who intended to continue the Qing Empire in the form of the Chinese Republic, the Chinese Communists did not pledge allegiance to the KMT's state building. They preferred to refer to China with the generic name *zhongguo* (middle kingdom or state) and suggested a "free union" principle for redefining the relationship between the Han-dominated state and the non-Han groups. This did not mean that the CCP identified any political group within the non-Han peoples with which to work. But, for the moment, it was more important for the CCP to satisfy Moscow by stating its support of these peoples' right to their own "democratic self-governing states."[21]

The early 1920s was a period during which both the CCP and the KMT competed for Moscow's endorsement. Moscow identified Sun Yat-sen's party as its principal collaborator in China and instructed the CCP to cooperate with the KMT.[22] Unable to compete with the KMT for the number one position in receiving Moscow's assistance, the CCP, by becoming a full-fledged Comintern branch, nevertheless gained an ideological edge over the KMT, which had a nationalist orientation.

By any account, Moscow was the real beneficiary of the CCP's Bolshevization, which made the CCP an obedient instrument of Moscow's policies. In late 1923, when commenting on a KMT program, the CCP leadership lectured the KMT that its "nationalism" should include both an external aspect opposing foreign imperialism and an internal focus on "removing our own repression of the small and weak nationalities of the colonies (such as Mongolia and Tibet)."[23]

This CCP critique of the KMT was made at the time in coordination with Moscow's pressure on the KMT to change its orientation toward China's "domestic" nationalities, especially Outer Mongolia. However, when Moscow's separate dealings with the CCP and the KMT are evaluated together, it becomes clear that the Bolsheviks were far from seeking a revolutionary solution of China's "national question" by the Chinese themselves.

Containing the Chinese Revolution

There is a general agreement in the field that despite the Bolsheviks' claims for historical departures, Soviet foreign policy in the Far East continued tsarist Russia's objectives and tactics.[24] Along with the United Kingdom and Japan, revolutionary Russia retained tsarist Russia's image in the Chinese Nationalists' eyes as one of China's principal foreign adversaries. Yet in certain aspects, Soviet Russia did make a departure from its predecessors and was unique among foreign powers in China. During China's republican period (1911–49), the Soviet Union was the only foreign power that could continually reverse the Chinese statecraft of "using barbarians to control barbarians" and play one organized Chinese force against another. In the short run, Chinese political groups' desperate need for foreign support provided the Soviets with opportunities for manipulation. In the long run, however, Moscow's cynical policy behavior was bound to collide with the interests of its temporary Chinese collaborators.

The ascendance of Bolshevism in Russia did not alter but intensified the geopolitics of Eastern and Central Asia. After taking power in Russia, the Bolsheviks only briefly flirted with a "new diplomacy" toward China. In July 1919, Moscow issued a declaration renouncing all the old treaties between tsarist Russia and China. Three years later, however, Joseph Stalin told Soviet representatives in China in a telegram: "In the [Soviet Communist Party] center's opinion, when negotiating with China, the general declaration of 1919 and 1920 must not be allowed to serve as the basis of direct policy directives, [because] then the Chinese government did not react correspondingly to the declaration."[25]

In the 1920s, as Moscow pursued a buffer-zone strategy with regard to China's borderlands in the north and northwest, it had an opportunity to sport a triple play. Its official diplomacy engaged in negotiations with the nominal central government in Peking, which since the fall of the Qing had a revolving door used by different groups of military strongmen. In the meantime, Moscow provided political advice and military assistance to the KMT that openly challenged the legitimacy of the Peking government. This policy was further supplemented with the CCP's united-front orientation under the Comintern's direction, which could apply pressure on the KMT leadership from within.

The Kremlin's recent residents paid close attention to the "national question" in the Chinese revolution neither because they valued the revolution's "theoretical correctness" nor because they believed that the revolution urgently needed a nationality-sensitive strategy. Instead, they worked to foster a revolutionary movement in China that could follow an orientation compatible with Soviet foreign policy agenda in Asia. China's "national question" was particularly relevant to the Soviet strategy in Central Asia. As far as China's "minorities" were concerned, Soviet leaders were interested only in the three prized territories of the old "Great Game": Mongolia, Chinese Turkestan (Xinjiang), and Tibet. That is why the Comintern beseeched the CCP to form a "correct attitude" toward China's peripheral "colonies" but had nothing to offer to enlighten the CCP's understanding of China's ethnic conditions as a whole.

In the early 1920s, the revolutionary "spillover" from Russia to Mongolia and Xinjiang provided opportunities to the Bolsheviks. They sent troops into both regions in "hot pursuit" of counterrevolutionary Russian forces and eventually fostered a separate state in Mongolia. Nor did the Bolshevik leaders overlook Tibet. The Lamaist government received communications from Russia's atheistic new rulers, who were interested in sending "scholarly delegations" to the Buddhist land. Moscow even promised support to Lhasa in the event that Tibet, an "apparently independent" state, was attacked by its "certain neighbor."[26] The certain neighbor could meant either British India or China. In Moscow's endeavors, the Bolshevized CCP became a useful assistant, whereas the nationalistic KMT remained an obstacle.

Whereas the CCP's interest in the "national question" remained doctrinal, the KMT leadership harbored a genuine intention to extend their revolution into the non-Han borderlands. Operating from a nationalist premise, the KMT leaders were much more susceptible than the CCP to the situation of China's borderlands. They were not enchanted at all by Moscow's intentions about Mongolia and Xinjiang. Having grown out of an originally racial revolution against the Manchu rule of China, the KMT was no novice to China's ethnopolitics. When the Bolsheviks tasted state power in Russia, the KMT's "five-race republic" formula was already six years old. Therefore, when entering into cooperation with the Bolsheviks in the early 1920s, the KMT leaders only sought tangible assistance to gain the state power that had eluded them since 1911 but not foreign ideas to redefine China. Prompted by their weak position in southern China, the KMT leaders contemplated a strategic plan to use Mongolia and Xinjiang as the party's new bases in the power contest with China's warlords. This presented the Soviet leaders with a problem of balancing their objectives *within* and *on the verge* of China.

Sun Yat-sen himself was an enthusiastic advocate of the northwestern strategy. Between 1920 and 1923, he more than once discussed the plan with Soviet agents in China and in his communications with leaders in Moscow. He contended that Mongolia and Xinjiang were the doorways for the Chinese revolution to receive material or even direct military assistance from the Bolsheviks.[27] The most serious effort to enlist the Russians' support for the idea was made by Jiang Jieshi, Sun's trusted military aide at the time. From early September to late November 1923, on behalf of Sun, Jiang led a military delegation to Moscow.

Soon after his arrival, Jiang told his hosts that his mission was to discuss with Soviet leaders a plan for a geostrategic relocation of the Chinese revolution. In a lengthy memorandum titled "The New Prospect of the Chinese Revolution," Jiang summarized the strategy conceived by Sun and his military staff. The plan was to move the headquarters of the Chinese revolution from the Western powers' sphere of influence in southern China to the close neighborhood of Soviet Russia in Mongolia or Xinjiang. Depending on which of the two regions was selected as the KMT base, the Chinese revolutionaries would need two to five years to make military preparations with Moscow's assistance.

Afterward, decisive southward expeditions could be launched from the KMT base to destroy the warlords and reunify China. Sun personally preferred the Mongolian option. The advantages of Mongolia, according to Jiang's presentation, included its geographic proximity to China's political centers, especially Peking, and its less complex "national question" than the Muslim issue of Xinjiang. Although mindful of possible British and Japanese reactions to KMT–Soviet cooperation in Xinjiang or Mongolia, Jiang dismissed any likelihood that these powers would intervene.[28]

Although the KMT plan seemed to provide a perfect scenario for KMT–Soviet cooperation as well as for implementing the "national liberation" scheme for the ethnic groups in the borderlands concerned, Jiang had to wait two months before receiving a negative response from the Soviet leadership. To Jiang, the development was both disappointing and surprising. Before Jiang's trip to Moscow, Sun had discussed the plan with Adolf Joffe, the Soviet representative in China. Joffe had embraced the idea of forging a KMT–Soviet partnership in northwestern China and also sent his opinion back to Moscow.[29]

Yet Joffe had fallen out of step on this matter with his leaders in Moscow. Specifically, Joffe and Moscow had different ideas about Mongolia. In reality, after World War I, when turning their attention from the reactionary West to the revolutionary "Orient," Bolshevik leaders opted to view China and Mongolia as two separate arenas. Thus, when the "Oriental work" was first created by a "department of Oriental nations" under the Siberian Bureau of the Russian Communist Party, it set up one office on China and another on Mongolia and Tibet. This approach proved to be in concert with the Soviet government's foreign policy and would be continued by the Comintern in later years. By the time of Jiang's mission, the Soviet government had already decided to maintain Mongolia's de facto separation from China so that Mongolia could serve as a buffer against Japanese influence in North China and Manchuria. An extension of the KMT's influence into Mongolia was therefore viewed by Soviet leaders as highly inconvenient to their objectives.[30]

But such a selfish consideration was not presentable in dealing with the KMT delegation. Before the formal rejection was delivered to the Chinese,

Georgi Chicherin, Russia's people's commissar for foreign affairs, approached Jiang and suggested that the KMT should probably postpone its plan for now because the Mongols were scared of the Chinese. Jiang responded by contending that the KMT's nationalism was for cooperation between equal nationalities but not for national separation. He also stated frankly that one of the objectives of the KMT's northwestern plan was to solve China's "national question." On November 12, when the Soviet military authorities received the KMT delegation to comment officially on its northwestern plan, a different line of suasion was tried. Jiang was told that the KMT should follow the Bolsheviks' model of making long-term, patient political preparations before taking any military action in China.

Accordingly, the Soviets explained, the KMT at present ought to devote its energy mainly to indoctrinating and mobilizing the working class and the peasants in China proper. A few days later, when G. Ye. Zinoviev, chairman of the Comintern Executive Committee, and several other Comintern officials conversed with the KMT delegation, the same line was applied again. On that occasion, Jiang was quizzed about the situation of classes and the land question in China. Zinoviev complained that the KMT had so far neglected China's working-class movement and urged the Chinese to put Sun's "Three People's Principles" into "more concrete and more unequivocal" terms.

After the meeting, annoyed but undaunted, Jiang sought to salvage his plan in an interview with Leon Trotsky, then chair of the Soviet Revolutionary Military Council. But he only got an uncalled-for encore of the same Soviet performance. Trotsky told Jiang that "a good newspaper is superior to a poor army division" and that at present the KMT "must firmly and sharply turn the wheel of its political direction" by "focusing all its attention on political works and reducing its military activities to the necessary minimum." When the political conditions of China became ready, Trotsky promised, the Soviet government would then be able to provide assistance to the KMT. But even then, Trotsky added, the KMT should "launch military operations from the territory of its own country but not from Mongolia."[31] The last remark betrayed the Soviet leader's true concerns.

Clearly, at the time the Soviet intention was more anti-Japanese than anti-Chinese. Nevertheless, the incongruity between what Moscow did with its left hand and with its right hand is dumbfounding. In the 1920s, the CCP and the KMT were two wings of the same Chinese revolutionary movement. Though the former learned from Moscow that it must assume the task of national liberation not only for China but also for the non-Han peoples at China's peripheries, the other was told not to extend the Chinese revolution to the borderlands at all.

For Moscow's purposes, this double play had a consistent objective. The CCP was then just a party of political ideas but not a force of military substance. Its adoption of the Comintern formula on the "national question" allowed the Soviets to inject an idea onto China's political arena that supported the non-Han peoples' right to self-determination. It was hoped that this could somewhat soften Chinese resistance to the Soviets' maneuvering with the ethnic groups in China's borderlands.[32] As for the KMT, the party capable of military-political actions, it must be told where to stop. In the "Great Game" for Central Asia, Moscow did not want any Chinese force, whether revolutionary or warlord in character, to disturb its delicate balance with Japan and the United Kingdom.

To later developments in China, Jiang's mission had three significant consequences. First, the encounter between Jiang and Soviet leaders in Moscow led the latter to intensify their effort to "correct" the KMT's attitude toward the non-Han peoples in China's borderlands. On November 28, the day before Jiang's mission returned to China, the presidium of the Comintern Executive Committee passed a resolution on the KMT and the Chinese revolution. The resolution directly suggested that the KMT reinterpret its "Three People's Principles." Among the three principles, the Comintern devoted the better part of its "concrete and unequivocal" advice to the "nationalism" doctrine.

For the external aspect of Chinese nationalism, the Comintern urged the KMT to develop a "healthy anti-imperialist movement" based on solid work with China's laboring classes. For the internal aspect, the Comintern reminded the KMT that because of the Chinese authorities' suppressive policy in the past, the "minority nationalities" of China were suspicious of even the KMT's intentions. Therefore, "the KMT must not rush to establish cooperation with the minority nationalities in an organizational form, and, for the present, it should limit its work to propaganda and agitation." The resolution urged the KMT to openly support China's minorities' right to self-determination and to pledge to put the principle into practice when the victory of the Chinese revolution would allow "the nationalities of the former Chinese empire" to form a "free Chinese federation of republics."[33]

Sun, still anxious to cooperate with the Soviet government, decided to heed Moscow's advice despite Jiang's misgivings. In January 1924, the KMT held a national congress to reorganize the party and to launch officially a united front with the CCP. A new KMT program was proclaimed by the congress, and principles from the aforementioned Comintern resolution were incorporated into the program. With CCP members' active participation in its drafting, the proclamation became the first official document in Chinese history that referred to China's non-Han peoples as "minority nationalities," a conception coined by the Comintern.[34]

Thus, at least on paper, Moscow seemed to be successful in Bolshevizing the KMT's stand on the "national question." The expedient nature of the move on the KMT's part, however, did not escape the eyes of Soviet agents in China. Soon after the KMT congress, Michael Borodin, Sun's Soviet adviser and the architect of the new KMT–CCP coalition, noted in his report to Moscow that Sun personified the "worst contradiction" of the Chinese nationalist movement. In Borodin's opinion, Sun on the one hand saluted Lenin's creed but on the other continued to flirt with Western imperialism and to display Chinese chauvinism against the "minority nationalities." So Borodin did not stop goading the KMT leaders to put their words into deeds.[35]

The second result of Jiang's trip to Russia was to turn him into an anti-Soviet zealot. Before his mission, Jiang had been a staunch advocate of forging a KMT–Soviet military partnership in the northwest. In Moscow, he first felt belittled by the Soviet leaders' tardy response to his proposed plan and then felt cheated after learning about Moscow's true intentions in Outer Mongolia.[36] After returning to China, Jiang wrote a letter to Liao Zhongkai, a left-wing leader of the KMT, contending that the Soviet policy was to promote the CCP in China but not to seek honest cooperation with the KMT. But his bitterness against Moscow was more nationalist than partisan:

As for its [Soviet Russia's] China policy, the purpose is to turn Manchuria, Mongolia, Hui [territory], and Tibet into its soviets, and probably to have a hand in China proper as well. . . . Its so-called internationalism and world revolution are not different from Caesar's imperialism except their deceiving names.[37]

During the rest of his life, Jiang would continue to regard the Soviet Union as China's most dangerous threat. After Sun's untimely death in 1925, Moscow's effort to coax the KMT into its orbit during and after Jiang's mission began to harvest counterproductive results. Jiang soon outmaneuvered all his competitors in the KMT and became a predominant figure in the party. To launch the Northern Expedition to unify China, for a while Jiang kept intact the KMT's united front with the CCP and cooperation with Moscow. These, however, were no longer needed in the spring of 1927, after Jiang reached Shanghai and made contact with Western influence and the Chinese capitalists there.[38] Overnight, Jiang turned his army against the CCP. Moscow not only failed to Bolshevize the KMT but also created a life-long adversary in Jiang.

The third consequence of Jiang's mission to Moscow was that the exchanges between Jiang and the Soviet leaders also had a significant impact on the CCP. Up to that point, the CCP had upheld China's reunification as a goal of the Chinese revolution, even though the timing and form of the unification were blurred by the CCP's pledged support for the frontier minorities' right to secession from China. Jiang's mission brought the issue of Mongolia into sharp focus. To the Chinese revolutionaries, Moscow's negotiations with the Peking regime over Outer Mongolia could still be interpreted as a tactic for coping with China's counterrevolutionaries. Moscow's outright prohibition of the Chinese revolutionaries' "organizational contacts" with the Mongols was an entirely different matter. The CCP could not avoid taking a stand on the dispute between its domestic ally and its international sponsor.

Befitting KMT–CCP cooperation in China, Jiang's four-member delegation to Moscow had included Zhang Tailei, who held a dual membership in the CCP and the KMT and was also a member of the Executive Committee of the Comintern's Youth League. After the Jiang–Soviet skirmish over Mongolia, Zhang's immediate reaction was to let his Soviet hosts know that Moscow's rejection of Jiang's northwestern plan could affect the KMT positively by significantly weakening its militarist faction, meaning Jiang and his associates. In Moscow, Zhang also argued with Jiang in defending the Soviets' Mongolia policy.[39] Back in China, though, it was not as easy for the CCP to maintain a consistent stand on Outer Mongolia.

Outer Mongolia was an issue in the CCP's relationship with Moscow from the outset. In late 1921, the Soviet government signed a treaty with Outer Mongolia without regard for China's objections.[40] Chen Duxiu, then in charge of the Executive Central Committee of the neonatal CCP, soon let the Comintern know that the party was prepared to rally other political groups in China to promote China's recognition of Mongolia's independence and Soviet Russia.[41] Yet the alienation of China's borderlands after the Qing's fall was a very emotional issue in Chinese politics and required delicate treatment. Therefore, at its Second National Congress in the same year, the CCP adopted the flexible formula of recognizing the minorities' right to self-determination but working for their free reunion with China. In the next few years, when debating with the KMT over the issue of Outer Mongolia, constantly mindful of the national emotion within China, the CCP's approach was to defend the Mongols' right to secession but not to promote their actual separation.[42]

Nevertheless, from the end of Jiang's mission until the Comintern-sponsored KMT reorganization in January 1924, Outer Mongolia became one of the issues that sharply pitted the CCP against the KMT. In the first few months of 1924, when the Moscow–Peking negotiations over Outer Mongolia entered their key stage, the CCP took further actions to coordinate the Soviet diplomacy. At one point, Li Dazhao led a group of intelectuals to the Ministry of Foreign Affairs in Peking to show their support for the Soviet policy on Outer Mongolia. Wellington Koo (Gu Weijun), then the foreign minister, was dumbfounded on the occasion by Li's proposition that Outer Mongolia could be better off even if it were put under the Soviet control.[43]

By May, Soviet and Chinese diplomats finally hammered out a face-saving formula for the Peking regime that maintained China's de jure sovereignty over Outer Mongolia but did not restore its actual control. The development also eased the CCP's predicament between Soviet foreign policy and China's public opinion and allowed it to take a more politically defensible stand in China on the issue of Outer Mongolia.[44] Actually, after settling the Mongolian question with the Peking government, the Soviet leaders ceased urging the Chinese revolutionaries to pay attention to China's "national question." For instance, in late 1926, when making a speech on the Chinese revolution at a Comintern conference, Stalin did not even mention the question of China's "minority nationalities."[45]

This is not to say that in this period the CCP only passively echoed the voice from Moscow with respect to China's interethnic problems. In the mid-1920s, Li Dazhao wrote some essays on reorganizing China into a federated state that would allow the harmonious coexistence of diverse cultures and give equal rights to different social, political, religious, and ethnic groups. Li apparently wrote these essays with conviction.[46] Moscow's prescription for China's "national question" was also questioned within the CCP. Significantly, Mao voiced his doubt in early 1924, soon after the Comintern successfully persuaded the KMT to support the minorities' right to self-determination. During a meeting between Borodin and a few CCP members, Mao questioned the wisdom of applying the self-determination principle to all of China's borderlands. He pointed out that in Tibet, where the

CCP and the KMT had no influence at all, national self-determination could only serve the interests of British imperialism.

However, Mao agreed to apply the self-determination principle in Mongolia and Chinese Turkestan (Xinjiang), because in these regions the Chinese revolutionaries and Soviet Russia had a common front. In addition, Mao took it for granted that in Mongolia and Xinjiang the minorities' right to self-determination should be granted by the Chinese authorities, not by any foreign force.[47] It would be an exaggeration to suggest that on the occasion Mao intended to make a serious objection to Soviet policy. Yet Mao's nationalist instinct and pragmatism brought him to see the same thing as Jiang had: These borderlands were problems for the Chinese themselves to solve, and the Chinese revolutionaries had to reach these places first before any solution could be tried.

Go among the "Minorities"?

Mao's remarks to Borodin touched upon a fundamental question regarding the relationship between China' revolutionaries and the minorities: the former's ability to reach the latter in both physical and ideological senses. In the wake of the May Fourth Movement of 1919, a movement of "going among the people" was started by politically motivated intellectual youths. The movement helped initiate a connection between the elite vanguards of the Chinese revolution and China's vast rural populace.[48] The CCP's ability to reach China's peasants would eventually guarantee its victory in the power contest with the KMT. In the 1920s, of course, no one in China or Russia considered comparing the importance of China's minorities and peasants.

Nevertheless, the fact that the northern and western borderlands were beyond the revolutionaries' reach highlighted the regional and ethnic limitation of the Chinese revolution. For some time, China's "national revolution" was meaningful only to the Han populace living in the eastern and southeastern part of China. There were certainly non-Han ethnic groups living in China proper, but they were either "invisible" to or ignored by China's partisans. In 1923, when Li Dazhao predicted that in a new federated China "all old hatred and grievances would melt like ice," he had in mind only the officially recognized "five great nationalities" (Han, Manchu, Mongolian, Hui, and Tibetan).[49]

The CCP's limited knowledge about China's ethnic situation reflected a general condition in the Chinese, or Han, society at the time. Aside from certain prejudices bequeathed from history, including the socioculturally constructed Hua–Yi dichotomy, commonly accepted categories for ethnic identification did not exist in China.[50] During the first two decades of the twentieth century, ethnology and sociology were just being introduced into China from the West. The beginning of China's own ethnology actually over-lapped with the CCP's formative years. At the time, most scholars in the field were motivated by the Chinese–Western confrontation and concerned themselves mainly with the conditions and historical evolution of the "Chi-nese nation (*zhonghua minzu*)."[51]

Qu Qiubai, a leading CCP member in the 1920s, was one of the pioneer scholars in the field. Yet his relevant writings and lectures were typically in-troductions and interpretations of the Marxist–Leninist dogmas on the "na-tional question." As far as China's own ethnic conditions were concerned, Qu, like many of his contemporaries, insisted that the Han populace made up the "Chinese nation" and the Han "commoners" made up the leading class of the Chinese revolution.[52] In this period, the only exception made by the CCP that went beyond the five-race formula was its identification of the Miao and the Yao in Hunan's peasants' movement as "the same-state-and-alien-race peasant compatriots" (*tongguo yizu de nongmin tongpao*).[53]

During its formative years, in cooperating with the KMT and focusing on the mobilization of the laboring masses in China proper, the CCP could hardly develop a connection with China's ethnopolitics, which was most restless along China's northern and western frontiers. At the time, the KMT was a force based in Guangdong Province. China's industrial workers were also concentrated in the southeast. These conditions gave a decided south-ern emphasis to the CCP's activities. The CCP leadership began to redress the south–north imbalance after the Northern Expedition was launched and, especially, in the wake of the May Thirtieth Movement of 1925. The move-ment originated with a labor dispute in Shanghai but expanded into a nation-wide protest against the United Kingdom and Japan. When the political con-ditions in northern China became increasingly tense, the CCP leadership made a series of policy readjustments to strengthen the party's work in the region. These steps also led to the CCP's first, though brief, effort to "go to the minorities"—the Inner Mongols, in this case.

The CCP's groundwork among the Inner Mongols had an earlier begin-ning. In 1923, Li started to indoctrinate some Inner Mongolian students in the Peking Mongolian and Tibetan School.[54] The result was to enlist the CCP's first group of Inner Mongolian members. In the spring of 1925, Li sent these new recruits back to Inner Mongolia. Their task was to develop the CCP's working connections in the area in the name of the KMT.[55] In October 1925, the CCP central committee set up a regional committee for northern China under Li. A "resolution on the Mongolian question" was adopted at the same time, signifying the party's new attention to the ethnopolitical factor in northern Chinese politics. The document directed the party to take advantage of the "special situation of Inner Mongolia," meaning the Inner Mongols' revolutionary potential wrought by a dual exploitation by the Mongolian princely classes and Chinese commercial capitalism. To involve the Inner Mongols in the Chinese revolution, the CCP supported the organization of an "Inner Mongolian People's Revolutionary Party" (IMPRP) that should be in close cooperate with a CCP-guided "peasants–workers–soldiers grand alliance."[56]

At the time, however, the Inner Mongolian partisans were by no means the only force in Inner Mongolian politics. The Chinese Nationalists, Outer Mongols, the Comintern, and a local warlord named Feng Yuxiang pursued different aims in Inner Mongolia and tangled with the CCP and one another in extremely intricate political alliance relationships. In the final analysis, Inner Mongolia's political ambiguity was typical of a "border zone" as defined by Owen Lattimore.[57] The late Qing followed a policy of "divide and rule" among the Mongols and identified the "Inner" Mongols as its closer constituents, in contrast to the Mongols in the "outer zone."

Until 1902, the Qing's policy of separating the Mongols from the Han allowed the former to maintain their political and demographic predominance in Inner Mongolia. Afterward, however, to prevent Russia from "nibbling the Mongolian frontier away" (*canshi mengjiang*), a new policy of "migration and frontier substantiation" (*yimin shibian*) was enforced. As a result, the ethnopolitical and ethnocultural conditions of Inner Mongolia were significantly altered in the direction of "sinicization." The ensuing governments of the Chinese Republic continued the Qing policy. In 1914, Yuan Shikai's government simply erased Inner Mongolia from China's political map by dividing the region into three "special districts."[58]

To use Lattimore's "double-edged sword" analogy for China's border zones, the policy since the Qing for sharpening the sword's outward striking edge only caused centrifugal effects among the Inner Mongols.[59] In the immediate post-Qing years, thirty-five of the forty-nine Inner Mongolian banners proclaimed their participation in Outer Mongolia's quest for independence from China. After Outer Mongolia gained its de facto separation from China with Soviet Russia's assistance, it became the Eden for Inner Mongolia's revolutionary youths.[60] The "inner" and "outer" halves of Mongolia would, however, remain divided in the years to come, and the situation seemed to suit both Moscow's and Japan's power politics well in this part of the world.[61]

That was why, after signing an agreement with the Peking regime on Outer Mongolia's "autonomy" under China's de jure sovereignty and explicitly ordering the Chinese revolutionaries not to develop any "organizational contact" with the Mongols, Moscow was willing to allow the KMT and the CCP to extend their influence into Inner Mongolia. In the Inner Mongolian project, not surprisingly, the Comintern was never neglectful of its responsibility to give "guidance."

According to information that has recently surfaced from the Russian archives, in early July 1925, G. N. Voitinsky, head of the Comintern's Oriental Department, traveled to China from Outer Mongolia. Before proceeding to southern China, he met with a group of Inner Mongols and discussed with them the possibility of setting up an Inner Mongolian party after the model of the People's Revolutionary Party in Outer Mongolia. In the meantime, a Comintern agent, a Buriat Mongol named A. I. Oshirov, also worked among the Inner Mongols to get the different fractions to agree on the organization of a unified Inner Mongolian party.[62]

Then, on October 12, under the observation of KMT, CCP, Comintern, Outer Mongolian, and Feng Yuxiang's representatives, the IMPRP held its inaugural congress in Zhangjiakuo (Kalgan). The program adopted by the congress directed Inner Mongols' struggle against Mongolian princes' "feudal privileges," Japanese imperialism, Chinese warlords, and exploitative Chinese merchants. The program set "self-determination by all the nationalities within China" as the first goal of the Inner Mongolian revolution and also pledged cooperation with the KMT and the Han populace in completing the Chinese revolution.[63]

The CCP's name was typically missing in the IMPRP's program. Even though the CCP participated actively in the preparations for launching the Inner Mongolian movement and there were CCP members in the IMPRP's leading group, the new Inner Mongolian party took the KMT as its Chinese counterpart. Three conditions made the CCP an almost invisible, though very much present, agent in Inner Mongolia's ethnopolitical front. First, under the general framework of KMT–CCP cooperation, the CCP's operatives carried out all the public organizational works in the name of the KMT. They assumed double or even triple identities, but their CCP membership was always kept underneath the other garments.

Second, beginning in 1925, Moscow's policy in China gave great importance to Feng's Northwestern Army (a.k.a. Guominjun, or "citizen's army"); the CCP consequently also devoted its main effort to achieving

Feng's cooperation.[64] The CCP's strategic goal in the region, according to Li, was to "break through to the Soviet Union and Outer Mongolia via Zhangjiakou and the Peking–Suiyuan Railroad, and to achieve international cooperation and assistance in advancing the revolution."[65] At the time, this could be achieved only through the region's military strongman, Feng. In comparison, the CCP's effort with the Inner Mongols was just part of the supplementary work of mass mobilization.

The third reason for the CCP's anonymity in Inner Mongolia's ethnopolitical front, however, was the class orientation in the party's mass work. To the newly Bolshevized CCP, such categories as "peasants," "workers," and "soldiers" made more sense than "Inner Mongols." When the CCP indeed considered the issue of the Inner Mongols, as in the aforementioned party resolution on the "Mongolian question," the issue was treated as one on the "Mongolian peasants." As a matter of fact, before the KMT–CCP split in 1927, the CCP avoided any direct organizational contact with the IMPRP.[66] In its mass work in Inner Mongolia, the CCP preferred to take a supraethnic approach through its front organization, the "peasants–workers–soldiers grand alliance," though most of the alliance's members were Han.

Although the CCP wanted Inner Mongols' cooperation with the "grand alliance," in its brief existence the alliance concerned itself mainly with winning over the armed elements in Inner Mongolia. The militarist line was soon criticized within the CCP. In February 1926, after dissolving the alliance, the CCP decided that in Inner Mongolia the peasants were the "most important mass" and they could be most effectively mobilized through "peasants associations." At the same time, the CCP further retreated from the ethnopolitical front by considering the IMPRP a KMT responsibility.[67]

The CCP's circuitous way of dealing with the Inner Mongols reflected a reality that within the revolutionary hierarchy centered in Moscow, the CCP could not yet comfortably put the Inner Mongolian movement under its own wing. Organizationally, the CCP would rather defer the interethnic aspect of the Inner Mongolian question to the KMT and the Comintern. Perhaps sensing the lack of direct Chinese involvement in the IMPRP, suh Comintern officials as Voitinsky considered the organization of the IMPRP as a matter "beside the China question."[68]

Therefore, during the first year after its establishment, the IMPRP expanded despite the CCP's aloofness. By the end of 1926, the Inner Mongolian party grew into an organization of 6,000 members. Interestingly, it was Oshirov who brought the burgeoning IMPRP to the CCP's attention. In December 1926, the CCP central committee decided that the work in Inner

Mongolia "deserved our close attention" because the IMPRP could be useful to the ongoing Northern Expedition. Still, the CCP center cautioned its northern apparatuses against "exaggerating and fancying its [Inner Mongolian work's] potential for development" on the one hand and "underestimating its possible effect" on the other. More important, the CCP simultaneously agreed with a request made by the expanding IMPRP that the KMT's headquarters in Inner Mongolia be abolished and "all affairs of the Mongolian nationality" be handled by the IMPRP.[69]

Thus, in the years before the KMT–CCP split of 1927, the CCP's work reached the Inner Mongols but did not really "go among" them. In the wake of Jiang's bloodbath against the CCP in the spring of 1927, the CCP had to cease all its earlier efforts in Inner Mongolia in the name of the KMT. The intricate political alignment in China and Inner Mongolia during the heyday of multilateral collaborations was now replaced by a relatively simple contest between the right and the left wings of the Chinese revolution. In 1928, the CCP belatedly decided to take complete control of the "real and military power" of the IMPRP. But by this time, the IMPRP itself had already disintegrated beyond salvage.[70] The CCP would have to wait for another seventeen years before it could get a second chance to incorporate the Inner Mongolian movement into its fold.

"Class struggle by the proletariat" and the "national question" were the two dogmas central to the Bolshevik brand of Marxism. These themes, which theoretically defined Bolshevism, also proved vital to the Bolsheviks' revolutionary practices. When introduced into China, however, these creeds met different receptions from the Chinese Nationalists and the Chinese Communists. Determined to blend China's diverse social and ethnic groups into "one nation" and "one state," the KMT rejected any applicability of the class-struggle idea to China's conditions. During the heyday of KMT–Moscow cooperation, the KMT leaders briefly paid lip service to minorities' right to self-determination, but they were never blind to the fact that the principle was serving the Soviets best in China's borderlands. The CCP's unconditional embrace of both doctrines made it a different force from the KMT in the Chinese revolution.

Although the CCP's agitation for class struggles in China's cities and countryside began to create a social basis for the new party's contest for national power, its indoctrination in the "national question," however, remained superficial. In this period, because of the CCP's southeastern and urban focus and its open cooperation with the KMT, the party's Bolshevization in the "national question" was more about its submission to Moscow and differentiation from the KMT than about its relationship with China's ethnic minorities.

The CCP's first opportunity to "go to the minorities" in Inner Mongolia merely proved its inability to handle the inherent contradiction between the class-struggle doctrine and the "national question" conception in the Marxist-Leninist system. But doctrines can be adhered to in the abstract; in the abstract, one's doctrinal devotion can become impeccable. In the post-1927 years, forced into isolation in China's southern countryside and thus becoming even more distant from the ethnopolitical struggles in China's northern and western borderlands, the CCP created its own "soviet state" to reflect an idealized Bolshevism. This is the story for the next chapter.

3

Sovietization: A Rebellious Option

In the history of the Chinese Communist Party (CCP), there were disastrous turns of events that in the long run proved fortunate for the party's power struggle. Its split with the Kuomintang (KMT, or National People's Party) in 1927 was one of these. The development forced the CCP to make certain drastic policy readjustments. These measures, necessitated at first by the need for survival, eventually put the CCP on its way to national power. During the first few years after the CCP–KMT split, the CCP was not only forced underground but also out of the cities. An urban-oriented movement for mobilizing industrial workers was consequently transformed into a rurally based regime sustained by a peasants' army.

During this process of transformation, Chinese Communists discarded in practice, if not in theory, the Bolshevik model of revolution that stressed workers' and soldiers' uprisings in urban centers as a winning strategy. A Chinese Communist heterodoxy was thus created by Mao Zedong and other like-minded CCP leaders. This variant of communism identified the peasantry as China's principal revolutionary force and designated the countryside as the CCP's threshold to power. Yet Mao and his associates were certainly not apostates against Marxism, which continued to serve as the CCP's guiding ideology. A most ironic phenomenon happened to China's communist politics of the late 1920s and the early 1930s: While abandoning the Bolshevik urban strategy and essentially practicing a Chinese warlord's approach of "armed separatist regime" (*wuzhuang geju*) in the countryside, the CCP formed its military-political regime as a "Chinese soviet republic," as if to escalate the party's Bolshevization to a higher level.

The "sovietization" of the Chinese Communist movement in this period

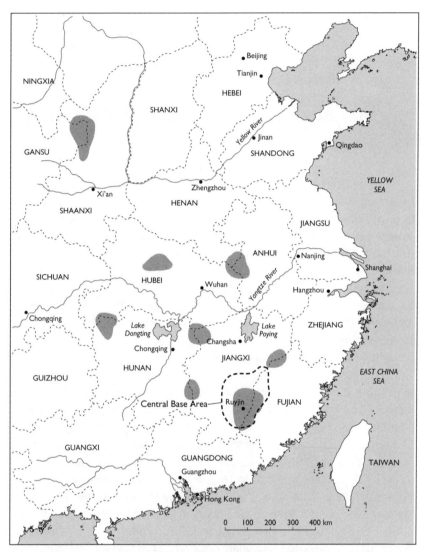

Map 1. Chinese Communist Bases in Southern China before the Long March

indeed reflected the CCP's continued drive to achieve its ideological identification with Moscow. This should, however, not obscure a fundamental change of the CCP's identity in China's political life. Sovietization marked the beginning of the CCP's "incipient state" within China's then-chaotic political system. On the surface, the KMT–CCP split did not seem to alter in any significant way China's divisive warlord politics of the 1920s; the event just resulted in the further fragmentation of multilateral competition in China. This condition itself, as argued by Lucian Pye, might be a necessary antidote to China's aged monolithic society.[1]

However, the political divisiveness itself could not provide any direction to China. The competition between the two "ideological warlords," the KMT and the CCP, would. In this sense, the two parties' falling-out in 1927 for the first time made China's warlord politics a meaningful pluralistic contest. As for the CCP, for the first time since its birth, the party was no longer merely conducting an amorphous "movement" but was obliged to undertake concrete measures in "state building." The policies and practices of the "Chinese soviet republic" would assume a pioneering significance for the CCP's state-building efforts in the years to come.

The CCP's assumed statehood provided a new context for the party's relationship with China's "national question" and induced the transformation of the question from one of ideology into one of policy. By nature, the policy significance of the "national question" could be derived from either a power holder's or a power contender's stand. Before its split with the KMT, the CCP was neither. Shortly before Jiang Jieshi's bloody purge of the CCP in April 1927, Zhou Enlai defined the CCP's position in these words:

> At present, our work is mostly limited to helping the National Government and the KMT. Therefore, we actually do not have any plan for democratic dictatorship and for seizing the power; the party has always taken a stand of not raising the question of seizing power. The party does not control the government, meaning that other people have ruled at the top and we have worked at the bottom, . . . and this is the party's stand.[2]

"He who holds no rank in a state does not discuss its politics" (*buzai qiwei, bumou qizheng*). So goes a motto on China's ancient statecraft. The CCP, of course, did not achieve this level of aloofness in its relations with the KMT's burgeoning state before April 1927. The CCP was part of the KMT's state-building enterprise and did "discuss" KMT politics from its partisan point of view. Yet in the meantime, the CCP did not hold an independent share in any of the KMT government's policies, even though its "work at the bottom" was contributing to certain aspects of the KMT's policies. The "Chinese soviet republic" ended the CCP's calculated "disinterest" in state power.

In 1931, the "Chinese soviet republic" issued an "outline constitution" that formulated the first version of a Chinese communist state. The inclusion of the "national question" in this instrument indicated that the CCP's involvement with the question had evolved from an initial, ideological stage to the next, policy stage. Without question, such a transition could not be accomplished only in paper. As will be shown in this chapter, the outline constitution of the Chinese soviet republic was only the documentary reflection of the geographic, political, and ideological readjustments that were made by the CCP in the years following the April 1927 purge.

"Advanced South" versus "Backward North"

In the study of Chinese history, there are two well-known thematic contrasts, one between "Maritime China" and "Continental China" and another between China proper and Chinese Inner Asia.[3] Although Chinese civilization emerged in the "cradle of the Yellow River," in the past 1,000 years, its cultural and political center shifted southward to the Yangtze River Valley. Ever since, southern China has served as China's economic dynamo and has also produced most of China's talented minds.[4] In modern times, China's intellectual reservoir in the south has played a vital role in pushing China's modernization by absorbing and digesting Western influence. Not surprisingly, it was the so-called Maritime China, consisting of the overseas Chinese diaspora and China's southeastern coastal provinces, that produced the leading core of the Revolution of 1911. The Nationalist Revolution of the 1920s was also characterized by a Canton-based revolutionary attack from the south against the Beijing-based conservative warlord regime in the north.[5]

Yet during the first half of the twentieth century, the dichotomy between the "progressive, pluralistic south" and the "conservative, centralistic north" had some twists. In 1928, the KMT decided to install its "Nationalist Government" in Nanjing on the Yangtze River. The choice of capital proved unfortunate. In Chinese history, most of the strong and unified dynasties established their capitals in northern China, manifesting a determination to keep a constant vigilance on the non-Han peoples of Inner Asia. By contrast, weak monarchs during China's divisive times would be content with maintaining their sovereignty only in the southern part of China. The site of Nanjing facilitated the KMT government's access to the capitalist sector of the Chinese economy, which was more developed in the south than in the north, and kept a safe distance between the new Nationalist state and the Russo-Japanese menace to the north. Yet the choice also manifested the KMT's political conservatism and strategic timidity.

Eventually, the KMT would fall to the same fate as many southern dynasties in Chinese history and would be overcome by a more vigorous political force: the northern-based CCP. The KMT's southern character also decided its rigidity in China's ethnopolitics. After its northwestern strategy was rejected by Moscow in 1923, the KMT leadership lost any incentive to develop an imaginative policy in dealing with China's interethnic problems. A sharp contrast between the KMT's affection for Maritime China and its neglect of Chinese Inner Asia can be seen in the fact that during the Northern Expedition in the mid-1920s, the KMT leadership created an Overseas Chinese Affairs Commission but not a single agency in charge of ethnic and frontier affairs.[6]

Beginning its revolutionary undertakings as part of the Nationalist revolution, for a period the CCP also followed a southern strategy. The CCP's political geography during its first decade can be illustrated by following a paper trace. During the period, the CCP's central committee produced many resolutions, decisions, directives, and public statements.

A recent official CCP documentary publication, *Zhonggong Zhongyang Wenjian Xuanji* (Selected documents of the CCP Central Committee), provides a clue about the shifting geographic realm of the CCP's activities. From 1921 to 1925, the CCP center and the party's congresses received reports from its branches in both southern and northern provinces. A "Beijing district" was one of the few places that made special reports to the party center. This reflected Beijing's importance as the state's capital as well as Li Dazhao's presence in the area. Then the KMT–CCP northern expedition against the Beijing government was launched, and this led to a significant increase in CCP documents bearing on North China.[7]

Although indicating the CCP's active involvement in northern China politics, however, these documents could not prove that in this period the CCP's strength existed evenly in the south and the north. As a matter of fact, according to a CCP report dated December 5, 1926, at the time the party had a total membership of 18,526, but only 3,314, or fewer than 18 percent of these, were in northwestern, northern, and northeastern China. The report especially criticized the party's work in Rehe, Chahar, and Suiyuan (the three special districts of Inner Mongolia) for its failure to produce enduring party organizations.[8]

In Inner Mongolia, the CCP had been able to establish some organizations at all only through cooperating with Feng Yuxiang, a so-called enlightened warlord based in northwestern China. After mid-1925, Feng's "Nationalist Army" and the KMT became the two military forces separately supported by Moscow in northern and southern China.[9] The CCP's relationship with Feng in the north was therefore similar to that with the KMT in the south. In April 1927, after taking Shanghai with the assistance of the CCP and organized laborers in the city, Jiang Jieshi ordered the massacre of his left-wing collaborators. The end of the KMT–CCP honeymoon in southern China also brought the CCP–Feng cooperation in the north to a conclusion. From 1927 to 1930, the paper trace of the CCP documents concerning North China was interrupted.[10] In these years, the party leadership was overwhelmed by its survival problem in southern China and could not afford to give much attention to the north. Soon after Jiang Jieshi's anticommunist attack, the CCP held its Fifth National Congress and decided that "the southeastern provinces are the most advanced and richest [in China] and we must not give them up to the bourgeoisie."

In stressing the south's socioeconomic superiority over the rest of China, the party actually reaffirmed its strategy focusing on China's modern urban sectors. In the next few years, however, the CCP was gradually forced out of the cities and had to act increasingly in some newly created rural bases in accord with Mao's aphorism, "power comes from the gun barrel." The CCP would remain in southern China for a period, but it was compelled to find a new way of life.[11]

As an ideo-political movement, the CCP could not easily find a way of life not prescribed in the idealized Bolshevik model. During the first half of 1930, Li Lisan became the principal leader of the CCP, and the so-called Lisan line began to dominate the party's strategic thinking. Like the previous CCP leadership, Li viewed southern China, especially the urban areas, as the center of the Chinese revolution. The revolution that had originated in the south would bring in the north, and the eventual combination of the revolutionary activities in the two areas would lead to a new "revolutionary upsurge" in China. With this expectation, Li's strategy was to achieve "victory first in one or several provinces" that would in the end result in the CCP's seizure of power throughout China. Within the party, opponents criticized Li for his blind and dangerous optimism; they instead supported a more patient approach, starting with consolidation of the CCP's military bases in southern China's countryside.[12] Neither did the Comintern endorse Li's inflated estimation of China's revolutionary situation.

Yet Moscow's displeasure was principally vented against the northern half of Li's proposed stratagem. To compensate for the CCP's weakness in northern China, Li contended that the Mongolian People's Republic (MPR) should reunite with a Chinese soviet republic and that the MPR and the Soviet Union should launch military expeditions into China in coordination with the Chinese revolution. To the leaders in the Kremlin, this scheme constituted an outrageous revival and amplification of the KMT's northwestern plan that they had rejected several years before.[13] Given the Comintern's attitude, the Linsan line was doomed to collapse in the CCP. In 1931, a reshuffled CCP leadership endeavored to purge Li's influence within the party organizations, especially those in the north. Thus, Li's basically south-centered strategy was repudiated because of its allegedly north-oriented adventurism.[14]

Unexpectedly, Japan's aggression in Manchuria in September 1931 forced the CCP to reconsider the south–north dichotomy in its political strategy. In the next two years, the paper trace of the CCP documents bearing on North China became increasingly thick.[15] Japan's military action in Manchuria and the resultant threat to North China created a tremendous diversion to the CCP's south-tilted strategy. The national outrage against Japan would not allow the CCP to continue to keep the north on the back burner of its strategy. At the same time, Moscow also began to sound the alarm. In early November, the Comintern exhorted the CCP that Japan was conducting a war not against Jiang Jieshi and the KMT but against the Chinese people and the Soviet Union. The CCP had to respond to the pressures at home and from Moscow.

In 1932, the CCP leadership told its organizations in the northern provinces that the party's ignorance about conditions in North China must not continue. These organizations must now work hard to eradicate the influence of those "theories on the backwardness and uniqueness of the north" and intensify aggressively their military and political activities. The party's northern work, the CCP center advised, must be undertaken as an effort of "armed-protection of the Soviet Union."[16]

Such an orientation, however, was largely a hollow talk at the time. While professing unrealistically its internationalist loyalty to the revolution of the Soviet Union, the CCP, including its leading body and principal apparatuses, was under the KMT's fierce attack in the south. Under the circumstances, the party first strove to save its southern roots and was unable or unwilling to make any organizational restructuring or strategic shifting toward North China.

"Red Banner" versus "Black Banner"

When contemplating their China policy, Soviet leaders never lost sight of where the power was. Amid the unpredictable political trends in China, the Kremlin's strategists found it useful and necessary to support revolutionaries on the one hand and to deal with the power holders on the other. In the early 1920s, while conspiring with the KMT and the CCP against the warlord regime in Beijing, the Soviet government continued to maneuver with the latter. The rationale, according to the Soviet commissar for foreign affairs, Georgi V. Chicherin, was that "Beijing is the symbol of national unification and we should associate with Beijing before anything else."[17]

Moscow's game plan was to maintain a functional relationship with Beijing while working for the warlord regime's overthrow by the KMT and then the KMT's replacement by the CCP. After this game plan was interrupted by the events of 1927, Moscow blamed the CCP for its frustration. A few months after the April 12 incident, Stalin blamed the CCP leadership for not carrying out the Comintern's directives. He raised a rhetoric question to other Soviet leaders: "What is the current Central Committee of the CCP?" He answered his own question: "[It is] nothing but an 'amalgamation' of general phrases gathered here and there, not linked to one another with any line or guiding idea."[18]

Yet the Comintern itself was a site of ideological and power contentions. The repeated reshuffling of the CCP leadership in the 1920s and early 1930s just reflected the turmoil in Moscow's own China strategy. After being forced out of the KMT's shadow by Jiang Jieshi, the CCP could survive only if it had the ability to dispense with Moscow's harmful directives and retain the useful ones. While the CCP was juggling its policy options, Stalin became impatient, complaining that "there is not a single Marxist mind in the [CCP] Central Committee capable of understanding the underpinning (the social underpinning) of the events now occurring" in China.[19] But there was one mind among the CCP leaders, not necessarily Marxist according to Stalin's standard, that understood the rules of the power struggle in China. Mao, though not yet in the position to dictate the CCP's policies, saw a way out for the besieged party: independent military struggle sustained by a land revolution in the countryside.

In late July 1927, Joseph Stalin published a three-phase theory on the Chinese revolution, suggesting that after the KMT–CCP split, the Chinese revolution had entered its third phase, or a transitory "soviet revolutionary" phase preceding the proletarian dictatorship.[20] This dogmatic formula still fell into the established framework of urban-oriented revolution. Though forced to admit the CCP's new situation, Stalin's mere invocation of "soviet revolution" did not specify a practical political strategy for the Chinese Communists. At the time, the more urgent significance of the subject to Stalin was how it could be used in his power struggle with Leon Trosky. The feasibility and timing of the soviet formula for the Chinese situation could be argued differently by Stalin to suit his purpose within the Kremlin.

As for the rural revolution in China, Stalin regarded it as most useful if a red peasants' army could be created to be used by the urban working class.[21] Thus, after the April 1927 massacre, the CCP for a while continued the old approach and did not even stop seeking cooperation with the KMT. In the next a few months, the CCP continued to recognize the KMT's leadership in the revolution, hoping to maintain a working relationship with the KMT's "left wing." In August, when the CCP finally learned to appreciate the military logic in China's politics and began to arm itself through a series of military uprisings, these military actions were undertaken in the name of the KMT revolutionary committee to "deal with diplomatic problems."[22]

Although the CCP leadership was slow to develop a new political strategy, Mao—who had earlier chosen not to work at the city-based party center and had gone to the countryside of Hunan to "make friends among the outlaws"—got an inkling of Stalin's idea.[23] On August 20, 1927, a Comintern agent arrived in Hunan and told Mao that the Comintern wanted the CCP to establish works-peasants-soldiers soviets in China.[24] Mao's instinct for power, not any indoctrination in Bolshevism superior to the rest of the CCP leadership, let him to grasp immediately the potential of the message. Enthralled (in his own words, he "jumped 300 *chi*"), Mao wrote to the CCP central committee without delay and suggested that the CCP discard the KMT's "black banner" at once and raise its own "red banner" by setting up a soviet government in China. Mao also made it clear that he was ready to do so in Hunan Province.[25]

The party center's first reaction was to censure Mao by citing recent directives from the Comintern. These instructed the CCP to continue to use the KMT's name in supporting the "peasants' and workers' democratic governments," asserting that a "soviet government" was still premature in China. About a month later, the Comintern seemed to have resolved its obvious self-contradiction on the issue of a Chinese soviet, and consequently, the CCP Central Committee acknowledged the merit in Mao's August letter and decided to "change banners." Meanwhile, however, the center rendered Mao's idea a heterodox by deciding that soviet governments should be organized only in cities.[26]

Indeed, Mao's rural approach bore little resemblance to Stalin's China strategy. In Stalin's view, the value of China's peasants' movement was to provide the fodder for the Chinese Red Army, but any political accomplishment of true revolutionary significance could only be achieved in the cities. But at the end of 1927, a CCP effort to launch a city soviet through an armed uprising in Guangzhou only resulted in a fiasco.[27] Mao had no intention of rushing back to the cities. By the summer of 1928, in a period of less than a year, his military base in the Jinggang Mountains of the Hunan–Jiangxi border region had expanded to an area of more than 7,000 square kilometers with a population of 650,000.

Mao's idea was to use the favorable physical features and the "political vacuum" of the region to consolidate the Red Army but not conduct any outward expansion before the next round of warlord warfare broke out. He also attached important political significance to the base area. Borrowing the territorial-occupation tactic from the warlord regimes, Mao named his base as an "armed regime of workers and peasants" (*gong nong wuzhuang geju*). At that time, such autonomous regimes could exist because of China's divisive conditions; but in the long run, the gradual development of this kind of rural bases would bring the revolution closer and closer to a nationwide victory.[28]

To the CCP center, Mao's effort in the countryside was not only conservative but also suicidal. In early 1929, while it itself was forced to go underground in KMT-controlled Shanghai, the CCP center asked Mao and Zhu De to leave their "dangerous area" immediately. Writing a letter on behalf of the central committee, Zhou Enlai warned Mao and Zhu against making the Red Army a successor to the failed peasants' Taiping Rebellion of the nineteenth century.[29] Mao's countercriticism of the center's sole focus on the cities was but a weak dissenting voice. In the next year, while Mao was perfecting his stratagem of "using the countryside to encircle the cities," the CCP center, with the Comintern's endorsement, was pushing the Bolshevik type of soviet building. In late February, 1930, the center issued a directive to the party that the expansion of the existing soviet areas must be done through city-centered local uprisings. In September, the CCP center began to plan for the establishment of a central soviet government in an urban center. Its local apparatuses were instructed to make preparations for city uprisings and the expansion of the existing bases toward Wuhan.[30]

Thus by late 1930, although the CCP had discarded the KMT's black banner for some time, its leading members could not achieve a consensus on where the party's red banner should be erected. By the late summer of 1930, the soviet movement had grown deep into southern China's rural areas. "Soviet governments" existed in more than 300 counties with a total population of 50 million. To Mao and the like-minded, these "soviet areas" should be maintained as strategic bases where the revolution would grow. To the urban-oriented CCP center, these constituted just an overture to ushering in the main event, a general uprising in the cities. But at this time Mao's unorthodox achievement began to catch Stalin's imagination, and *Pravda* openly praised the Chinese Red Army's guerrilla warfare in the countryside. In January 1931, the Comintern instructed the CCP to establish as soon as possible a provisional government for a "Chinese soviet republic" in southern Jiangxi. In November, the government was launched in Ruijin, a rural town of Jiangxi, with Mao as the chairman.[31]

Unlike the previous soviet regimes, which had controlled territories of different sizes and in many cases had only been peasants' associations with a new name, the "Chinese soviet republic" in Jiangxi resembled serious state building. Using the Soviet Union as its model, the central soviet government adopted the people's commissar system and established a whole set of administrative branches, including a committee for national defense and another for foreign affairs. In contrast to the allegedly "feudal" administrative division of the Republic of China, the "soviet republic" was run with a new, "democratic-centralized" system, though its current territorial domain was not clearly defined. The state formation also included the adoption of a "national emblem" and a "national color."[32] In its first public proclamation, the central soviet government declared:

> From now on two completely different states will exist in the Chinese territory. One is the so-called Republic of China, a tool of [foreign] imperialism and a state of the warlords, bureaucrats, landlords, and bourgeoisie that suppresses the workers, peasants, soldiers, and other laboring classes. . . . Another is the Chinese Soviet Republic, a state of the workers, peasants, soldiers, and general laboring masses under exploitation and oppression. It raises a banner of ousting imperialism, eliminating the landlord class, overthrowing the KMT warlord government, and extending the soviet government throughout China.[33]

This proclamation was intended more for domestic mobilization than for international recognition. Indeed, even the Soviet Union would not pretend that the Chinese soviet republic was a state entity for diplomatic treatments. In the combustible international atmosphere of the early 1930s, Moscow maintained its traditional double-dealing approach toward China. In 1930 and 1931, when the Comintern was promoting the CCP's soviet movement in China, the Soviet government engaged the KMT government in diplomatic negotiations to normalize their relationship. In December 1932, when the CCP's "soviet republic" had just celebrated its first birthday, Moscow and the KMT government in Nanjing fully restored their diplomatic relationship.[34] But a legalistic perception would overlook the fact that by assuming the position of a state, the CCP rid itself of the last trace of KMT influence and achieved a "revolutionary independence" from China's "legitimate" central government.

By separating itself from the Chinese government but not receiving formal recognition from the international community, the Chinese soviet republic entered a status comparable to the Tibetan government in Lhasa and the Mongolian government in Ulaanbaatar. These, of course, were not identical phenomena. The Chinese soviet republic was a rebellious enterprise, remaining part of the mainstream Chinese politics and intending to seize power in China. Its "independence" from the Republic of China was political and ideological. By contrast, Lhasa and Ulaanbaatar were two separatist forces that were seeking to transform themselves from China's peripheries into the sovereign centers of their own peoples. Their estrangement from China was indeed historical and cultural-ethnic, but what irritated the Chinese authorities most was their physical separation.

Iconoclastic Hunanese and the "Marvelous Georgian"

At the time, when debating among themselves about the soviet strategy, the CCP leaders did not compare their cause with those of Tibet and Mongolia. Although the CCP often mentioned the two regions together as objects of foreign and Chinese imperialist oppressions, it assigned a revolutionary identity only to Mongolia. In term of revolutions, Mongolia seemed to have surpassed China in ridding itself of foreign imperialism and achieving a new society. That was why in late 1929, in a letter to Chinese workers in Mongolia, the CCP urged them to support the government in Ulaanbaatar and to "naturalize themselves enthusiastically into the Mongolian nationality."[35]

But when the CCP was struggling in southern China for its own survival, the "national question" appeared peripheral to the party in both physical and tactical senses. In other words, the "national question" never achieved a constant importance in the CCP's political agenda as it did in the Bolsheviks'. Praising Stalin's theoretical work on the "national question," Lenin once called him the "marvelous Georgian."[36] Russia's ethno-demography made the "national question" a vital issue for the Bolsheviks' political strategy, and it was fitting that Stalin, a Bolshevik of non-Russian origin, assumed a leading role in the Bolsheviks' "nationality affairs."[37] Neither China's demographic composition nor the CCP's ethnopolitical character could put the "national question" on the front-burner of the Chinese revolution and produce a top CCP member of non-Han origin. What these conditions fostered was an iconoclast Hunanese, Mao, whose background provided little quality for him to become the CCP's own "marvelous Georgian." Along with the expansion of the CCP influence, the party would eventually add some prominent non-Han members to its ranks. But the process could not alter the party's overwhelmingly Han character.

In her insightful study of the provincial origins of Chinese Communism, Wen-hsin Yeh argues that radicalism in the provinces differed from that of the intellectual elites based in Beijing and Shanghai in that the latter were able to make "informed cultural choices." Provincial radicalism was rather a "consequence of the dialectical interaction between the quickening pace of modernization and the petrifying weight of traditionalism."[38] In China's modern history, Hunan, Mao's conservative home province, was an arena of intensive contest between traditional and new forces. Before Mao's time, it had produced such figures as the Confucianist official Zeng Guofan, who buttressed the "last stand of Chinese conservatism" in the mid–nineteenth century, and the radical reformer Tan Sitong, who chose to shed his blood for the abortive "Hundred-Day Reform" of 1898 to make it meaningful.[39] In Mao, the "dialectical interaction" was a continuous process.

Despite his rebellion against China's traditional society, Mao was culturally less radical than many of his contemporaries. As a young intellectual, he was suspicious of the fashion in his time of seeking solutions to China's problems by going abroad, believing that most of the foreign-trained Chinese students were "still muddle-headed and still baffled" when they returned to China.[40] Among the CCP principals, Mao was the only one who did not travel abroad before 1949. Mao—never able to master a foreign language in his lifetime—chose to believe that Western ideas could be learned more efficiently by reading translated works. His knowledge of the West in general and of Marxism in particular was thus rather limited. His acceptance of Bolshevism appeared a much less "informed choice" than those of many of his comrades who had received training in Moscow. To him, communism was first and foremost one of several "methods" that could be used to solve China's problems. In Mao's words, among all the available approaches, only "radical communism, or the worker-peasant orientation with a method of class dictatorship, can achieve expected results and is therefore most usable."[41]

Intellectually, however, Mao's understanding of Marxism–Leninism as a theoretical system had a rather feeble start and would attain an capricious character in the rest of his life. According to his own reminiscences, he became a Marxist by studying three Marxist works. In reality, before he became a founding member of the CCP, he was converted to Marxism by reading only one mimeographed pamphlet, *The Communist Manifesto*. At the time, the "Marxist" Mao was no closer to Marxism than the "Christian" Hong Xiuquan, founder of the "Heavenly Kingdom of the Great Peace" in the mid–nineteenth century, had been to Christianity. Mao himself was very conscious of his lack of familiarity with Marxist theories. Many years later in Yanan, even after he already occupied the top position of the CCP leadership, he still tried to avoid engaging his Moscow-trained comrades in polemics on Marxism.[42]

Nevertheless, Mao's self-conscious inadequacy in Marxist theories did not diminish at all his insurmountable self-righteousness. He actually turned the inadequacy into an advantage against his more "Bolshevized" and therefore, in his eyes, "muddle-headed" colleagues. His revolutionary career proved that his iconoclasm was directed against not only China's traditional society but also the Bolshevik orthodox. Yet his renowned revisionism must not be exaggerated. His alleged indigenization of Marxism-Leninism was neither a comprehensive nor an instantaneous accomplishment. Actually, he left many Bolshevik dogmas unchallenged. He took some of these dogmas, such as the class-struggle doctrine, to his heart. As for the Bolshevik formula on the "national question," he did not have any compelling reason to modify it. Therefore, while staging a rural guerrilla strategy to challenge the Bolshevik model of urban proletarian uprisings, his iconoclasm fell flat on the "national question."

In China's sociopolitical environment, the degree of a person's ethnopolitical sensibility depended on his personal experiences with or theoretical interest in ethnic affairs. Throughout his formative years, Mao did not show any particular interest in ethnicity. His home province, Hunan, was also the home of the Miao, Yao, and Tong peoples. But these peoples seemed so marginal to Hunan politics that his pre-1921 writings completely neglected their existence. His lack of interest in ethnicity would continue until the time of the CCP's northward Long March in the mid-1930s.[43]

Although he was an erudite and astute scholar of Chinese history and political culture, Mao, like many of his contemporary southern intellectuals, did not have much knowledge about China's ethnopolitics. From his revered teacher Yang Changji, a reform-minded Neo-Confucianist, Mao learned about a modern Chinese cliché that throughout history China had treated its tributary "dependencies" (*shuguo*) much more "generously" (*shen kuan*) than foreign powers had their colonies.[44] Mao probably first became aware of the notion of national self-determination from the Allied Powers' rhetoric in World War I. But he quickly became disillusioned with the *realpolitik* of the Paris Conference and began to view the principle as an index to the powers' shameless hypocrisy.[45]

Yet by the end of World War I, "national self-determination" had become an unerasable part of Asian revolutionaries' lexicon. China's political activists of different persuasions could not help but notice the doctrine's implication to the status of Manchuria, Mongolia, Tibet, and the Muslim areas of northwestern China. Mao's aversion to imperialism, both foreign and Chinese, led him to sympathize with these "weak and small peoples . . . on the verge of extinction." Even before becoming a CCP member and getting any wind of the Comintern program on the "national question," he already favored the idea of letting China's frontier ethnic groups exercise self-determination. In late 1920, discussing with his associates ways of reforming China and the world, he suggested that Chinese revolutionaries should "help Russia complete its social revolution, help Korea and Nanyang [meaning Southeast Asia] gain independence, and help Mongolia, Xinjiang, Tibet, and Quinghai achieve self-government and self-determination."[46]

Unlike his northerner mentor Li Dazhao, who viewed China's interethnic relationship as part and parcel of the Chinese revolution, Mao did not spend time on exploring the related practical and theoretical questions. For a while, Mao allowed himself to be limited to a tunnel vision, focusing on the class relations within Han society.[47] His early endorsement of the frontier groups' self-determination just indicated that when the Comintern formula on the "national question" arrived in China, it did not have to convince Mao and like-minded.

This is not to say that in the 1920s Mao had no encounter with China's ethnopolitics at all. His first known exposure to the non-Han peoples probably occurred during the Northern Expedition. Between May and September 1926, he was the principal of the sixth class of the Peasants Movement Training Institute in Guangzhou (Canton). The class's curriculum covered various "theoretical" and "practical" problems, but the "national question" was not among these. During this period, he offered twenty-three hours of lectures, focusing on the subject of the peasant movement in the Chinese Revolution. The class had about 300 trainees, including 7 Inner Mongols—all of whom were Tumed Mongols from the Guisui (Hohhot) area.

Allegedly, Mao gave some personal attention to these Mongolian trainees, interviewing them and probing into the social and political conditions of Inner Mongolia. Merely stressing to the Inner Mongols that the Han and Mongolian laboring masses had identical interests, Mao's first interethnic contact did not provide him with any insight either on the Mongolia issue or China's "national question." After completing their four-month training program, these Inner Mongols returned to their home areas to start a peasant movement but not to engage in any "nationality work" (*minzu gongzuo*).[48]

Soon Mao had another opportunity to become involved with the "national question." In December 1926, the peasants of Hunan held their First Congress in Changsha. As a CCP expert on the peasant question, Mao was invited to the conference to "provide guidance." One of the congress's resolutions was on the liberation of Hunan's Miao and Yao peoples. The document identified these ethnic groups as the Han peasants' "compatriots" of the "same country but different nationalities" (*tong guo yi zu*). Criticizing ordinary Han people's bigotry and blaming the "Han feudal rulers" and "local chieftains" for the Miao's and Yao's dire conditions, the resolution called upon revolutionary Han peasants to help the Miao and Yao join their movement on an equal footing. Mao participated in the drafting of the congress's final documents, but his contribution to this particular document is unclear.[49]

In 1930, Mao wrote in one of his social investigation reports: "Constant outsiders to the internal operations of commerce cannot make anything but mistakes if they try to decide a policy for dealing with the commercial bourgeoisie and winning over the urban poor masses."[50] This statement carried a central conviction behind his empirical and pragmatic tactics: policies had to be based on a solid mastery of facts derived from the investigation of pertinent problems[51] In this sense, he was an effective organizer of the peasants and an accomplished military strategist but by accident or choice remained a lifelong "layperson" on the issue of ethnicity.

Between 1928 and 1931, while fighting a heterodox guerilla war in the countryside, Mao developed no independent thinking about the "national question." During these years, his separation from the urban-based CCP center created tremendous difficulties for the communications between the two sides. Mao's resultant freedom of action tended to set him on a collision course with the center's policy preferences. Yet as far as the "national question" was concerned, he dutifully adhered to the party's established rhetoric. This can be seen from the propaganda operations of the "Red Fourth Army" under him, which occasionally made reference to the frontier ethnic groups. Such slogans as "the Manchus, Mongols, Hui, and Tibetans decide their own rules [*zhangcheng ziding*]" were included in the Red Army's public notices and handbills.[52] Except for professing Mao's group's ideological affinity with Bolshevism, such slogans had little meaning for the Han peasants in the Hunan–Hubei–Jiangxi border regions whose support was the key to the Red Army's daily struggle for survival.

Thus, although Mao's practice in the countryside established a "soviet state" context for the evolvement of the CCP's stand on the "national question," his creativity had nothing to offer to the question per se. It was therefore the work of the theory-oriented CCP center to place the "national question" into the new context. Without a "marvelous Georgian" of its own, however, the CCP would not gain its benchmark theory on the "national question." Aside from dutifully repeating the Comintern formula, the CCP was left to do only one thing—to make ad hoc policy adjustments constantly, according to its ever changing political environment.

International or National Minorities

The disastrous turn of events in 1927 inflicted tremendous losses on the CCP organization. The "Bolshevized" CCP center—obsessed with the survival question—for a moment even forgot the "national question." For more than a year, the subject almost disappeared from the CCP's policy deliberations.[53] Then the "national question" returned to the CCP agenda only when the party held its Sixth National Congress in Moscow in the summer of 1928. The congress adopted several detailed resolutions on the political conditions of China and the party's military and political strategies. The resolution on the "national question," however, included just one short paragraph that stressed the "enormous importance" of the subject. In reality, the resolution indicated the marginal significance of the subject to the CCP at the time, for a consideration of the "national question" was relegated to the party's next congress. Such a resolution was adopted at all probably only because the CCP congress was held in the Bolsheviks' capital.[54]

Otherwise, the resolution did include some noticeable features. In referring to the non-Han peoples, it replaced such terms as "alien race" (*yizu*) and "nationality" (*minzu*) with the conception "minority nationalities" (*shaoshu minzu*). As indicated in the previous chapter, the term had a Comintern origin and was first borrowed by the KMT in its 1925 proclamation on the issues of Mongolia, Xinjiang, and Tibet. In the 1928 resolution, the CCP expanded the application of the conception to the Koreans, Taiwanese, and "primitive nationalities" such as the Miao and Li in southern China.[55]

What remained primitive, however, was the CCP's understanding of the conception of "minority nationalities." The conception had been adopted by the Soviet Russian government in 1920. In that year, a "Department of Minorities" was added to the structure of the Commissariat of Nationalities to represent the nonterritorial ethnic groups' interests. Thus the Bolsheviks made a careful ethnopolitical distinction in naming Russia's territorial, autonomy-seeking ethnic groups as "nationalities" but its nonterritorial, access-seeking ones as "minorities."[56] The CCP, unaware of this extremely important distinction, used "minority nationalities" to encompass all the non-Han groups of China. Since then, the CCP has stuck to the usage and has assigned only a numerical significance to "minority."[57]

The CCP's actual understanding of the conception in the late 1920s was even more problematic. In June 1929, when the Second Plenum of the Sixth National Congress convened, the party center decided to solicit information about "minority nationalities" from its local organizations to facilitate its policy deliberations. The question was defined as one concerning "the nationals of Britain, America, and Japan in Shanghai, the peoples of India, Annam [Vietnam], Korea, and Taiwan, the Koreans and Japanese in Manchuria, the Mongols in Shanxi and Shunzhi [today's Beijing and Hebei areas], the Tibetans in Sichuan, the Hui people [*Huimin*] in Gansu, and the Miao nationality [*Miaozu*] in Yunnan," plus the Chinese nationals in Annam, Malaya, and the Philippines.[58] Under such a definition, the CCP strayed even farther than before from achieving a realistic understanding of China's own ethnopolitics. In the CCP's perception, the question of "minority nationalities" went beyond China's national boundaries, and the party became just an agent of the Comintern's international scheme. This perception, of course, was endorsed by Moscow.[59]

After the 1927 debacle, the CCP center became even more reliant on Moscow in policymaking. In the next three years, it echoed the Comintern's analyses of China's political conditions. In preparation for the arrival of the next "revolutionary high tide" in China, the CCP center tried to restore its severely damaged urban apparatuses. Yet before such a "tide" could come, in July 1929 Moscow and the Chinese government suffered a serious diplomatic rupture over the Chinese Eastern Railway in Manchuria.

This dispute soon led the two sides into an "undeclared war." To coordinate Soviet military actions in northern Manchuria, Stalin contemplated a "Manchurian revolutionary uprising" that should be conducted by a Chinese brigade secretly supplied by Moscow. If such an "internal event" of China could successfully capture Harbin and replace Zhang Xueliang's warlord power with a revolutionary regime in Manchuria, then the Soviet Union would be able to obtain a friendly eastern flank without provoking any international outrage. The uprising did not happen, but there is evidence that the Soviets indeed carried out political agitation within Chinese troops during the conflict. While the CCP received Moscow's request to intensify its pro-Soviet propaganda in Harbin, its organization in the area learned about the Soviets' military sabotage only indirectly.[60] This is early evidence for how Moscow could pursue its private interests outside its international alliances.

This is not to say that Soviet leaders overlooked how the CCP might assist their own foreign policy. While depicting the Manchurian situation as a "joint imperialist offensive against the Soviet Union," the Comintern instructed the CCP to stage an "armed-defense of the Soviet Union."[61] To Soviet leaders, Japan's influence in Manchuria was especially menacing. Thus, under the direction of the Comintern, the CCP center moved to intensify the party's activities in Manchuria and Inner Mongolia. The CCP's Inner Mongolia operations in the late 1920s were even less consequential than Li Dazhao's efforts a few years before.

A departure was made, however. Differing from Li's approach for launching a supra-ethnic, laboring-class movement in Inner Mongolia, this time the CCP adopted the typical Leninist ethnopolitical strategy, using the ideal of "national independence" to agitate Inner Mongols' struggle for establishing an "Inner Mongolian National [or People's] Republic" (*neimeng minzu*—or *pingmin*—*gongheguo*). The party propaganda contended that

Inner Mongolia be confirmed as a "national unit" (*minzu danwei*) and that only the Inner Mongols have the right to decide whether their state should be unified with Outer Mongolia or should join a Chinese soviet federation (but never the Republic of China).[62] Aside from Moscow's tightened supervision, the CCP's new rhetoric about Inner Mongolia also reflected the party's new position in Chinese politics after its split with the KMT in the spring of 1927: It was no longer obligated to pay homage to the KMT's official China.[63]

Also during this period, the CCP incorporated the Korean Communists in Manchuria into its own organization and began to regard communist activities in Korea as part of its own responsibilities. Soon a similar orientation was also adopted for Annam (Vietnam).[64] Given the fact that most of the CCP leaders at the time tied the fate of the Chinese revolution to a Moscow-centered world revolution, it was small wonder that they did not differentiate the "minorities" in the international scene from those in China. As Zhou Enlai once contended, the CCP was responsible for the "minority nationalities" *within* and *around* China because its important position in the world revolution was to lead the revolutions in colonies.[65] The CCP center's consideration of the "national question" attained a "domestic" focus only after it came out of hiding in Shanghai and arrived in the CCP's own "state" in Mao's guerrilla bases.

In early November 1931, a delegation of the CCP center reached the "central soviet region" in Jiangxi to launch the soviet republic. Mao, founder of the rural base, was pushed aside by these leaders from the cities. Mao's frustration was evident in his referring to these newcomers, in private, as "Messrs Western-style house" (*yangfang xiansheng*).[66] From November 1 to 5, a party conference of the soviet region was held with the "Messrs" presiding. The better part of the conference was used to "correct" Mao's military and social policies. Pejorative labels such as "rich-peasant line," "guerrilla-ism," and "narrow empiricism" were piled on Mao. These, however, did not prevent Mao from being placed in the leading position of the Chinese soviet republic. This arrangement had been foreordained by Moscow, which seemed to have more confidence in Mao's creative political-military faculty than in the other CCP figures' borrowed Marxist dogmas.[67]

Yet because Mao's "narrow empiricist" practices did not include any program on the "national question," the Comintern demanded that "the [Chinese] soviet government ought to implement a Bolshevik nationality policy toward the minority nationalities in accordance with the principles of equality and national self-determination."[68] During the inaugural conference of the soviet republic, Wang Jiaxiang, a returnee from Moscow, made a report on the "national question." A resolution on the subject was adopted afterward. The subject was also included in the "soviet outline constitution" drafted by Zhou.[69]

The "outline constitution" was one of the "landmarks" in the evolution of the CCP's "nationality policies," though previous studies have attached different significance to this historical document.[70] Yet the historical process of the CCP's ethnopolitics is not only made up of a series of documented terms and conceptions. The outline constitution was a product forged by at least three political trends in China at the time. First, the inauguration of the soviet republic in rural guerrilla bases but not in any urban center ended the debate between Mao and the CCP center about where the CCP's power base should be. In the spring of 1931, the security of the CCP center in Shanghai finally cracked. This led to the arrest of CCP secretary general Xiang Zhongfa, who then rallied to the KMT authorities. The remnant CCP center had no choice but to retreat hastily to the countryside.[71]

Second, in September 1931, the Japanese military in Manchuria engineered the Mukden incident and thus began Japan's formal colonization of the region. The worsening of China's national crisis did not immediately propel the CCP to consider a national reconciliation with the KMT. To the contrary, the situation further convinced the CCP leadership that a revolutionary and anti-imperialist alternative had to be created to replace the KMT regime, which seemed to have been compromising and collaborating with foreign imperialists.[72]

Third, facing with a domestic and a foreign enemy, the CCP's predicament was compounded by a continual "party-line" struggle within the CCP center orchestrated by a visible hand from Moscow. The friction involved different interpretations of China's political conditions conceived with the same set of Bolshevik dogmas. From late 1929 to the fall of 1930, the CCP leadership under Li Lisan quarreled with the Comintern's Far Eastern Bureau over tactics in the Chinese revolution. This, however, could not qualify Li as a forerunner for his similarly quarrelsome fellow Hunanese Mao in challenging the Soviet model of revolution. Though Mao used his unorthodox approach to open rural bases for the CCP, he never directly quibbled with Moscow. Li—not feeling inhibited in faulting those by now rather cautious

Comintern agents for not supporting his grandiose and risky schemes—did not offer the CCP any feasible way out of its plight.

In August 1930, Stalin finally lost his patience with what he called Li's "idiotic and dangerous tendency." Afterward, the Soviet leadership and the Comintern decided to remove Li from the CCP leadership and ordered him to come to Moscow.[73] In its effort to purge the influence of the so-called Lisan line, the new CCP leadership, consisting of young returnees from Moscow such as Wang Ming (a.k.a. Chen Shaoyu) and Bo Gu (a.k.a Qin Bangxian), blamed its predecessor, among other things, for neglecting altogether the "national question."[74] Thus, when the "Chinese Soviet Republic" was set up in Jiangxi and adopted its "outline constitution," the CCP ideology was a strange combination between heterodox Maoism and the borrowed dogmatic Bolshevism, and between a China-centered revolutionary nationalism and a Moscow-oriented internationalism.

This is the context in which the Chinese soviet republic's stand on the "national question" must be understood. The outline constitution and several other soviet documents bearing on the question were crafted first and foremost to sever any of the CCP's connections to the KMT in the past. Therefore, despite the CCP's earlier endorsement of KMT programs in Sun Yat-sen's time, now the Chinese soviet asserted that beginning with Sun Yat-sen, the KMT's programs on the non-Han peoples represented the bourgeois and landlord interests and did not bring the slightest improvement to China's "minority nationalities." Otherwise, the Chinese soviet's pledge on its "absolute and unconditional" support of the minorities' right to national self-determination, including the right to secession from China, just repeated the CCP's constant commitment to the Comintern formula.

What was new was a more elaborate interpretation of that right to secession. Now, supposedly, the "minority nationalities" in Mongolia, Tibet, Xinjiang, Yunnan, Guizhou, and other areas where they made up the local majority could choose one of three options: (1) to "separate from the Chinese Soviet Republic and establish their own states," (2) to "join the [Chinese] Soviet federation," or (3) to "establish autonomous regions within the Chinese Soviet Republic."

To attract these peoples' allegiance, the Chinese soviet republic was defined as a fully accessible workers-peasants' state "without national barriers." Meanwhile, complete political and legal equality and positive cultural and economic progress were promised to the minority peoples living among the Han majority. Again, Outer Mongolia was made a case in these documents to attest to the CCP's sincerity—its independence was "unconditionally recognized" by the Chinese soviet republic.[75]

As a rebellious force restrained to a small rural region, the Chinese soviet assumed more symbolic than substantive significance. The symbolic character of the soviet regime was best manifested in its declaration of a "national revolutionary war" on Japan on April 15, 1932. Despite the "constitutionalization" of the issue of ethnicity by the Chinese soviet republic, in the next few years the CCP was more insulated from China's ethnopolitics than in any other period of its history. The main force and leading core of the CCP were forced out of cities and confined to southern China's countryside, where non-Han groups were either nonexistent or invisible. Five of the CCP's ten bases, including the "central soviet region," were in Jiangxi. The only non-Han population of the province, the She people, would not be identified as a distinct "nationality" until after 1949. The same is true of the Tujia group in Hunan and Hubei, where CCP bases also existed.[76]

Only in two remote and isolated soviet regions in Shaanxi and Guangxi, the Mongols and the Hui in the former and the Yao in the latter constituted a significant policy issue for the local CCP organizations. Meanwhile, CCP apparatuses in areas controlled by the KMT, the Japanese, or regional warlords (e.g., Yunnan, Sichuan, Gansu, Manchuria, and Inner Mongolia) had to deal with non-Han peoples of their regions on a daily basis. Only indirectly, the CCP center in Jiangxi learned about the interethnic problems facing these struggling local organizations. These organizations might not be able to find any solution at all for their problems with the Chinese "soviet constitution."[77]

Neither did the Chinese soviet's minorities programs demonstrate a better comprehension of China's ethnic affairs than the CCP's earlier cliché borrowing from the Russian Bolsheviks. Typically, the Chinese soviet was launched on November 7, 1931, to manifest its adherence to the model of Soviet Russia. Its three-option formula on the minorities' right to self-determination constituted another borrowing from Moscow. The formula was adapted, probably by Wang Jiaxiang or Zhou Enlai, from Stalin's discussion of the issue in 1913.[78] In sum, the importance of the Chinese soviet's programs on the "national question" should not be overestimated; they neither provided practical guidance for the party's actions in the field nor made any breakthrough in the party's understanding of China's ethnopolitics.[79]

A real departure was made, however. It was not the content of the Chinese soviet's new minorities programs but the way in which they were proclaimed. Along with other "government programs," they helped unveil for the first time the CCP's alternative, the "soviet state," to the official Chinese state under the KMT, the Republic of China. The real mission of the "soviet republic" was not "state building" but "state destruction." It posed an open challenge to the "legitimate" official state with a rebellious mechanism.

Such a contender's scheme had many precedents in Chinese history. In this context, the red Jiangxi regime's "nationality policies" were designed less for attracting the non-Han peoples toward the "soviet state," which would require much effort to overcome too many barriers in terms of space and time, than for encouraging these peoples' alienation from the official Chinese state. Earlier, in the mid-1920s, while still cooperating with the KMT, the CCP had struggled against the warlord regime in Beijing but not the entity of the Republic of China.

The CCP's attitude toward the frontier "alien races" at the time indicated a passive acceptance of China's divisive conditions (China's unity was seen as "infeasible" and "undesirable"). In the 1930s, now that the KMT monopolized the Republic of China as its own party-state and was poised to unify all of China, the CCP leadership began to appreciate, though only still in theory, the Leninist maxim that the "national question" was a revolutionary "yeast." Borderland peoples' alienation from the Republic of China was therefore positively encouraged.

The result of the Chinese soviet's experiment with the Leninist strategy was, however, disappointing. Early in 1934, when reporting to the Chinese soviet's Second National Assembly, Mao could mention only one achievement of the CCP's "nationality policy" in the soviet regions: these regions' serving as asylums for expatriate revolutionaries from Korea, Taiwan, and Vietnam.[80] Mao pointed out that "the starting point of the soviet's nationality policy should be to rally all suppressed minority nationalities around itself and to increase the anti-imperialist and anti-KMT revolutionary forces."[81]

Although these Korean, Taiwanese, and Vietnamese revolutionaries' "rallying" to the CCP bases reflected a function of the Comintern's international network, China's non-Han peoples' not rallying indicated the extremely limited outreach of the Chinese "soviet republic." Mao's contention also reflected an assumption generally held within the CCP leadership that when the old China had lost its luster to attract the non-Han and the remote to rally to itself, the CCP's revolutionary alternative could enlist these peoples' support like a magnet. Soon after Mao's speech, the CCP made a breakthrough to reach the non-Han peoples in the borderlands and thus got a chance to test the hypothesis on the natural alliance between the CCP and the minorities.

Ironically, the "breakthrough" and the "chance" came only after Jiang Jieshi's deadly "annihilation campaigns" deprived the CCP of its own "soviet state" in southeastern China, the supposed rallying center for the minorities. As a result, the ethnogeographic relationship between the CCP and the non-Han peoples changed drastically. Before the party could draw the "minority nationalities" toward itself, it was forced to embark on a strenuous migration toward the northwestern frontiers and to seek sanctuary in areas where "minority nationalities" constituted a significant portion of the local population.

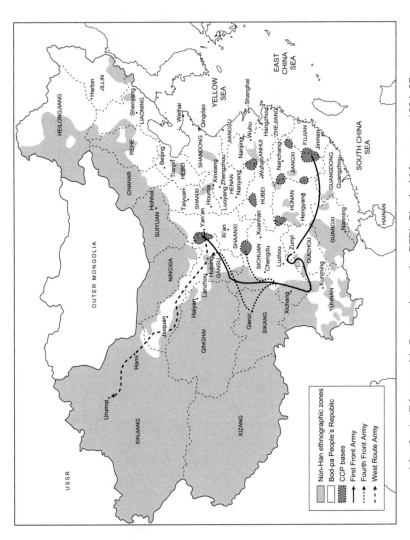

Map 2. An Ethnographic Perspective on the CCP's Physical Movement, 1934–37

4

Northernization:
The Search for a Peripheral Strategy

Sima Qian, the famous chronologist of ancient China, once asserted that all great causes in Chinese history "originated in the south but eventuated in the north (*qu yuan yu nan, shou gong yu bei*)."[1] Because he lived in the Han dynasty when China was chronically troubled by the Xiongnu in the steppes, Sima Qian obviously ranked pacification of the northern frontier as the crowning accomplishment of China's rulers. Interestingly, the Chinese Revolution of the twentieth century also demonstrated a northward tendency in certain pivotal events like the Northern Expedition and the Long March. A difference between these and the Grand Historian's dictum is that they were episodes in China's civil wars: The Northern Expedition was the Nationalists' key step to overcome China's warlords; the Long March salvaged the Chinese Communists from the Nationalists' deadly encirclement.

Yet the Communists' experience did bear some resemblance to the situation depicted by Sima Qian. Their cause not only moved physically to the north but was also redefined by the frontier environment. In the mid-1930s, after completing a 6,000-mile lurch from the Yangtze River Valley in southern China to the Yellow River's embrace in the northwest, the Chinese Communist Party (CCP) was able to launch a "Yan'an way" of revolution and to lay the foundation for its final victory in China.[2] The new base area in the northwest, adopted only reluctantly by the CCP, eventually proved advantageous. Geostrategically speaking, during China's war against Japan from 1937 to 1945, the base served as a sanctuary for the CCP on the flank of Japan's military thrust and also as a nerve center for the party's guerrilla operations. Then, during the Chinese Civil War from 1946 to 1949, the base was well situated to facilitate the CCP's contest for North China and Manchuria. Sociopolitically, in this remote rural area the CCP perfected its

77

mass-line tactics and mobilized the Chinese peasantry to join China's military and political struggles. There was yet one more consequence of the CCP's northward movement: The process of the Long March and the relocation to the northwest helped reshape the CCP's ethnopolitics.

As has been shown in the previous chapters, during the early years of the Chinese Communist movement, the CCP leadership considered the "national question" largely in isolation from China's ethnopolitical realities. Until the time of the Long March (1934–35), none of the CCP principals had had any extensive experience in dealing with ethnic affairs. In adhering to the Marxist class-struggle doctrine and the Leninist anti-imperialist thesis, the CCP leaders adopted two fundamental assumptions about the "national question." First, "national antagonism" (*minzu chouhen*) in China existed principally between the suppressive central government and the ethnic minorities.

Second, among the laboring masses of all China's nationalities, there was a genuine common class interest with which their respective ethnic identities could not compete. Accordingly, if there appeared to be any intergroup animosity between two different peoples, involving the Han or not, it had to be a consequence of the Chinese government's or foreign imperialists' "divide and rule" schemes. As far as the CCP's own relationship with the non-Han groups was concerned, the CCP leadership saw the party in an invincible position: Because the CCP was a revolutionary movement committed to overthrowing imperialism, the Chinese central government, and the minority groups' own "backward systems" all at once, the party was "naturally" on the side of the non-Han laboring masses.

Furthermore, viewing the Soviet Union as a model that solved the "national question" successively, the CCP leaders were confident that their own policy, informed by Bolshevik doctrines and Soviet experience, would appeal to the Han and non-Han populace alike. In a word, before their extensive contact with China's non-Han groups during and after the Long March, the Chinese Communists saw an natural ally in the non-Han peoples.

This assumption, however, was shattered along the way of the Long March. The disillusionment befell to the CCP at a bad time, when the party needed support from the frontier ethnic groups more than ever. When the Long March ended in northern Shaanxi, the center of the Chinese Communist movement became situated along the fault line between Han society and the frontier, non-Han cultures. For the first time, the CCP was compelled to develop a functional ethnopolitical strategy. Yet though the party leadership was seriously troubled by the recent findings about the frontier ethnopolitical conditions, it could not get any ready remedy from the Marxist-Leninist dogmas. This dilemma forced the CCP to begin a process of conceptualizing the "national question" as a concrete problem for China.

"Upper-Stratum Line"

The Long March—wrought by the Red Army's military defeat—began as a disorderly retreat. Its tortuous course went through areas in southwestern China inhabited by the Miao, Yao, Yi, and Tibetan peoples and ended in northwestern China where the Hui and Mongols made up a considerable portion of the population. Inevitably, the Red Army's relationship with these peoples became a vital condition for its daily operations. In June 1935, when the Red Army entered Sichuan, its general political department demanded that all high-level political officers prioritize the issue of gaining minority peoples' support.

This message was also conveyed to the foot soldiers through the Red Army's official organ, *Hongxing Bao* (Red Star), then under Deng Xiaoping's editorship.[3] One of its editorials exhorted: "One does not qualify for the party membership and is not a good red soldier if he cannot understand the party's nationality policy, cannot see the importance of the work to win over the minority nationalities, and does not participate in the work!" The Red Army headquarters sternly warned against the "foolish bigotry of Great Hanism (*da hanzu zhuyi*)" among the troops that would alienate the minorities. The troops were told to take advantage of the local peoples' hatred of the Han rulers and to gain their support for the Red Army.[4] The tricky part, of course, was how to convince the non-Han locals that the Red Army was different from the "Han rulers."

In viewing the "national question" through a class-struggle lens, the CCP always blamed the "Han rulers" for the dire situation of China's non-Han groups. To the Chinese Communists, a genuine interethnic relationship in China could only involve a confrontation between a laboring-class alliance and an upper-class alliance, each encompassing all the ethnic groups concerned; any other kinds of interethnic relations that blurred the class division would be viewed as fabrications by the reactionary Chinese or foreign ruling classes. Until the beginning of the Long March, this perception hadpropelled CCP officials to work to turn negative "national antagonisms" into positive "class antagonisms." A "lower-stratum [*xiaceng*] united front" transcending ethnic barriers was deemed an attainable device against the

Kuomintang (KMT, or National People's Party) government and its alleged non-Han collaborators.[5] Meanwhile, any notion that the CCP should cooperate with the ruling elites of the non-Han peoples would be repudiated within the party as unprincipled and opportunistic.[6]

During the Long March, the Red Army had to modify its class-struggle doctrine as far as interethnic contacts were concerned. Although the "Han government" would continue to be named as the main cause of minorities' sufferings, its alleged accomplices across the ethnic division, the non-Han ruling elites, were for now acquitted of any class crimes. In November 1934, shortly before the Central Red Army entered the Miao and Yao areas in northern Guangxi, its political department adopted a few "working principles" to guide the troops in the forthcoming interethnic encounter. The Red Army was required to "develop an intimate relationship with the upper-stratum representatives [*shangceng daibiao*]" of the local non-Han groups by forging a political or military alliance with them. This drastic reorientation was pragmatic, not doctrinal. The circumstances compelled the CCP to put the class-struggle orientation in abeyance only temporarily. Neither did the proposed new course imply that in the eyes of the Chinese Communists the "minorities" obtained an enhanced status.

To the contrary, in the CCP's own ideological context, the upper-stratum approach had a pejorative connotation for the non-Han peoples. According to the directive of the Central Red Army political department, the non-Han peoples were "extremely backward in economic and cultural developments" and their socioeconomic conditions had not allowed class struggles to unfold; therefore the ruling elites or headmen were still the "sole representatives of their national interests."[7] Nevertheless, no matter how the CCP leadership reasoned and justified its new orientation, the reality was that the party now had to squarely face China's ethnic relationships.

The most famous development stemming from the CCP's new orientation was the "blood alliance" between Liu Bocheng, commander of the Central Red Army's advance column, and Xiao (meaning "younger") Yedan, the head of the Guji clan of the Yi in western Sichuan. In May 1935, Liu concluded the alliance with Xiao Yedan according to Mao Zedong's specific instruction that, in the Yi area, the advance column's task was not to fight but to propagate the party's nationality policy. The stratagem paid off. The Liu–Xiao Yedan accord allowed the Central Red Army to prepare a daring operation in the Yi area so that it could cross the Dadu River and thereby escape a deadly encirclement by Jiang Jieshi's forces.[8]

The expedient alliance making with the "upper stratum" was useful to the Red Army only to a certain degree. Its effectiveness hinged on the circumstances in which the contact between the Red Army and the local ethnic groups took place.[9] When the Red Army was only passing through the non-Han regions, ethnic incidents between the two sides could possibly be reduced to the minimum. This was not always the case, however. There were instances in which some Red Army troops looted the locals exactly because these troops were travelers and did not see the need to cultivate a long-term relationship with the non-Han peoples.[10] Otherwise, when the Red Army attempted to create permanent bases in non-Han areas and did pay close attention to foster a functional relationship with the local populace, it was often faced with various types of resistance.

Consequently, to the Red Army, the resistant local peoples became "Yi bandits" (*yi fei*) or "Tibetan reactionaries" (*fan fan*).[11] The numerous ethnic incidents indicated that the Red Army was unable to achieve the non-Han peoples' cooperation simply by adjusting its own political orientations. The ethnic antagonism in China's west was too entrenched to be appeased by the Red Army's propaganda. The overbearing character of the issue plagued the CCP leadership's decision making on the eventual destination of the marching Red Army.

Where To?

The CCP conference in Zunyi, Guizhou Province, in January 1935 has been known as a turning point in the CCP's history because it established Mao's practical leadership in the party's military affairs.[12] Mao's leadership, unlike the CCP's official histories would like to suggest, did not immediately provide the Red Army with a definitive strategic destination. Until that point, he had advocated for a new base area in the Sichuan–Guizhou border region. At the Zunyi conference, however, those present modified his suggestion and decided to strive for a new soviet region in western Sichuan. Yet the decision was not final. In the following months, the location designated as the Red Army's new home would be changed several times. Not until mid-June did Mao and his associates come to a decision that the remote northwest, not the relatively close southwest, was a better strategic option.

Now the Red Army had to make a really long-distance migration. Accordingly, the Red Army's military task was to "occupy the Sichuan, Shaanxi, and Gansu Provinces, establish provincial soviet governments, and at a proper time organize an expedition army for taking over Xinjiang."

The strategy was confirmed by a meeting of the central politburo in late June (the Lianghekou conference). Because of the strained Chinese–Japanese relations in North China, the CCP leaders also decided to issue a Red Army proclamation against Japan.[13] These developments finally established for the Red Army a strategic goal under the slogan "Marching up to the north to resist Japan" (*bei shang kang ri*). Unfortunately for the Red Army, the developments also would soon lead to a serious split within the CCP leadership.

A few months later, still in the middle of the Long March, Mao wrote these words in his poem, "Mount Liupan":

Agreed that he who fails to reach the Great Wall could hardly be the hero;
Reckoning up, already we had come twenty thousand li!
. . .
Ready this day the long tassel in our hands—
When shall we truss up that Grey Dragon?

The "Great Wall" clearly indicated the destination of the Red Army's northward march. But the "Grey Dragon," or the designated enemy, as Mao explained many years later, was meant to be Jiang Jieshi rather than the Japanese.[14] Therefore, irrespective of the Red Army's propaganda then and the CCP historical literature's claim many years later, at the time "resistance against Japan" was mainly public rhetoric rather than an intended or realistic goal for the Red Army's military operations. When deciding the Red Army's destination, the CCP leaders constantly considered two factors: (1) what area or areas in western China had the best conditions for the survival and growth of the Red Army, and (2) what area would be most convenient for the CCP to receive the urgently needed assistance from the Soviet Union. Still in a general retreat, the CCP leaders did not prioritize those conditions of a given area that might facilitate the Red Army's future attacks on the KMT regime or the Japanese. To most of the CCP principals, the combination of the two cardinal factors pointed in the direction of the northwest.

Until this time, the Chinese revolution, either under the KMT or the CCP, had followed a certain geo-ethno-political logic. When the revolution was on the offensive against China's power center, it mainly tapped into the Han populace in China proper and confronted the influence of the Western powers in eastern China. When in retreat and seeking a sanctuary for recuperation, however, the revolution tried to reach the close neighborhood of China's ethnic frontiers and attempted to establish direct contact with the Soviet Union though northwestern China.

It has been mentioned earlier in this study that the KMT in the mid-1920s had conceived a northwestern strategy just to be discouraged by Moscow. The CCP, at another difficult time before the Long March, had also contemplated a northwestern strategy. In 1928, an opinion within the CCP favored the northwest as a place for the party to nurture its wounds inflicted by the KMT's recent attacks. The idea was immediately dismissed by Moscow. For a while, even a discussion of the northwestern option would be repudiated in the party as a retreating opportunism.[15]

The summer of 1928 also began a transitional period for the political situation in Xinjiang. In July, Yang Zengxin, the warlord who had controlled Xinjiang since the end of the Qing Empire, was assassinated. The next enduring warlord regime under the notoriously tyrannical Sheng Shicai would not emerge until five years later. In between, Xinjiang was under the crisis-laden administration of a mediocre local bureaucrat named Jin Shuren. At the beginning, Moscow deemed Xinjiang's internal weakening as its own advantage. The Jin era soon became the heyday of the Soviet Union's "trade without treaties" in the region.[16] The expansion of Soviet interests also increase the stake.

In early 1931, the Comintern began to contemplate organizing "people's revolutionary parties" among the Muslim populations of Xinjiang and Gansu, two provinces defined by the Comintern as "typical colonies" of China. Especially in Xinjiang, Moscow's purpose was to safeguard the Soviet Union's dominant trading position and to preempt any British anti-Soviet scheme. In Moscow's plan, both the CCP and the Mongolian People's Republic were expected to play a role in agitating and organizing the local people.[17] Yet the turmoil in Xinjiang came too quickly for the schemers in Moscow. A popular rebellion broke out in Hami, a county of eastern Xinjiang, while the Comintern was still considering how to import a controlled revolution into the region. Caught by surprise, for many months Moscow could not ascertain the "character" of the rebellion and whether or not Uigur members of the Soviet Communist Party should be dispatched to Xinjiang.[18]

By the summer of 1932, the situation had become further complicated by a colorful Muslim warlord named Ma Zhongying, who moved into Xinjiang forcefully from Gansu and threw the whole region into chaos. Amid the new uncertainty, Moscow began to use the territory and personnel of Outer Mongolia to keep a hand in the situation. In the meantime, Moscow seriously considered using the CCP's military force to regain the upper hand

in Chinese Inner Asia. In February 1933, the Comintern Executive Committee telegraphed Zhang Guotao, whose Fourth Front Army had just retreated into Sichuan, and asked him to extend his new base into Xinjiang.[19]

In still focusing on eastern China, at the time the CCP leadership was
cautious about Moscow's proposition for extending its force into the northwest. When Zhang entered Sichuan, on the one hand the CCP center hailed
the development as an opportunity to "light the torch of revolution throughout the Northwest"; on the other, it was worried that any further action by
the Red Army in the areas west of Zhang's current position would likely
provoke a joint attack from the British, Tibetan, and Sichuan warlord forces.
In the summer of 1934, when the central soviet region in Jiangxi was on the
verge of collapse, the CCP center had to make plans for the worst scenario.
Anticipating a dispersion of the Red Army forces, CCP strategists divided
China into six military districts. A "northwestern military district" was demarcated to include Sichuan, Shaanxi, and Gansu, but no area in the far west
was included.[20]

In other words, the CCP's initial plans for dealing with its worsening crisis did not go beyond the fault lines between the Han and non-Han cultures.
Moscow, however, believed that the CCP might need to move further west
to save itself. In mid-September 1934, urged by the Comintern leadership,
Wang Ming, then the CCP representative residing in Moscow, wrote to the
CCP leaders in China and urged them to embark seriously on a northwestern enterprise. The party was required to strengthen its leadership over the
existent soviet bases in Sichuan and Shaanxi and to "breaking through" (*datong*) to Xinjiang. Wang's letter, however, took a long time to reach the CCP
in China. Between October 1934 and November 1935, the CCP center also
completely lost its communication with Moscow. The CCP leaders did not
even know about the existence of a CCP base in northern Shaanxi until they
read about it in KMT newspapers in the late summer of 1935.[21]

The loss of communication with Moscow proved fateful for the CCP, because there was a serious policy disagreement in its leadership during the
same period and Moscow could not possibly serve as an arbitrator between
the two sides. The disagreement led to a momentary split of the Red Army
between the Fourth Front Army under Zhang and the First Front Army under Mao and the rest of the CCP's central committee.[22] The quarrel was about
the final destination of the Long March. In June 1935, the CCP center decided on a northward movement at the Lianghekou conference. But soon
Zhang challenged the decision with a proposed southwestern venture. Before the Lianghekuo conference, Zhang had established a Provisional Government of the Northwestern Federation in northern Sichuan.

The proclaimed purpose of this government was to "recover Tibet and Xikang in the west, pacify Xinjiang and Qinghai in the north, and conquer Yunnan and Guizhou in the south in order to create a region that also includes the soviet bases in Shaanxi, Gansu, Sichuan, and Guizhou." In late June, when Zhang met with the rest of the CCP leadership, he did not conceal his preference to move southward, or, as a secondary choice, to move into Qinghai and Xinjiang as proposed by Moscow two years before. The CCP center's choice was to march northward and to establish a border region that could bridge Sichuan, Shaanxi, and Gansu. Although Zhang agreed at the meeting to accept the center's decision, his later actions indicated that he did not feel bound by the decision.[23]

In September, barely three months after the joyful meeting of force by the First and Fourth Front Armies in northern Sichuan, the two forces turned their backs on each other. Although the former continued to move northward and would arrive in northern Shaanxi in late October, the latter maneuvered southward and would enter Xikang in November. In early 1936, after communication between the CCP and Moscow was restored, the Comintern intervened in favor of the CCP center's position. But the physical reunion of the Red Army was not realized until October 1936, and the rift between Zhang and the rest of the CCP leadership would prove irreparable.[24]

During the controversy over the Red Army's destination, the two sides used similar labels to implicate each other. These included "rightist opportunism," "defeatism," "warlordism," "pessimism about the future of the soviet movement," "fleeing away from the enemy," "un-organizational activities," "splitting the party and the revolution," and so on.[25] These incriminating exercises were commonplace in the CCP's numerous internal "party-line struggles." But this communist jargon concealed a simple fact of life: Forced out of its hotbed in the eastern Chinese provinces and cut off from Moscow's guidance, the CCP had plunged into the unfamiliar western landscape and become hyper-anxious about its own fate.

This anxiety led to the Red Army's division over a *geostrategic* question. This particular character set the debate apart from all previous party-line struggles, which had been over doctrinal or tactical matters. When Zhang and the CCP center debated the pros and cons of the southwest and the northwest options, their assessments of the non-Han groups featured prominently. The debate was therefore about with whom the Red Army should join as well as about where the Red Army should go.

When CCP strategists considered an area's potentials as a base site, they closely examined the area's geographical features, its political connection to the rest of China, the enemy's situation, the local economy, and "mass conditions." Zhang and the CCP center respectively stressed how favorable were their own choices in these aspects. The command of the Fourth Front Army described the advantages of the western Sichuan area in the following words:

> The Song[pan]–Li [county]–Mao [county] region is a natural barrier in western Sichuan, which is shielded by the thousand-li range of the Min Mountain, close to Shaanxi and Gansu in the north, and dominant over the western Sichuan plain in the south; in the southern direction [we] can drive directly into Chengdu and water horses in the Yangtze River, and in the northern direction [we] can sweep Gansu and Shaanxi and gallop across the Central Plains. In addition, the area provides abundant products, such as cattle and sheep, grain, medical materials, gold, metal, and other resources. These will invalidate the enemy's attempt to blockade the area, and can also become the principal sources to strengthen the red region's economic basis. The physical features of the region deprives the enemy of any tenable defense position but enables us to concentrate forces from a commanding high position and attack the enemy in all the directions. In the west, the passage to Mongolia and Xinjiang is unimpeded, releasing our fear of disturbance in the rear. *Furthermore, suffering from the suppression and exploitation by Han officials, imperialism, KMT warlords, and unscrupulous merchants, the Hui [Muslim] and Fan [Tibetan] populace of the region has struggled . . .* [words missing] *fiercely. Everyone of them values martial qualities and masters horse riding and firearms, and therefore in this region the Red Army has the best basic condition for enlargement.*[26] [emphasis added]

In August, based on a report by Mao, the CCP center issued a document to justify the northern strategy. Though using less colorful language than Zhang's, the document was similarly comprehensive in discussing all the aspects of the issue. Its sharpest disagreement with Zhang was about the "mass conditions":

> In terms of the worker-peasant masses' conditions in this area [Shaanxi and Gansu], because of the deep agricultural crises in these years, famine, heavy taxation, and concentration of land, the preconditions for a great peasants' revolution have been growing rapidly. The peasants' struggles against taxation and for land and their guerrilla movement have already been unfolding. *These will enable us to organize and lead the*

spontaneous peasants' struggle among the region's basic Han masses, and to enhance their [political] consciousness for embarking on the road of soviet revolution. The Red Army's enlargement and growth can thereby be facilitated as well. [These developments] can also stimulate and advance national liberation of the non-Han masses (Hui, Mongol, and Tibetan) of this and neighboring areas to establish their own people's republics. Through our assistance, mobilization, and leadership, we will be able to win over this movement and channel it into the soviet torrent.[27] [emphasis added]

These documents clearly demonstrated a fundamental difference between the CCP center's Han-centered strategy and the Fourth Front Army's heavy inclination toward the non-Han region. When the debate continued, it became increasingly focused on the significance of the "minorities' region" to the CCP movement. Whereas Zhang criticized the CCP center for "using empty words to disdain the regions of the minority nationalities," the center contended that in such areas the Red Army "would only become worn and depleted but could not be replenished."[28] When the Fourth Front Army irreversibly turned southward, the CCP center made an appeal to the army's rank and file and painted a rather dire prospect for them:

For whatever reasons we must not return to where we came from, not cross the snow mountain and the marshland for a second time, and not go back to the minority-nationality areas where all the masses ran away. . . . Moreover, what is the way out to move down to the south? Down in the south there lay the marshland, snow mountains, and deep forests; the south is sparsely populated and lacks food; and the south is a minority-nationality region where the Red Army will be reduced but cannot be replenished. . . . To thrust down to the south, [the Red Army] can only reach Tibet and Xikang, but not Sichuan, and will have to suffer from coldness and hunger and sacrifice lives without any benefit to the revolution. To the Red Army, there is no way out in the south; a southward movement is to embark on a road to ruin.[29]

It needs to be noted that although the Mao–Zhang debate was characterized by their disagreement on "minority areas," there is no evidence that one was more "pro-minority" than the other. Although Zhang's depiction of the minorities' revolutionary spontaneity was overly optimistic, Mao also exaggerated the Red Army's difficulty with the ethnic groups. For instance, as was discussed above, not "all the masses" of these groups ran away when the Red Army arrived. The cruxes of the two leaders' varying stands were respectively these: Mao insisted that the Red Army's strength depend on its constant connection to the Han ethnographic region; Zhang believed that the Red Army's survival was possible only in areas where the KMT's influence was the weakest.

At the time, Mao predicted that by moving into Xikang, more than half of the Fourth Front Army would likely be destroyed. The Fourth Front Army indeed could not consolidate its position in western Sichuan, and, as predicted by the CCP center, was forced to move into the more remote Xikang. But in Xikang, the Fourth Front Army did not perish; it did not even suffer any serious loss. In mid-1936, when Zhang canceled his self-appointed party center and began to move northward to join with the CCP center, the Fourth Front Army remained the strongest unit among all the regular Red Army organizations.[30]

The preservation of the Fourth Front Army was a miracle that neither Zhang nor the CCP center seemed able to explain. Recently declassified KMT documents in Taiwan prove that the Fourth Front Army's survival in Xikang was an ethnopolitical phenomenon. The Red Army's Long March was not only a vital phase of the KMT–CCP struggle but was also a stirring agent for other political arrangements in southwestern China. At the tail of the Red Army, Jiang Jieshi's force for the first time was able to extend its influence into the region. As the Red Army entered Xikang, it also injected a disturbing element into a delicate situation between the KMT regime and the Lamaist government of Tibet. Since the collapse of the Qing Dynasty, the theocratic Tibetan government had sought secession from China. The successive "central governments" of the Republic of China had not been able to get a handle on the problem.

Then, in December 1933, the Thirteenth Dalai Lama died. The KMT government took the opportunity and sent a memorial mission to Lhasa. The real purpose of the mission, however, was to open discussions with the Tibetan authorities on mutual relations. Between August and November 1934, the mission under Huang Musong stayed in Lhasa and engaged Tibetan officials in several conversations. These indicated that although the Tibetan authorities harbored an ambiguous attitude toward China's claimed sovereignty in Tibet, it insisted that the two sides' territorial disputes involving Xikang must be solved first.[31] At the time, Chinese-controlled Xikang and Tibet were separated by a natural barrier, the Jinsha River, a convenient demarcation established as a result of much military friction. In the end, Huang's mission was unable to solve any of the standing issues between the Chinese and Tibetan governments. But by opening a dialogue, the mission did improve the atmosphere between the two sides.

The Red Army's moving into western Sichuan in 1935, however, threatened to ruin the new beginning of the Chinese–Tibetan relationship. The KMT regime had to consider whether or not its troops should follow the Red Army into Tibet if the army continued to move westward and to cross the Jinsha River. In June, Jiang Jieshi ordered Jiang Zhiyu, the Chinese representative in Lhasa, to ask the Tibetan authorities to strengthen its defense along the Jinsha River.[32]

The Tibetan authorities' response, however, was more enthusiastic than Jiang Jieshi had expected. In its answer to Jiang Jieshi, the Tibetan government not only promised to instruct its troops in eastern Tibet to cooperate with the KMT army in blocking the Red Army's advance but also indicated an intention to "reinforce the Tibetan Army at the front and to pursue the enemy."[33] Jiang Jieshi was immediately troubled by Lhasa's offer of assistance. Aside from telegraphing Lhasa and asking it not to violate the Jinsha River line, in mid-August Jiang also sent an order to Liu Wenhui, the KMT regime's military commander in Xikang:

In a June telegraph to Tibet we asked the Tibetan army to coordinate with the Central Army in Xikang in preventing the Communist army's westward flight. But we did not mean to move the Tibetan army away from its defensive position to pursue the enemy and even less to demand a reinforcement of the Tibetan army. Now the remnants of the northwestern bandits [the Red Army] are almost terminated and cannot possibly flee into Xikang. Thus there is absolutely no need for a Tibetan expedition army to move out. Another telegraph has already been sent to Tibet. It asks the Tibetan army to follow the June telegram and to stay in its current defensive position but not to cross the Jinsha River lest it cause misunderstandings. Liu Wenhui and Ma Bufang in Qinghai should keep a close surveillance [over Tibet] and warn Tibetan officials not to cross the Jinsha River.[34]

Obviously, at this point Jiang Jieshi was so confident about his ability to end once and for all the Communist question in China that he regarded a Tibetan eastward movement as a more troublesome scenario than the Red Army's westward plunge. By prioritizing the Tibetan question over the Communist question in southwestern China and ordering his generals there to focus on Tibet's movement, Jiang Jieshi unwittingly prepared a safe haven in Xikang for the Fourth Front Army, which at the time just started its southwestern venture. As Zhang later recalled:

> During our sojourn in Xikang from November 1935 to June 1936, there was almost no war in the front. Liu Wenhui's army stationed in Kangding and staged a confrontation with our army on the other side of the Zheduo Mountain, but the two sides lived together peacefully. Our army extended westward to the eastern bank of the Jinsha River, and a small number of Dalai Lama's British-trained Tibetan troops garrisoned on the western bank of the river. The two sides, however, never fired at each other.[35]

Like other local forces that submitted themselves to Jiang Jieshi only reluctantly, Liu had his own reasons to hold back in fighting the Communists. Still, Jiang Jieshi's order legitimized his peace with the Red Army in Xikiang. Thus, in the CCP's history, the Fourth Front Army's preservation became one of the early cases in which the Chinese Communist movement benefitted directly from China's official ethnopolitics.

In the meantime, the CCP's burgeoning ethnopolitics began to find its pragmatic pivot. An unmistakable point made by the CCP center and Mao in their debate with Zhang was that the party and the Red Army must not separate themselves from their own social and ethnic roots in China proper and must not become wanderers in the unfriendly non-Han frontier regions. All CCP leaders understood that the "mass line" was the lifeline of their movement. In learning from their encounters with the non-Han populace along the way of the Long March, for the first time the CCP leaders learned to pay attention to the ethnodemography of a given area. They became extremely uneasy when and if the Red Army was about to enter an area where the Han accounted for less than a half of the local population.[36] For such an area had no potential for the party's mass-line work.

In spite of their previous rhetoric about the importance of the "minority nationalities" to the Chinese revolution, most CCP leaders admitted in their debate with Zhang, indirectly at least, that their movement was ethnically limited to the Han people. Eventually, this weakness would have to be redressed, especially in light of the Red Army's destination, the ethnic-cultural fault line in the northwest. But even in the northwest, the Red Army must first foster a solid tie with the Han populace of the region. In other words, even in moving toward the very margin of Han society, the CCP never for a moment changed its Han-centric political strategy.

"Great Hanism"

Noting this continuing CCP Han-centric political strategy, however, is not to say that the CCP was more ethnocentric than other national Communist parties, including the Russian Bolsheviks. Yet the CCP's ethnopolitics during the Long March was different from the Bolsheviks' in an important sense. To the Bolsheviks, the domestic aspect of their "national question" involved an ascendant Russian proletarian movement's policies to placate and absorb the political aspirations of the other "nationalities" within the former tsarist empire. To the CCP in the Long March, the "national question" was part of its migrating Han peasants' army's search for asylum in the neighborhood of the non-Han peoples.

In other words, the Bolsheviks never needed to worry about their own ethnocultural identity, but the Chinese Communists were facing a real danger of being cut off from their own roots. The CCP's ethnocentrism in the 1930s must be understood in this context. Subscribing to the supranational ideology of Marxism, the CCP leaders never explicitly admitted that their movement had a unitary ethnocultural basis. Nevertheless, their ethnocentric concerns were betrayed by the aforementioned arguments on the ethnically selective mass line and on the necessity for the party to keep connected to the mainstream of the political life of China proper. Only when attacking one another did CCP leaders appear more frank than usual about the ethnic character of the CCP movement. In their debate about the non-Han regions' significance to the Red Army, the CCP center and Zhang used "Great Hanism" (or "Pan-Hanism," *da hanzu zhuyi*) to name each other's alleged offense against the "minorities."[37] In a twisted manner, the allegation about "Great Hanism" divulged a "frontier mentality" among the CCP leaders— an anxiety about losing their original ethnocultural ties because of the CCP's relocation to the fringe of Han society.

Despite its frequent appearance in the CCP's documents and literature, "Great Hanism" remains a conception of obscure origins. In its formative years, the CCP was categorized by the Comintern as part of the national revolution in the Orient. The party nevertheless differentiated its own "correct proletarian nationalism" from the KMT's "bourgeois nationalism." Thus the CCP was not necessarily opposed to Chinese nationalism. It was always important, however, for the CCP to identify who was the true representative of the Chinese nation.

For instance, in the mid-1920s, Qu Qiubai in one of his writings posted a rhetorical question about "who makes up the nation of China?" His "simple answer" was that "only the Han people make up the nation of the Chinese state [*zhongguo minzu*]." But Qu felt it necessary to take the answer one step further in identifying the "commoner class" of the Han as the true representative and leading class of the Chinese nation.[38] This line of argument conveniently attributed China's "old imperialism," "colonial suppression," and "slogans of great Chinese nation [*da zhonghua minzu de kouhao*]" to the ruling classes but not to any particular ethnic group.[39] Noticeably, however, at the time, the CCP did admit that any of the "five great nationalities" in China (Han, Manchu, Mongol, Tibetan, and Hui) could become a national suppressor and commit "Pan . . . ism."[40]

The CCP's earliest official application of "Pan . . . ism" to a situation in China seems to have occurred in the party's criticism of the "parochial nationalist ideas of Great Mongolism [*da menggu zhuyi*]" in 1930.[41] But the conception was not used to mean that the Mongols were becoming a suppressor group against the others. Rather, it meant that the Mongols were seeking an unreasonable status vis-à-vis the Chinese state. The CCP–KMT split in the late 1920s opened the door for the CCP to attack publicly the "Han ruling classes" represented by the KMT. For instance, in November 1931, in a program of the Chinese soviet government, the CCP explicitly named the Han ruling classes as suppressors of the other nationalities in China and accused the KMT regime of upholding "Sun Yat-sen's 'nationalism'" and becoming a contemporary anti-minority tyranny. Yet "Great Hanism" was not used in this occasion.[42]

The first appearance of "Great Hanism" in CCP documents occurred during the party-line struggle against the so-called Lisan line. In early 1931, Wang Ming started a polemic against Li, who was then responsible for the CCP's policymaking. Wang accused Li of totally ignoring the importance of the work among the "minorities" and therefore of committing a mistake of "great Han nationalism" (*da hanzu minzu zhuyi*). Wang diagnosed Li's "mistake" as a reflection of the "vestiges of parochial traditional ideologies." By putting his diagnosis in quotation marks, Wang seemed to claim the authorship of the term.[43]

From then on, the conception of "Great Hanism" became part of Chinese Communist jargon. A year later, when censuring its Sichuan organization for a condescending attitude toward the minority peoples there, the CCP center used "Great Hanism" in its critique. Interestingly, it was the CCP's Sichuan provincial committee, in a "sincere" effort to criticize its own mistake, that identified the KMT as the originator of "Great Hanism" and thus made its own alleged "mistake" a political problem, more serious than a mere "national prejudice."[44] In later years, the label would be used liberally in the CCP's commentaries on the KMT government's suppressive policies toward the non-Han peoples, CCP organizations' "mistakes" in the "nationality work," and ordinary Han people's bigotry in relation to the non-Han peoples.[45] In a word, in the CCP's discourses, "Great Hanism" assumed a generic significance and was used to brandish all negative thrusts of the Han vis-à-vis the non-Han groups.

If "Great Hanism" came to mean ethnocentric bigotry, it then was a congenital characteristic of the entire Red Army, which was made up mainly of Han peasants. This was true to its leadership as well. As the Red Army marched through the Yi region in western Sichuan, on one occasion Mao himself joked that when he became the emperor of China, the Yi people could send tribute to him. Such a mentality of "identifying oneself with the celestial dynasty" in dealing with the non-Han peoples was not rare among CCP cadres, and it had already been criticized within the party many years before.[46]

During the Long March, when Zhang and the CCP center wielded "Great Hanism" in their mutual attacks, more specific policy ramifications were implied. Zhang's usage of the conception was more or less in concert with Wang's original definition. He criticized Mao and the other CCP leaders for nullifying the nationality work because of their "excessive underestimation of the minority nationalities' revolutionary role" and their conviction about the "backwardness" of the minority regions. In his speeches within the Fourth Front Army, Zhang pointed out that so-called backward Tibet had twenty-four modern battalions, superior to the Red Army, and that the so-called backward Outer Mongols had successfully conducted their revolution ahead of the Chinese.[47]

As far as the alleged "backwardness" of the frontier regions was concerned, there was no real disagreement between Zhang and Mao. The real debate was about the compatibility between the Chinese Communist movement and a particular region, Xikang and beyond. In this regard, the CCP center and Mao did not maintain a consistent stand. On July 3, 1935, while making preparations for an operation in western Sichuan to open a passage to southern Gansu, the CCP center, without Zhang's participation, adopted a document calling for the Tibetans in Tibet, Xikang, and western Sichuan to start their own revolutionary movement. The document, in the form of an open letter to the Tibetan people, deviated from the party's "upper-stratum line" of the time in relation to the Miao, Yao, and Yi peoples. It left no room for interclass collaborations within Tibetan society.

As in the party's earlier documents bearing on Tibet, the open letter depicted the Dalai Lama as a running dog of British imperialism and the Lamaist government as a parasitic system that must be destroyed. The letter pointed out that a "Xikang–Tibetan national liberation movement" must strive for the Tibetans' "thorough independence from Britain and China" and for various internal reforms in Tibetan society. In the meantime, the CCP center contended that to be successful, the movement had to be an "inseparable part" of the Chinese soviet movement and the international proletarian revolution.[48]

At the time, there was no "national liberation movement" in Xikang and Tibet, nor was the CCP center prepared to make a serious effort to start one. Although the "lower-stratum" orientation was adopted particularly to politically ready the Red Army to cross the Tibetan areas, it cannot be verified how and whether or not the open letter was ever disseminated to the local populace. Any CCP propaganda among the Tibetan people would have encountered tremendous difficulties because the Red Army lacked the language personnel and the Tibetan language was incompatible with CCP jargon.[49]

One thing is clear, however: The Red Army's rough experience in the Tibetan areas hardened most of the CCP leaders' resolution to move northward. At a CCP politburo meeting in September 1935, Mao told those present that the Red Army had to move to the north, because, according to Mao, in the north "the Han and the Mongols live together and Mongolia is our brother," but in the south the CCP's "relationship with the *Fan* [Tibetan] people is extremely bad."[50] Despite the CCP's open letter to the Tibetans, Mao actually could not see even a slim chance for the CCP to collaborate with the Tibetans as an ethnic group. Therefore, when Zhang used "Great Hanism" to accuse Mao of avoiding the Tibetans, he was at least right about the fact.

At the time, the debate within the CCP leadership was about a practical policy question as to whether or not the largely Han movement of the CCP should throw its lot into the Tibetan areas. As was typical of the CCP's internal friction, however, the arguments of the two sides had to be made in association with "class" stigmas. "Great Hanism" was bourgeois by definition, and the stigma itself seemed forceful enough to overcome the other side. In such a debate, the actual policy contents in question were often ignored. Therefore, it is especially noteworthy that when returning the "Great Hanism" label to Zhang, the CCP center's repudiation was targeted at the Fourth Front Army's practices in the Tibetan areas that were actually in concert with the CCP center's own open letter mentioned above.

"Bod-Pa People's Republic"

The Fourth Front Army's ethnopolitical enterprise among the Tibetan population of Xikang lasted from the late fall of 1935 until the summer of 1936. It was the CCP's most extensive contact with a non-Han people up to that time. The experience, however, would afterward be dismissed by the CCP center as part of the so-called Guotao line. The sweeping verdict prevented the CCP leadership from examining carefully the value of the experience. This was unfortunate for the CCP, because the experience exposed certain problems that would continue to plague the CCP–minority relationship in the years to come.

The Fourth Front Army's experience raised a question about the extent to which the CCP could capitalize on the non-Han peoples' ethnonationalism. Detecting a strong anti-Han sentiment among the Tibetans, the Fourth Front Army advertised the "overthrow of the Han official ruling class" as the central item in its mass work. Propaganda was carried out to glorify Tibet's imperial past and to promise the CCP's support for restoring Tibet's "lost territories" in the east. Zhang himself explicitly argued that the CCP must support the establishment of a "greater Tibetan state" (*da xizang guo*) to win over the Tibetan nation.[51]

However, the discrepancy between this rhetoric and the Red Army's practice was enormous. To create a revolutionary base was not fundamentally different from any other type of political takeover. In the operation, population control was a basic requirement. The Fourth Front Army attempted to establish tight control over the local Tibetan populace by creating several Tibetan revolutionary regimes. Among these, the most important was a "Bod-pa People's Republic," which was launched in Ganzi in May 1935. "Bod-pa" was the ethnym used by the local Tibetans for themselves. By adopting the name, the Fourth Front Army presented the republic as a prototype of an independent Tibetan state.

In reality, from day one the republic was under the close supervision of Zhang's Northwestern Federation Government. Having been "authorized" by the republic, Zhang's security personnel acted through a "political examination department" against any "counterrevolutionary" activities in the republic's territory. Without exception, the republic's sixteen Tibetan county governments were mere appendixes to their Han counterparts in the form of the "Han people's autonomous committees," an interesting and ironic case in which a numerically smaller Han population dominated the local Tibetan majority through its "autonomy." To mobilize the local people's support, the Red Army used such slogans as "Resist the Han and expel the British" (*kang han qu ying*) and "Promote Tibet and annihilate Jiang [Jieshi]" (*xing fan mie Jiang*). But clearly, the leadership of the Fourth Front Army was realistic enough to know that a genuine, spontaneous Tibetan ethnonationalist movement would be difficult to control. Therefore, in Zhang's own words, most of the Tibetan autonomous governments supported by the Fourth Front Army were "only empty names."[52]

Another question raised by the Red Army's Tibetan experiment was about the usefulness of the class-struggle doctrine in the CCP's ethnopolitics. The Fourth Front Army did not limit itself to ethnopolitical agitations as the only means of enlisting local support. The doctrine of class struggle, a more familiar tool of mass work to the Red Army, was widely applied. The problem was that the doctrine could never be carried out consistently. The Red Army conceived a series of "antifeudal" policy measures to "liberating" the lower-class masses. Land redistributions were implemented with an expectation that the measure would most effectively gain ordinary people's support. Yet as far as the local ruling elites were concerned, they received contradictory treatment in different counties. In some places, they were politically excluded and socially banished; in others, they were not touched or even relied upon by the CCP's cadres. Both tendencies were viewed by the leadership of the Fourth Front Army as incorrect. But except for recommending "flexibility," the leadership itself could not articulate a clear guideline on the matter.[53]

There was also a question as to the conditions that defined the interethnic contact. The discrepancy in the Red Army's class policies happened because they were not conceived as part of a consistent and systematic social revolution for the sake of the local people; instead, they were seen as expedient measures to be implemented according to circumstances to benefit the Fourth Front Army itself. As a matter of fact, all the propaganda and organizational efforts were made just for a short-term purpose: to feed the Red Army. Social reforms or the status quo were alternative commodities that the Red Army offered to the local people, in rhetoric or action, if the army could in return get a tangible item: foodstuffs.

When the Fourth Front Army's 45,000 troops suddenly arrived in Xikang, they brought tremendous strains to the local economy. The army leadership admitted that "the main reason for the minority nationalities' hostility toward us was the contradiction between the question of the Red Army's provision and that of the masses' interests."[54] The need for supplies forced the Red Army to backtrack on some of its reform promises. For instance, at first the Red Army attacked the old local regimes for levying exorbitant taxes and promised to abolish all rents and taxes. This was soon changed into a policy of "tax reduction" and then again into one of "regular taxes only." The Red Army was eager to show the local people that it was better than all the old regimes in the past, Han or Tibetan. But its need for survival tended to undercut its public relation campaigns. In reality, the Red Army's "regular taxes" were only slightly lighter than the old ones.[55]

Always in preparation for military operations, the Red Army could not avoid putting irregular burdens on the local people either. To meet emergent contingencies, the troops often engaged in "purchase–search–confiscate" operations to get food. For instance, in April 1936, while making preparations for an attack on Kangding, the Fourth Front Army put a request through the "Bod-pa people's government" that the people of the Daofu area "lend" 3,000 *shi* (about 8,249 bushels) of "war grain" to its troops in two weeks. This kind of extortion was bound to alienate the populace concerned, which often resisted by running away or hiding what they had. Thus, despite the Red Army's stern disciplinary measures against reckless behaviors by its own personnel, frustrated troops could still sometimes go on a rampage.[56]

In the final analysis, therefore, the Red Army's relationship with the Tibetan people of Xikang was not determined by its stand on the issues of Tibet's autonomy or class struggles but by its food policy. The local people were often confused by the Red Army's behavior. To them, the army troops' friendly demeanor contrasted sharply with the other Han armies, but its "extortion [of food] was worse even than Liu Wenhui." Under such circumstances, an intimate relationship between the Red Army and the Tibetans could not grow. Zhang later recalled that in Tibetan areas the Red Army was like "living in a foreign land."[57] He himself was paranoid and distrustful of the Tibetans. In the summer of 1936, when the Fourth Front Army finally decided to give up its southern effort and to join Mao in the north, Zhang ordered the execution of the commander of a Tibetan division who up to that point had loyally served the Red Army. This Tibetan division would also be dissolved after the Fourth Front Army arrived in northern Shaanxi.[58]

The Fourth Front Army's failure to take roots in the Tibetan areas seemed to end the polemic between Zhang and Mao over the Tibetans' compatibility with the CCP movement. Yet the Red Army's Tibetan experience had a broader ramification. The Second Front Army under He Long and Ren Bishi did not participate in the controversy between the Fourth Front Army and the CCP center. In the summer of 1936, it became the last main force of the Red Army to pass through the Tibetan areas. Afterward, the army's report on its "nationality work" frankly admitted that "no experience and achievement were gained in the Fan [Tibetan] region." Meanwhile, the report listed many difficulties for the troops in getting along with the local people.[59] Therefore, after the first extensive encounter between the Chinese Communist movement and the Tibetan populace in western China, a negative consensus about the Tibetan region emerged among the CCP leaders as well as the rank and file of the Red Army. Although the Tibetan people's collective memory of the Red Army is difficult to document, it must have reciprocated the Red Army's feelings. In the early 1950s, when the Chinese Communists were ready to enter the Tibetan region for the second time, all these mutual memories would come to life again.

The impact of the CCP's "northernization" on its perception of China's "national question" cannot be exaggerated. The experience indicated that to the CCP, the real-life "national question" occurred in circumstances rather different from the Russian Bolsheviks', and that the Leninist-Stalinist doctrines on the question proved irrelevant to the Red Army's daily problems. A condition that the Russian Bolsheviks had to deal with after 1917 was a two-revolution situation in Russia: one was a "Russian revolution in the Russian ethnographic territory" with political and social aims, and the other was an "anti-Russian revolution in all the non-Russian ethnographic territories of the oppressed non-Russian nationalities with aims primarily national and social."[60]

In both polemical debates and policy practices in relation to the "national question," the Bolsheviks had socialists of different persuasions *and* ethnic backgrounds as their counterparts. To them, the question was always one concerning the "correct" theories and strategies within the ranks of the national and international socialist movements. In addition, before and after seizing power in Russia, the Bolsheviks constantly treated Russia's domestic "national question" from a central position vis-à-vis the peripheries.

By contrast, ever since the Mongolian revolution had been externalized to China by the Soviet foreign policy in the 1920s, the CCP had operated in a one-revolution environment in the Chinese ethnographic territory.[61] During the Long March, while moving into the non-Chinese ethnographic territories, the Chinese Communists became alienated from the ethnographic base of their own revolution. In the frontier non-Han societies, they could not find a situation of class confrontation in which they could apply the familiar mass mobilization tactics; in their daily operations, the most useful cross-ethnic counterparts were often the laboring masses' "class enemies"; physically and politically marching away from China's political center, they were seeking a tenable peripheral position of their own and tended to appear predatory rather than patronizing to the frontier peoples. Although the CCP's physical and political relations with the non-Han communities would later change again, its judgments on China's real-life "national question" were derived from the Long March, an interethnic contact that happened under conditions far from "normal" that would influence its policymaking for a long time.

During the Long March, in their relations with the non-Han frontiers, the CCP center and the Fourth Front Army followed respectively an "avoidance" and an "engagement" strategy. Zhang's abortive effort to communize the Tibetan areas in Xikang seemed closer to the Bolsheviks' sanguine strategy of treating the "minorities" as a yeast for revolution. But the lack of relevance of the Bolshevik doctrines and experiences to the Red Army would render a historical inquiry null if the inquiry is limited to the two strategies' connections to the Marxist-Leninist tradition on the "national question."

Instead, a necessary angle is to see the "avoidance" and "engagement" approaches in terms of China's long tradition of frontier affairs. The avoidance tradition has a most remarkable monument in the Great Wall, and the engagement tradition is characterized by a range of policies from outright conquests to "loose reins." Mao and the CCP center's prevailing over Zhang did not mark a conclusive victory for the avoidance approach. Having moved to the foot of the Great Wall, the CCP could not avoid dealing with the non-Han groups in the northern frontiers, just as the Great Wall had never been able to separate the "Chinese" from the "barbarians." Now, living in the close neighborhood of the Hui and Inner Mongols, the CCP had to come to terms with its new ethnopolitical environment in northwestern China. The process of the CCP's resettlement in ethnic China had the same long-term effect as the party's adaptation to the sociopolitical realities of the rural China: The process did more to reconnect the CCP movement to China's past and current realities than it did to further its Bolshevization.

5

Nationalization:
In Lieu of Internationalization

Having arrived in the northwest, the Red Army found a sanctuary in what was called the "cradle of Chinese civilization," or the big bend of the Yellow River that embraced part of Shaanxi, Suiyuan, and Shanxi. Another symbolic mark left by Chinese history, the Great Wall, demarcated the northern limit of the Chinese Communist Party's (CCP's) new base. In early 1936, Mao Zedong wrote a poem to express his impression on these monumental landscapes: "See the Great Wall, in and out, just one vast waste; the Great River, up and down, had its foam stilled."

In the same poem, Mao also disparaged the founders of some great dynasties in Chinese history and claimed that only his revolutionary associates could qualify as "truly great men."[1] The poem may have reflected Mao's "revolutionary romanticism" as asserted by the orthodox party history in today's China. But in Mao's case, the Hunanese's sentimental discharge could be triggered by the Yellow River and the Great Wall only when his cause had become marginalized from China's political and cultural centers. In history, two kinds of people had reached and crossed these landmarks—conquerors and refugees who moved either northward or southward. In the 1930s, the Red Army could hardly belong to the first category.

The Long March was an extremely arduous experience for the Red Army. The CCP center started the exodus from Jiangxi with an army 85,000 strong. Only about 4,000 of these troops survived the ordeal and reached northern Shaanxi in late 1935. In the next few months, the Red Army expanded rapidly and managed to increase its size more than five times. By the fall of 1936, after the Second and Fourth Front Armies also arrived in the area, the CCP center could again command a force of about 100,000 troops.[2] The Red Army's ability to tap into the peasant population in northwestern China seemed to vindicate Mao's Han-centered ethnostrategy, though at the time the bulk of the Red Army remained the Fourth Front Army that had survived the Tibetan encounter in Xikang.

Yet even this augmented force was ill matched against Jiang Jieshi's force of 300,000, which was moving in for the final kill. Mao and his associates had to decide what to do next. They had two options. One was to fight back into eastern China and to reenter the mainstream of China's political life; another was to break through to the international borders in the west or in the north and to get material assistance from the Soviet Union. Neither would be an easy undertaking, but both had to be tried. Eventually, the CCP would indeed be saved in the northwest, but not by these strategies. What saved the CCP was the upsurge in Chinese nationalism intensified by Japan's aggression.

Consequently, the CCP could not avoid embarking on a new course of action in suspending its class revolution against the Kuomintang (KMT, or National People's Party) regime and embracing China's national war against Japan. The significance of this development is that despite the lethal pressure from its domestic enemy, the CCP avoided the fate of internationalization and reliance on Soviet support. The external and no less lethal pressure from Japan compelled the CCP to make Chinese nationalism the central theme in its policymaking and to rely on its own resourcefulness for survival. Wielding the basically Han-centered Chinese nationalism, the CCP had to make drastic readjustments in its ethnostrategy.

"Breakthrough to the Soviet Union"

The national war against Japan in China after 1937 was a situation falling upon the CCP, not one created by its policies. On the contrary, after arriving in the northwest, CCP leaders pursued a strategy of reinforcing its anti-KMT struggle by reaching out to international assistance. In their war with the KMT, CCP leaders painfully suffered from the Red Army's inferiority in firepower. By the beginning of the Long March, the Comintern and the Soviet government had contemplated for some time the issue of sending material assistance to the CCP. But as indicated in Wang Ming's letter of 1934 to the CCP center, to get the assistance the Red Army would have to "break through" (*datong*) to the Soviet Union via Xinjiang.[3]

During the Long March, the idea of "breaking through to the Soviet Union" weighed heavily in the CCP's strategies. When the CCP center adopted the northward orientation, it was also decided that after the Red Army consolidated the new base in Shaanxi and Gansu, an operation would be launched to establish the CCP's direct connection to the Soviet Union.[4]

After the Zhang Guotao affair seriously weakened the Red Army, the CCP center became even more anxious to open a channel to Soviet assistance. In September 1935, Mao told the participants in a politburo meeting that after the Fourth Front Army split off, the original plan for the Red Army to create a soviet region in the northwest had to be replaced with a new "basic orientation" to "fight to the Soviet Union borders." Not expecting an easy reunion with Zhang Guotao, Mao considered it most urgent for the Red Army to "get instructions and assistance from the Comintern." The tasks of "rearranging, rejuvenating, and enlarging our force" should be fulfilled in the meantime. At the same meeting, Mao made an effort to enliven his depressed comrades, but the line he used was rather somber:

We can always seek help from others. *Our party is not independent and it is a branch of the Comintern.* Our revolution in China is part of the world revolution. We may first set up a base along the Soviet border and then develop toward the east. Otherwise, we can wage permanent guerrilla warfare.[5] [emphasis added]

In Mao's rather "national communist" career, this was a rare "international" moment. Eventually, these words would prove overly pessimistic. Yet they did reveal a conviction shared by top leaders of the CCP at the moment: if the besieged Chinese Communist movement was to be rescued by way of the Soviet assistance, it would have to "internationalize" itself by physically relying on the Soviet Union. Indeed, had later events developed along the course predicted by Mao, there would have been no "Yan'an way," a synonym for the CCP's self-reliant practice throughout China's war against Japan.

Soon after Mao's melancholy prognostication of the CCP's future, he and other leaders learned from the *Da Gong Bao* (Grand Public Daily) about the existence in northern Shaanxi of a red base area under Liu Zhidan. The news came as a pleasant surprise. Although the base included only about twenty counties, for the moment at least, it seemed large enough to accommodate the Red Army and to spare it from the fate of becoming roving rebels along China's borders.[6] Yet the CCP center did not give up the plan for establishing direct physical contact with the Soviet Union. At the end of November 1935, Mao laid out the new tasks for the Red Army. These included defensive preparations against the KMT's new offensives; the creation of a new soviet region bridging Shanxi, Shaanxi, Gansu, Suiyuan, and Ningxia; and "combination [of the soviet region] with the Soviet Union and the Mongolian People's Republic into one."[7]

By implementing these measures, the CCP would have to face the "national question" again. China's ethnic geography dictated that the CCP had to reach Soviet assistance by crossing the frontier regions in the north and northwest where the Mongolian and Muslim Hui population lived. In late November of 1935, the CCP center began to contemplate an operation to expand the current base area in the direction of Suiyuan. The purpose was to reduce the distance between the Red Army and the Mongolian People's Republic (MPR).

Because Suiyuan was part of the region historically known as Inner Mongolia, a propaganda campaign was first launched by the CCP to enlist the Inner Mongols' support.[8] It may be recalled that a similar effort had been made by the CCP among the Tibetans before its Long March entered the Tibetan areas. On December 10, 1935, a "Chinese soviet central government's proclamation to the Inner Mongolian people," undersigned by Mao, was publicized. Identifying Japanese imperialism and Jiang Jieshi as the "common enemies" of the CCP and the "Inner Mongolian nation," the document asked the Inner Mongols to fight along with the Red Army to "preserve the glory of Genghis Khan's time, avoid national extinction, embark on a road of national rejuvenation, and achieve independence and freedom in the same way as the Turkish, Polish, Ukranian, and Caucasus nations." Proclaiming that the "nation is supreme and all nations are equal," the CCP promised to support the restoration of the Inner Mongols' "original territory" and their right either to join with other peoples in a Chinese federation or to establish their own separate state. Disclaiming any intention to make an inroad into the grassland, the CCP invited Inner Mongolian leaders of all social statuses to forge an anti-Japanese and anti-KMT alliance with the Red Army.[9]

Two weeks after the proclamation was issued, the CCP politburo adopted a resolution on military strategy conceived by Mao. The strategy included three political measures and three military steps. The three political measures were: (1) to arm the Mongolian and Hui peoples' struggles against Japan and the KMT government and to incorporate these into the CCP's activities; (2) to take advantage of the internal contradictions of the enemy's camp and combine "our camp" and a "third camp" (anti-Japanese factions in the KMT) into a "unified national camp"; and (3) to combine the Chinese and Soviet Red Armies into one (at first in technological terms) on the basis of a common struggle against Japan. The military steps involved specific operations in Shaanxi, Shanxi, and Suiyuan in the next seven months, initiating separately an eastward expedition and a northward thrust toward the border of the MPR. Mao was confident that even if these measures and steps fell short of connecting the CCP with the MPR, the CCP's current base would be significantly enlarged and new opportunities would be created.[10]

As with the earlier propaganda toward the Tibetan population, the CCP's seemingly unequivocal support of Inner Mongols' ethnonationalist aspirations did not indicate that the CCP was prepared at this point to put its class-struggle doctrine in abeyance and to embrace the banner of nationalism. On the contrary, the CCP acknowledged the legitimacy of Mongolian nationalism exactly because its own contest with the KMT, construed as China's proletarian–bourgeois class struggle, had entered a most difficult phase. In this sense, the CCP's endorsement of Mongolian nationalism was expedient. It was made as a tactical concession to the Inner Mongols in the spirit of the Leninist strategy of using the "minorities'" ethnonationalism as a "revolutionary yeast" to undermine the "bourgeois" power structure.[11]

Not surprisingly, the CCP leaders' support of the Inner Mongols' ethnopolitical agenda was conditioned by the latter's participation in the CCP's current war against the KMT. Because of the existence of Japanese influence in Inner Mongolia, the CCP referred to Japan and the KMT regime in the same breath to define a "correct" direction for Mongolian nationalism.

In retrospect, the CCP's double-barreled orientation against both Japan and the KMT was politically difficult and strategically unfeasible. Yet the orientation appeared entirely logical to the CCP leadership at the time: The KMT regime remained the CCP's unrelenting internal enemy; Japan's penetration into Inner Mongolia might block the CCP's frontier strategy. More important, when Mao and other CCP strategists increasingly considered the Red Army's strategic position in the context of Soviet–MPR power, they could not avoid adopting a vantage point similar to that of the Soviets and the MPR. That was to view Inner Mongolia as a potential buffer zone against hostile forces from the south (the KMT) and the east (the Japanese). Thus the CCP's attitude toward Mongolian nationalism at the time was part and parcel of its "internationalizing" strategy.

In this sense, the context of the CCP's Inner Mongolian orientation differed from that of the Leninist strategy. Whereas the Leninist strategy was set at the "center" to cope with the "national question" of the "peripheries," the CCP's was the other way around and was a genuine peripheral strategy against the "center" of Chinese politics. In other words, depending on the directions of events, in the mid-1930s the CCP leaders could not rule out the possibility that their tactical support for Inner Mongols' political aspirations could turn into a substantial concession to Mongolian nationalism.

At the time, the Inner Mongols obviously occupied a prominent position in the CCP's military plan. According to Mao, the party had a relatively weak but workable relationship with the Inner Mongols. This attitude constituted a sharp contrast to the CCP center's utterly dismissive attitude toward the Tibetan populace in its controversy with Zhang Guotao. As mentioned above, due to its ideological affinity with the MPR, the CCP tended to view the Mongols as revolutionary "brothers." A positive appraisal of the Inner Mongols was also necessitated by the fact that to implement the strategy for a "breakthrough to the Soviet Union," the Red Army could not avoid going through Inner Mongolia.

Some recent developments in Inner Mongolia also helped to moderately resuscitate the CCP's confidence in working with the "minorities." In the summer of 1933, an autonomous movement emerged in western Inner Mongolia under Prince Demchugdongrob (Prince De), *jasag* (banner head) of West Sunid Banner. Complaining about the KMT government's failure to recover Outer Mongolia from Soviet control, to protect eastern Inner Mongolia from Japan's aggression, and to redress Inner Mongols' general grievances against the government's forced assimilation policies, the movement set up a unified Inner Mongolian government that would exercise Inner Mongols' "high-degree autonomy" for self-preservation.[12] The movement immediately challenged the KMT's administration of Inner Mongolia, which at the time was divided into several provinces.

Meanwhile, as the Japanese Army was trying to expand its influence from Manchuria to Inner Mongolia, Prince De's movement became a national security concern. The KMT government tried to manage the crisis by means of palliation. In the spring of 1934, it approved the establishment of a quasi-governmental body, named the Mongolian Local Autonomous Political Council, as a paltry concession to the Inner Mongols. But even this would be rescinded two years later. The KMT's rigid policy had a devastating effect on the Inner Mongolian autonomous movement. When it became clear that the Mongolian political council was merely a sham, Inner Mongolian nationalists split from within. Some continued to petition the KMT; some, like Prince De and his close associates, turned to the cryptically interested Japanese for help; and some made alliance with the CCP and the MPR for a radical change in China.[13]

As with any political landscape, that of Inner Mongolia was a divided one. What further complicated the situation were the region's cross-border ethnic and political links to the MPR and the influence of other international forces such as Japan and the Soviet-Comintern syndicate. The Inner Mongolian People's Revolutionary Party (IMPRP) of the 1920s became fragmented as well after the CCP–KMT split of 1927. When the CCP center and the Comintern, mainly through the MPR, worked without coordination to recover Communist influence in Inner Mongolia in the late 1920s and early 1930s, there were also some local rebellions under the leadership of a remnant left wing of the IMPRP. Among these, the better known was the military regime in Uusin Banner of Yekejuu League, which resisted the local Mongolian prince and Chinese local warlord between 1926 and 1929. Its leader was Sini (meaning "new") Lama (Ulijet Jirgalang). In the early 1920s, he spent a period in the MPR and received political and military training there. In 1925, he became a founding member of the IMPRP and of its Central Committee's Executive Committee.

As the founders of the MPR had done in Outer Mongolia several years before, Sini Lama started his rebellion with a traditional form of anti-authority organization in Mongolia, the *duguilong* (rebellion circle in which the participants signed their names in the pledge or petition in a circle so that the authorities could not identify the leaders). According to an official account in China, at certain point of the rebellion Sini Lama made contact with the CCP organization in northern Shaanxi for guidance. But his principal supporter was the authorities of the MPR, which supplied weapons and money to the Uusin regime until Sini Lama was assassinated in 1929. Then, between 1929 and 1931, another large-scale *duguilong* rebellion took place among the Khorchin Mongols of Jerim League under the leadership of Gada Meiren. Gada Meiren did not have Sini Lama's partisan background but led a struggle typical of the ethnic conflict between the Mongols and the Han authorities—a resistance against greedy Chinese warlords' land cultivation.[14]

To the CCP, these developments indicated that the Inner Mongols were politically motivated and that objective conditions did exist for the party's nationality work. The CCP's 1935 proclamation to the Inner Mongols indeed impressed many and would be well remembered in Inner Mongolia in the years to come. But in the short run, the implementation of the CCP's ethnopolitics hinged on the success of its strategy to establish direct contact with the Soviet Union. In the early months of 1936, the eastward expedition was launched but did not succeed. The planned next step to move the Red Army toward the MPR border thus could not be implemented.[15]

The frustration, however, did not immediately change the CCP's strategic goal. In late April, in a message to Moscow, the CCP center asked the Soviet government to provide the Red Army with "rifles and munitions, light and heavy machine guns, antiaircraft machine guns, modern equipment for bridge construction, and equipment for radio communications." If Moscow approved the request, the message stated, the entire Red Army was ready to move into Suiyuan to receive the materials in the fall of the year.[16] In mid-May of 1936, the CCP made another effort to reach the MPR border, but this time the expedition pointed to Gansu, Ningxia, and Qinghai in the west, a route that Mao had preferred not to take earlier.[17]

The three provinces in the west were within the so-called Quran Belt of China and were inhabited by a great number of the Hui people. Before the expedition was launched, the CCP repeated its established routine and issued a policy statement to the Hui. The statement was again signed by Mao and worded in the same vein as that to the Inner Mongols.[18] This time, the Red Army was able to penetrate into these provinces and to test the effect of the CCP leadership's proclamation-making exercise. The western expedition was implemented in phases between the summers of 1936 and 1937. Unknowingly, the Red Army stumbled into an extremely complicated web of domestic, ethnic, and international politics. The consequence was disastrous.

Because Soviet assistance was the main objective, the Red Army's action had to be coordinated with Moscow's intentions. At the time, however, the CCP was not necessarily the top priority for the Kremlin's China policy. The Japanese threat, the possibility of collaboration with the KMT, and the Soviet Union's long-term interests in the MPR and Xinjiang were all competing with the CCP question for Soviet leaders' attention. Between the spring and summer of 1936, leaders in Moscow became especially worried about the progress Japan was making in consolidating itself in northeastern and northern China. They urged the CCP to seek a cease-fire with Jiang Jieshi and criticized the CCP's selective united-front policy that rejected Jiang as a counterpart in China's national anti-Japanese struggle.[19] To the leaders in Moscow, at this moment, a CCP military thrust against the KMT military forces in the northwest was at least inopportune. When Moscow juggled these policy elements, the CCP suffered in China.

Regarding Soviet assistance as the most important precondition for the CCP to regain vitality in Chinese politics and not knowing about Moscow's complex power calculation, CCP leaders were troubled by what appeared to them Moscow's inability to decide in what direction the assistance should be delivered. After the CCP started its western expedition, Moscow wavered between the MPR and Xinjiang as the designated gateway for sending aid to the CCP. In November 1936, after Xinjiang was chosen by Moscow as the preferred location, the Soviets again became hesitant about whether or not the Chinese Red Army should be allowed to enter the region, which was then a Soviet sphere of influence.[20]

Moscow's vacillation certainly did not help the CCP center to clearly define its military strategy. In November 1936, after the Red Army failed to prevail in a "battle for Ningxia," the CCP leadership fell into a quandary as to what should be its next move. At a politburo meeting, Mao himself was atypically indeterminate. He told those present: "Our actions now are like straddling on two boats; it is better that the western expedition continues to move west and the eastern expedition continues to move east. If the westward movement cannot achieve its goals, of course we can turn to the east."[21] In this atmosphere, the CCP center allowed its "western route army" to stagger toward Xinjiang until it became too late to save the unit from being pulverized in the wasteland of the far west by the Hui warlords' troops.

The western route army was made up mainly of the original Fourth Front Army. When it joined the "battle for Ningxia" in October 1936, the army had 21,000 troops. By May 1937, only 437 of these had survived the ordeal of the "western expedition" and entered Xinjiang, which now served as a sanctuary for the survivors but no longer a gateway for the Red Army to receive Soviet aid.[22] In Moscow, Georgi Dimitrov, secretary general of the Comintern, suggested to Stalin that these survivors be admitted into the Soviet Union to receive training. However, this idea was rejected by Stalin's foreign minister, Viacheslav Molotov.[23] Clearly, in this case the interests of the Soviet state took precedence over the spirit of international communism in Moscow's policymaking. For all practical purposes, the failure of the western expedition marked the end of the CCP's strategy for a "breakthrough to the Soviet Union."

Genesis of a Failure

The western route army's failure cost about a third of the Red Army's regular troops, and the impact on the CCP was devastating. Because the western route army was mainly made up of troops from the Fourth Front Army, the CCP center conveniently blamed the "legacies of the Guotao line" for the failure. Zhang Guotao did not participate in the western expedition. Ironically, during the expedition, as a member of the CCP's central military council, Zhang sent telegrams to his former colleagues in the western route army and urged them not to question the center's strategic decisions, which, in his words, were "always correct."[24]

The leadership of the western route army was just a scapegoat for the disaster that resulted from many conditions. The most important was the hesitant strategy of the CCP center, affected by Moscow's unpredictable intentions, and the CCP's own negotiations with the KMT to forge a national front against Japan. The hesitance caused the western route army to waver at a key moment among the options of westward advance, eastward retreat, or base construction on the spot. After valuable time had been wasted, none of these could be undertaken. In the historiography on these events, there is a view that failing to use the western route army to open a passage to the Soviet Union, the CCP center decided to change its mission into a decoy to draw a great number of KMT troops away from the Red Army's home base. But this scenario cannot be sustained by evidence. If it was indeed the case, a question can be raised immediately about the CCP center's motive during the operation of sacrificing the better part of the former Fourth Front Army, which not long before had been Zhang Guotao's power base.[25]

The western route army's failure also indicated the bankruptcy of the CCP's ethnopolitics. In dealing with the conditions of the Quran Belt, the CCP's practices, including issuing nationality policy statements, observing special disciplinary codes in minority regions, and organizing minority nationalities' local governments, proved perfunctory. As a "people's army" that by nature relied on constant popular support for its operations, the Red Army, in thrashing into the Muslim areas in the west, was deprived of the key conditions for its existence. In comparison, the Fourth Front Army's earlier sufferings in a no-man's land in Xikang was more fortunate. This time, in Ningxia, Qinghai and beyond, the western route army was greeted by the local warlords with fierce resistance.

During its expedition, the western route army was supposed to "enlarge the Red Army vigorously." But its reports to the CCP center indicated differently: "After crossing the [Yellow] River, our side suffered many casualties and lost a great number of munitions, and these have not been replenished"; "two thousand eight hundred casualties, and six hundred missing, . . . [but] enlisted less than fifty into the Red Army"; "there are more Han people around Shandan city. . . and thirty have been enlisted into the Red Army." These same reports revealed a different situation for the enemy: "Ma's [Bufang and Ma Hongkui] forces have suffered very heavy casualties but still can concentrate new and picked troops to fight to the death"; "Ma's forces have suffered more than five thousand casualties but can get rapid replenishment from militias and flocks of able-bodied men."[26] Mao's earlier ominous prediction about the Fourth Front Army's extinction in a minority region had finally materialized in the fate of the western route army. But this time the CCP center itself, not Zhang Guotao, was responsible.

In the CCP's preexpedition statements toward the Hui people of the northwest, Han–Hui unity was promoted on the basis of a common struggle against the Japanese and the KMT regime, the principle of national self-determination was reaffirmed, and respect for Hui cultural and religious practices was vouched.[27] The policy indeed achieved certain results on the eastern side of the Yellow River. For instance, in 1936, during the "battle for Ningxia," a Hui autonomous government was set up by the Red Army in the Yuhai and Haiyuan area of Ningxia and managed to last for a few months.[28] But when the western route army pushed further west along the so-called Hexi (west of the Yellow River) corridor in Gansu, the Hui people's cooperation became exceptional rather than common. In injecting its force deeply into the Quran Belt, the CCP leadership did not seem to realize that the move threatened to topple a delicate balance of ethnopolitical power in the region.

By the time of the western expedition, the four Mas of the northwest (Ma Hongkui and Ma Hongbin in Ningxia, Ma Bufang in Qinghai, and Ma Buqing in western Gansu) had dominated the local affairs and had managed to keep Jiang Jieshi's government at arm's length. While pledging nominal allegiance to the KMT regime and Jiang Jieshi himself, the Ma families consolidated their local power by maintaining large personal armies. Jiang did not want to tolerate the existence of such semi-independent regimes within China; he tried to debilitate these Hui strongmen by using other warlords' forces, KMT organizations, secret police, and political pressure. But until the time of the Red Army's westward advance, Jiang had not been successful.[29] Tyrannical, autocratic, and exploitative as the Ma regimes were, they were Muslim in life and autonomous in their relationship with the KMT's central government.

These Ma regimes were far from being popular even among the ordinary Hui people, but they controlled the population efficaciously by combining the factor of fear with those of ethnic and religious ties. The Mas used clan, regional, and religious identities as the standards for selecting army and government officials. Although people of other ethnic origins did get appointed, they had to be absolutely loyal to the Ma families. The KMT's party organization was allowed to exist in the Mas' domains only because it was tightly controlled by the Ma families as well. Even the widely dreaded and supposedly omnipresent secret police under Dai Li, the Juntong (Military Bureau of Statistics and Investigation), could not compete with the Mas' local power. In Ningxia, Juntong agents became active after 1936. But, after a few confrontations with Ma Hongkui's own "special police," the Juntong was forced to go underground.[30]

Therefore, on the western side of the Yellow River, while poised to inflame the Hui populace with anti-Jiang and anti-Japanese slogans and enlist their support to the CCP, the western route army in reality posed a direct challenge to the well-organized military camp controlled by a few Hui regimes. By means of ethnic, religious, and brutal force suasion, these regimes had already effectively controlled the local population and could use them in a ferocious fight to keep the Han influence out of their land. The Hui warlords differed from the other warlords of the republican period in the fact that they combined their own interests with the local people's ethnic identity and historical memories. Reminders of a special kind of historical memories were indeed not lacking. Names of places in the region, such as Jingyuan (meaning "pacify the remote"), Pingfan (suppress the babarians), Anxi (secure the west), Wuwei (military might), and Hulangguan (pass of tigers and wolfs) recorded a history of bloody suppressions waged by China's central authorities against the local people.

More than a half-century before, the Ma brothers' grandfathers had laid the foundation for the Ma families' rule in the area by assisting the Manchu court to suppress their own people's uprisings.[31] Since that time, these ethnic autocracies had used local stability and their feudalistic loyalty to Jiang Jieshi to exchange the central government's noninterference in their rule of the region, and thus they had succeeded in shifting the arena of the center–periphery contest from the region to the "court." To the Muslim population, the tyranny of the Ma families was at least a tyranny of their own.

Now, the injection of the Red Army politics threatened to change the arrangement. The Red Army only tentatively tried the united-front approach with the Ma brothers but most of the time agitated for the overthrow of the Ma regimes.[32] Either way, the Ma regimes would not be able to maintain their relationships with the local populace and the KMT government that had until that time worked for themselves. In fighting the western route army, the Mas were not merely resisting the Chinese Communists; they were also blocking the extension of the KMT influence into the area in the form of anticommunist campaigns. After they won the war against the western route army, the Mas believed that the status quo of their relationship with the KMT regime was consolidated.

In early 1937, in a report to Jiang Jieshi, Ma Bufang boasted that because of the Mas's effort to defeat the western route army and their continuous support of Jiang Jieshi, "the [KMT] center has achieved a profound understanding of us. Now not only our army has gained a glorious reputation, but even the status of the Gansu and Qinghai populace has also been enhanced significantly."[33] Therefore, in a sense the guns in the war for the Hexi corridor echoed the ancient ethnic conflicts in the region as well as the warlord warfare in modern China.

Only afterward did the CCP learn the event's complicated connotations. Chen Changhao, political commissar of the western route army, was impressed by the "unity of the [Hui] nationality and the savage valiancy of the people's morale." His postdefeat "self-criticism" within the CCP touched upon the ethnopolitical elements of the western route army's debacle. About the "objective reasons" for the defeat, Chen had these words to say:

(1) Ma Bufang and Ma Buqing occupied Qinghai and northern Gansu for many years with their Hui army. They relied on the advantageous geographic conditions, the [economic] miracles based on exploitation, and the unity of the indomitable and barbarous [*yeman*] Hui people; they harbored a hatred caused by Han rulers' massacres in history, were affected by the "annihilate and prevent communism [propaganda]" in the past ten years, and were fearful of the nonsense about [our] "breakthrough to the Comintern." They regarded the CCP and the Red Army as bitterly hated enemies, and equated our invasion of their territories with an attempt to overthrow their rule. It should really be expected that, with the encouragement and assistance from Japanese imperialism, pro-Japanese cliques, and Jiang Jieshi, they would mobilize all national, political, military, and various "anticommunist" forces in the society to resist us actively and fiercely to the end.

(2) Objectively there was no possibility to achieve cease-fire and a united front [with the Mas]. The Hui people is a minority nationality and they view northern Gansu as the source of their life. The enemy has the regional advantage, but we have all the unfavorable social conditions. At the time we were promoting "peaceful unification" and "resist Japan to save the country," and proclaimed not to fight unless for self-defense. To the Hui nationality, we pledged forcefully against violation of its interests

and for an alliance with the Hui to resist Japan. But our move toward northern Gansu led the Hui army to believe that we invaded its area, abandoned peace, went back on promises, and intended to seize northern Gansu and to destroy the Hui army. Holding this narrow political view, the two Mas were impervious to our explanations and [efforts for] alliance and united front, and were determined to fight us with their main force.

(3) . . . In China the two Mas' cavalries are not the largest or the strongest, but they created a situation of regional domination and followed a policy of self-strengthening. . . . Their purpose was not just to deal with us; they also wanted to keep their territories for coping with the [KMT] center and for fending off Xinjiang and Mongolia. The magnitude of their strength was indeed beyond our expectations. . . . [The two Mas'] light equipment, fighting effectiveness, fast movement, familiarity with the terrain, inexhaustible supply of materials and manpower, . . . plus [the Hui's] national unity and the ferocity of the local people, these are exactly the conditions needed for military operations in northern Gansu.[34]

Chen Changhao's remains the only known statement by a senior CCP cadre on the ethnopolitical aspect of the western route army's failure. Clearly, in Chen's view, although the western route army had been fighting the warlord troops under the Mas, it had really been involved in an interethnic struggle and fighting with the Hui "nation." It should be noted that despite the ethnic character of the local politics in Gansu, Qinghai, and Ningxia, the Hui, unlike the Tibetans and Inner Mongols, did not at the time pursue a separate national identity from the Han Chinese. Instead, ever since the beginning of the Republic of China, the Hui elites had followed "strategies of integration" to position themselves in the existent Chinese system.[35]

Whatever insights were offered by Chen on the ethnic facet of the western expedition, these did not receive any serious attention from the CCP center because, at most, an ethnopolitical situation was just part of the "objective" conditions. What concerned Mao and associates most was the "subjective" reason for the failure, which by definition was the "Guotao line" presumably still helped by officers of the former Fourth Front Army. A campaign to criticize Zhang Guotao began within the CCP in early 1937. It was conducted to set a verdict on Zhang's "mistake" in splitting the Red Army during the Long March.

It was simply convenient for Mao to lay the responsibility for the western route army's failure on Zhang's shoulders as well. Zhang's "mistake" in relation to the minority nationalities was indeed mentioned in the criticism, and he was accused for prematurely and chauvinistically imposing a federal system on the Tibetans. But the real disagreement between Zhang and Mao over the Tibetans' "revolutionary quality" was completely forgotten.[36] In this circumstance, the CCP's ethnopolitical failure in the western expedition was also ignored. It was Chen Changhao who criticized himself briefly for not paying enough attention to the "mass work" among the Hui people.[37] But this did not lead to the CCP center's careful deliberation on the matter. It can only be inferred that after they misjudged the Hui people's condition on a massive scale, CCP leaders' already feeble confidence in working with the non-Han peoples was further eroded by the western expedition fiasco.

The extinction of the western route army would have put the CCP in an even worse position had it not taken place concurrently with a nationwide KMT–CCP truce. In early 1937, the KMT–CCP negotiations for a national united front against Japan were making progress. This development, however, only highlighted the western route army's misfortune; although the prospect of KMT–CCP cooperation did not move Jiang Jieshi to restrain the Ma brothers, who were slaughtering the disintegrated western route army, the prospect did influence the CCP center's decision on suspending a rescue operation to save the isolated western route army in the Hexi corridor.

The truce with the KMT constituted a fateful alteration of the CCP's living environment and opened many new opportunities for the party. Indeed, after this point, the worst time was over for the CCP. The desperate "internationalization" orientation, as represented by the "breakthrough to the Soviet Union" idea and actions, came to an end. Now the party turned its eyes inward and held a "nationalization" program for enlisting the vast Chinese populace to join its side.

"Trap of Nationalism"

While the western route army was still struggling to escape a fate of extinction, Mao telegraphed its commanders that Soviet aid would not come soon and "at present you must rely completely on yourselves to struggle in unison and to create a new situation."[38] At the time Mao probably knew that his prescription for the western route army would have to be applied to the entire CCP as well. What he could not foresee was that the Chinese Communists would not receive any assistance from the Soviet Union in the next decade. During that period, the CCP would have to develop the self-reliant "Yan'an way" to keep its movement alive. It is this self-reliance that finally made the CCP a distinct Chinese Communist movement independent from Moscow.

In view of the aforementioned serious efforts made by the CCP to become reliant on the Soviet Union, a big "what if" question in the CCP's history may be asked. What would the movement have become if its strategy for a "breakthrough to the Soviet Union" had succeeded? In that event, the CCP would have been further "Bolshevized" and "sovietized" in its ideological, political, and organizational orientations, and it would have become more marginalized in China's political life. It is also conceivable that the CCP would have developed a closer relationship with the local population either in Mongolia or in Xinjiang. Such a scenario would probably not have provided the CCP with the best chance to reenter China's highly nationalistic politics after 1937. In actual history, from the late 1930s to the mid-1940s, the CCP not only learned to decide its own policies despite its continued ideological affiliation with the Soviet Union but also reemerged in Chinese politics as a formidable challenger to the KMT regime. In this sense, the devastating defeat of the western route army was a blessing for the CCP in the long run.

Yet the key historical agent that turned the CCP's fiasco in the west into a blessing was Japan's aggression against China, a development termed by some as a "fortunate catastrophe" for the CCP.[39] However, the CCP—alarmed and angered by Japan's every aggressive move in northeastern and northern China since 1931—had adhered to its counterpart orientation to Jiang Jieshi's much criticized policy of "internal pacification must precede external resistance." Namely, to the CCP leadership, the anti-KMT revolutionary war had to take precedence over a national war of resistance against Japan. Or, in Zhou Enlai's words: "Resistance against Japan may need Jiang [Jieshi], but one must not sacrifice himself to Jiang even for the sake of resistance against Japanese."[40]

As early as in December 1931, a few months after Japan's occupation of Manchuria, the CCP center acknowledged that the party lagged behind the Chinese people's anti-imperialist demands because it feared to "fall into a trap of the KMT's nationalism." At the time, the party's weak relationship with Chinese nationalism was also reflected in a criticism within the party that the soviet movement in rural China "knew only about the land revolution but nothing about the national revolution." Yet as long as the CCP was trying to turn itself loose from the KMT's killing claws, the CCP center was only able to issue hollow directives to its organizations in North China on making preparations for a "national revolutionary war" against both Japanese imperialism and the KMT regime.[41] These were hollow because, as a rebellious movement, the CCP could not simultaneously wage a revolutionary war to overthrow the Chinese government and conduct a national war to defend the motherland.

Eventually, China was overwhelmed by its national crisis, and the KMT regime was compelled to ease its pressure on the CCP. But it took a mutiny by Jiang Jieshi's two generals, Zhang Xueliang and Yang Hucheng, in Xi'an on December 12, 1936, to turn the KMT regime around. During the process of solving the Xi'an incident, for the last time the CCP acted according to Moscow's intentions and helped bring the incident to a peaceful conclusion.[42] This paved the way for the second cooperative effort between the CCP and the KMT, and hence for China's national war of resistance against Japan.

It needs to be noted, however, that the "fortunate catastrophe" thesis alone cannot explain the drastic policy reorientations by the two Chinese parties. The CCP's relocation to northwestern China and the Comintern's "popular front" orientation after the mid-1930s were as important. The CCP's moving to the northwest, as discussed above, did not result in its securing a safe haven or obtaining Soviet assistance; the move, nevertheless, altered the party's geopolitical relationships with the KMT, the Japanese Army, and the northwestern non-Han peoples. As the distance between the CCP and the KMT increased, the CCP bases and the intruding Japanese army in North China became much closer than before. The situation made it easier for the KMT regime to tolerate a temporary coexistence with the CCP in order to fight the Japanese invader first.

In addition, in the summer of 1935, to resist the fascist tide in Europe, the Comintern adopted a popular-front policy for its European branches. During the sudden commotions in China caused by the Xi'an incident, the Comintern also urged the CCP to seek a peaceful solution of the crisis. These developments not only facilitated the critical formation of the CCP–KMT cooperation but also removed a question within the CCP that such a cooperation would constitute a desertion of Marxist orthodoxy on class struggles.[43]

During the Sino–Japanese war in the next few years, the CCP's relationship with the official Chinese state changed drastically. Before the war, the CCP implemented revolutionary programs wrapped in a dogmatic coat imported from the Comintern, maintained a rebellious status against the KMT central government, and incited China's non-Han groups to exercise their right to national self-determination vis-à-vis the Chinese government. During the war, the CCP openly brandished the banner of Chinese nationalism, committed itself to the defense of China's territorial and sovereign integrity in cooperation with the KMT, and urged all peoples in China, Han and non-Han, to unite in a common struggle against Japan. By the war's beginning in 1937, in reciprocating the KMT government's legalization of their regime in Yan'an, CCP leaders had basically identified themselves with the goals of the KMT's official nationalism.[44]

After reaching a rapprochement with the KMT, the CCP could mend its relationship with Chinese nationalism without much difficulty. In early 1937, Liu Shaoqi, then in charge of the CCP's work in KMT-controlled areas, wrote a letter to the CCP center. In the letter, Liu criticized the party for constantly emphasizing "support and protection of the Soviet Union" but neglecting Chinese people's demands in the past decade. Soon Mao personally endorsed the letter.[45] In the war years, the CCP would never fail again to stress its Chineseness. The most authoritative testimony on the CCP's national roots and loyalty was made by Mao himself. During the war, when asked by an American journalist which came first for the CCP between "China" and "Communist Party," Mao answered that the question was tantamount to asking who came first between a father and his child. "We Chinese have to use our own brains to think and decide what can grow from the soil of China," he remarked.[46]

The "nationalization" reorientation by the CCP was not just limited to rhetoric. Substantive policy changes were made to defer to Chinese nationalism. A fundamental change involved the CCP's suspension of its class-struggle strategy. According to the CCP's wartime reasoning, in an independent nation different classes ran into conflicts of interest but shared no "common interests for the entire nation"; because China was not such a nation and was on the verge of "national subjugation and racial extinction" (*wangguo miezhong*), the Chinese nation as a whole had an "identical interest" in survival.[47] Therefore, class struggles had to be suspended in favor of national unity. This new party line on China's domestic unity had a direct impact on the party's stand on China's interethnic relations.

Although the CCP's domestic class peace had the first KMT–CCP cooperative effort in the 1920s as a precedent and the Comintern's "people's front" orientation in Europe of the 1930s as an example, the readjustment of the CCP's ethnopolitics proved a much more difficult task for the CCP in both theoretical and practical senses. In this regard, the Bolshevik clichés and precedents became irrelevant because they basically pertained to the value of the "national question" in class struggles, not to the question's ramifications for a class peace. In other words, after the CCP nationalized its political orientation in favor of the official Chinese state, for the first time in its history the party could no longer define its nationality policy by merely citing Bolshevik jargon. The CCP had to develop a new set of definitions for such basic conceptions as the *Chinese* state, the *Chinese* nation, and China's "minority nationalities"—and the relations among these nationalities.

Earlier, in late 1935, when the CCP center just began to contemplate a national united front strategy, it took "state" to mean the "soviet people's republic" and "nation" to mean *zhonghua minzu* (literally, "central hua nation") excluding the non-Han groups. Under these definitions, the soviet republic represented both the "identical national interests" of the Han Chinese in a struggle against Japan and a revolutionary model for China's other "suppressed nationalities" to fight against the current Chinese central authorities. Despite its asserted "national" and anti-Japanese character, in practice this orientation continued the CCP's anti-KMT class struggle and interethnic agitations.[48]

Such a formula became passé in 1937. In May, Zhang Wentian (a.k.a. Luo Fu), then a leading member of the politburo, published an article to indicate the CCP's acceptance of Sun Yat-sen's Three People's Principles as the basis for the emerging national united front. An important leap of faith was made in the article in recognizing the Republic of China, no longer the "Chinese soviet state," as the territorial realm of the new national unity. Soon, in a report to the Comintern, the CCP center explained that under current circumstances, the principle of nationalism in practice meant nonrecognition of Japan's occupation of North China, the Northeast, and Inner Mongolia; protection of China's territorial and sovereign integrity; support for the minority peoples' rights of national equality and self-determination; and a reorganization of the Republic of China on the basis of a free union of all China's nationalities.[49]

On this occasion, CCP leaders did not bother to clarify the relationship between the non-Han groups' rights to "national equality" and "self-determination," or to explain the apparent inconsistency between the party's traditional support of the Mongolian People's Republic's independence and the official conception of the Republic of China that claimed China's sovereignty over Outer Mongolia. By the time, the CCP had already modified its attitude toward the MPR. Not long before, in a conversation with Edgar Snow, Mao asserted that when China became a democratic republic, Outer Mongolia would voluntarily join China in a federation.[50]

"Chinese Nation"

Although a multinational Chinese federation was not a novel idea and still reflected the Soviet model, the CCP's acceptance of the official Chinese Republican state as the territorial prototype for such a federation did represent a new commitment. The CCP's transition from the soviet state to the Chinese state was made relatively easily, but the redefinition of the "Chinese nation" proved more difficult. Unlike the CCP leadership in the early 1920s— which, to qualify the CCP for Comintern membership, had simply adapted the Bolshevik conceptions of "nation" to China—the leaders in Yan'an earnestly sought a workable definition of the Chinese nation that could meet the party's political need in China as well as its by now laxer understanding of Communist orthodoxy.

In the summer and fall of 1938, the CCP leadership held a series of lectures especially designed to help high-ranking party cadres clarify the question. The lecturer was Yang Song, a Soviet trained cadre and a frequent participant in the politburo meetings during this period.[51] Because the KMT was an ally now, Yang chose a theme from Japanese propaganda as his debating opponent, one suggesting that China had never been a nation but belonged to the same race and shared the same culture with Japan (*tongwen tongzhong*). Informed by Joseph Stalin's notion about the "modern nation," Yang argued that a modern Chinese nation indeed existed. It was *zhonghua minzu* (central hua nation). The conception was exchangeable with the political "modern Chinese" but not the ethnic Han.

The "modern Chinese nation," according to Yang, was a dynamic entity that had come into existence and continued to be configured during the "semifeudal and semicolonial" period of Chinese history (since the Opium War of 1840). Despite China's backwardness, the "Chinese nation" possessed all the principal characteristics of a modern nation in the Stalinist sense. In other words, it could pass all the linguistic, territorial, economic, and cultural-psychological tests for a modern nation. The "Chinese nation" should not be equated with the Han because the former also included members from non-Han groups who, through sinicization (in Yang's words, "assimilation with the Han people") in history, had lost their original racial (*zhongzu*) identities but had not become Han persons (*hanren*). The *zhonghua minzu* was therefore a common identity shared by these peoples and the Han. Thus, despite its inclusion of different historical stocks, the "modern Chinese nation" was a unitary ethnic entity. Yang, however, did not mean to suggest that all citizens of the Chinese Republic were members of the "Chinese nation." In China, there were minority nationalities and groups that could not yet qualify as nationalities under the Stalinist tests. China was therefore a multinational country with the "Chinese nation" as its leading core.

What, then, should be the CCP's policy toward the minority nationalities in the current national crisis? Yang argued that although the CCP's understanding and interpretation of the national self-determination principle must not be corrupted for political expedience, the principle should not be practiced by the minority nationalities during the current crisis lest their separatist tendency lead them into Japanese arms. In the future, Yang suggested, China would not follow many Western countries' examples of changing themselves from single-nation states into multinational entities via colonial conquests. China had been a multinational state from the outset; the "Chinese nation" would neither use force to conquer and assimilate the minority nationalities nor abandon its "nucleus role" in unifying these into a "modern independent and democratic country."[52]

It needs to be noted that in defining the "Chinese nation," Yang was careful to follow Stalin's formula and did not use *zhonghua minzu* in an all-encompassing manner to include every nationality in China. He also remained "Bolshevik" enough to maintain the theoretical link between the principle of national self-determination and the right of secession, insisting that the principle must not be distorted to mean merely minority nationalities' "cultural or local autonomy."[53]

This kind of theoretical subtlety appeared too tedious for Mao. When taking over the "Chinese nation" theme in his advocacy of national unity in China, he adopted a big-stroke approach. In mid-October 1938, when talking to an enlarged meeting of the CCP central committee, he declared that "the Chinese nation has indeed stood up!" Halfway through the monologue, he listed the nationality question as one of fifteen "urgent tasks for the whole nation." He put forward a plural conception, *zhonghua gezu* (various Chinese nationalities), contending that like all political parties and social classes, all nationalities of China should be included in the united front. They must be unified into one to be able to resist Japan's divisive schemes.

Politically, Mao favored self-government, the definition of which was rather ambiguous, by those non-Han nationalities who had their own communities, *provided* that they join the rest of China in the anti-Japanese war and align themselves with the Han in a unified Chinese state. Such a state, Mao elaborated, would assume the form of a democratic republic.

As for those nationalities that lived together with the Han in mixed communities, Mao argued that they should be given opportunities to participate in local administrations. In these communities, committees specialized in mediating internationality relations should be established. With regard to social policies, Mao was against forceful sinicization and for the development of the minority peoples' own languages and educational enterprises. The Han people must correct their "great Hanist" tendencies and stop using language or behavior derogatory to minority peoples' cultures, religions, and customs.[54]

This was the beginning of what has been termed by June Dreyer the CCP's "accommodation" approach to the national question, in contrast to the KMT's "assimilation" approach.[55] Yet at the time, Mao's policy statement made a sharper contrast to the CCP's own previous policies. Obviously, his intended audience was first and foremost the Han people. His declaration of the Chinese nation's standing up had a strong Han undertone. The CCP's wartime nationalism was in actuality to use a Han-centered national salvation program to replace the previous social revolution scheme centered on the laboring class. Although the earlier orientation had encouraged the minority peoples' rebellions against the Chinese authorities, the current one would not tolerate any action on the part of a minority people that might threaten to split China. Mao did not use Yang's blurred diagram of internationality relations in China; instead, Mao simply imposed the name *zhonghua* on all nationalities.

A year later, when elaborating further on the conception of the "Chinese nation" in a tract for instructional use within the CCP, Mao completely departed from Stalin's definition of the "modern nation" and made *zhonghua minzu* and the Han nationality two almost interchangeable terms throughout the Chinese history. As for the histories and cultures of the other nationalities, Mao had nothing to say except for their being part of *zhonghua minzu*.[56] In a Comintern forum, Yang's definition of the "Chinese nation" would appear more defensible than Mao's. But in Chinese politics, Mao's was certainly a more useful tenet for mobilizing the Han masses. Not surprisingly, in the war against Japan, the CCP followed Mao's formula in its mass work and political indoctrination among its troops. The conception of *zhonghua minzu* was invoked as a double-edged sword against the Japanese propaganda belittling the Chinese nation and against any minority people's separatist tendency endangering the motherland.[57]

In about 1937, the CCP undertook a reorientation—from class struggles to national salvation and from seeking Soviet assistance as a means of survival to tapping into the "Chinese nation" as the fountain of its strength—that was no minor effort. The reorientation considerably affected the CCP's nationality policy but did not change the policy's overall significance for the party. The policy was always devised not for the sake of the non-Han groups but for the need of the CCP's own strategies. To borrow the "awakening China" cliché, depending on the densities of the "international" and "national" components in its strategy at a given time, the CCP would fine-tune the dosage of its nationality policy so as to have the desired effect on the presumably torpid state of the minority nationalities. During the war against Japan, the CCP "nationalized" its strategy on a monumental scale and therefore did not wish to further awake the minority nationalities' ethnonationalism. The question is, of course, whether or not these peoples' ethnonationalism was something for any outside group to awake or hypnotize.

This is not to say that in the war years the CCP became identical with the KMT in its attitude toward the nationality question. The principle of national self-determination did not completely disappear from the CCP's rhetoric on the nationality question. Yet, unlike in the prewar years, the CCP no longer used the principle as its trademark vis-a-vis the KMT in the arena of ethnopolitics.[58] Politically, the principle became inconvenient because it promised to change the political foundation of China's ethnic relations. Now itself a defender of the foundation, the CCP nevertheless tried to differentiate its stand from the KMT's in defining the status quo of China's ethnic relations.

Thus, the CCP continued to criticize the KMT's nationality policy but with a changed focus. The issue of national self-determination no longer demarcated the fault line between the two parties. Instead, the CCP now chose to make the KMT's definition of the "Chinese nation" its main target. The criticism had a twofold task: one was to accuse the KMT of using such slogans as "nation first" and "state first" to suppress the CCP and other political parties, and another was to expose the KMT's Han chauvinism in its denying the very existence of non-Han nationalities in China.

The exercise constituted an important part of the CCP's wartime contest with the KMT for the role of representative of China's national interests. A well-known effort in this regard was the critique of Jiang Jieshi's notorious book, *China's Destiny,* issued under the name of Chen Boda, Mao's secretary. At the center of the debate was a question as to whether the Han and non-Han peoples of China were different "clans" of the same nation, as Jiang asserted in his book, or different nationalities, as the CCP literature had always claimed. Jiang stressed the blood ties among these "clans" as the basis for the formation of *zhonghua minzu,* but the CCP totally rejected the bloodline theory as racism and based the construction of *zhonghua minzu* on the long-term intercourse and association among all the nationalities involved. Following Mao's line of reasoning, Chen Boda contended that the "Chinese nation" really meant "various Chinese nationalities" (*zhonghua zhu minzu*).[59]

However, the CCP's disagreement with the KMT's definition of the Chinese nation was limited. Having embraced many of the goals of the KMT's official nationalism, the CCP could not conceptualize a Chinese nation too different from the KMT's. Actually, the two parties' presentations of *zhonghua minzu* shared these features: This was an entity that occurred in history long before the modern era; the Han was its magnetic nucleus; its formation involved other ethnic groups' ("clans" or "nationalities") assimilation with the Han; the official boundaries of the Republic of China demarcated the territorial domain of *zhonghua minzu; zhonghua minzu* was the common political identity for all members of the Republic of China; and the right to equality, not that to secession implied in "national self-determination," should be the ultimate goal pursued by all ethnic groups in China.

Indeed, the KMT and the CCP viewed the issue of equality differently. Since Sun Yat-sen's time, the KMT had believed that equality between the Han and the non-Han peoples could be achieved by treating and making the latter the same as the former. But the CCP attacked the idea of equality through assimilation as the very reason that the KMT regime refused to treat the non-Han peoples as equals of the Han.[60] Of course, in the war years, the two parties invoked the notion of *zhonghua minzu* more for unity within the Han than for equality between the Han and non-Han peoples. Their shared conviction was that only Chinese nationalism, not citizenship in the fragmentary Chinese Republic, could inspire a fervent fighting spirit against the Japanese among the vast majority of the country, the Han Chinese. Associated with *zhonghua minzu* was the image of a great nation with one of the world's richest cultures and a long and glorious past.[61] In comparison with this purpose, the political mobilization of the non-Han peoples using a lure of "equality" was secondary in the CCP's case and nonexistent in the KMT's.

An ambivalent relationship between the conception of *zhonghua minzu* and China's multinational reality was easily recognizable. Ethnologically, the conception was unwieldy in depicting and explaining China's interethnic relations. But neither the KMT nor the CCP was concerned with social scientific accuracy. To wartime leaders in China, the ethnopolitical name was too appealing to be put aside. Internationally, the image of the "Chinese nation" could justify China's right to survive as a nation-state and also invoke support from the overseas Chinese diaspora. Politically, the conception was absolutely necessary to bring all nationalities of China under one ceiling. A Han nationalism would have been too narrow to encompass all these cultural, historical, diplomatic, and ethnopolitical messages.

Surely *zhonghua minzu* was not a new term in China's political vocabulary. But during the anti-Japanese war, for the first time China's two principal parties reached a fundamental agreement on how the term should be defined. In this sense, if the official "Chinese nation" had been invented during the early years of the Chinese Republic, it was during China's war against Japan that this "imagined" Chinese community gained wide acceptance in China and abroad—hence the political guarantee for the notion's continuation to this date.[62]

To conclude this chapter, it is fitting to consider how the discussion here destabilizes some of the established interpretations in the field. It has been argued that the CCP's consistent promise of national self-determination to the minority peoples and the KMT's constant suppression of these peoples together gave life to the ethnonationalisms of China's non-Han nationalities.[63] The argument overlooks the confluence of the KMT's and CCP's nationality policies during China's war with Japan. As was indicated in discussions above, the CCP's "nationalization" after 1937 took much of the "pulling" power out of the CCP programs toward the non-Han groups. Moreover, the CCP's influence on non-Han peoples in the frontier regions, even after the party's relocation to the northwest, was always minimal. Therefore, while the KMT policies continued to "push" or alienate the frontier groups, it was the Japanese, Soviets, and British that exerted separately strong "pulling" influence on the local peoples' or regimes' tendencies toward autonomy in Inner Mongolia, Xinjiang, and Tibet.

It has also been argued that, during China's war against Japan, the CCP seized the national crisis to mobilize China's peasant masses and that the resultant "peasant nationalism" would eventually enable the CCP to win the struggle for national power.[64] Although this insight helps explain the rapid expansion of the CCP's popular basis, it does not present a complete picture of the CCP's national politics in the war years. If nationalism is to be viewed as a type of "opposition politics" targeted against a particular socio-political environment, during the anti-Japanese war the CCP's national politics embarked on a vital phase that brought about the conflation of "official" nationalism and "popular" nationalism in China.[65] In other words, the CCP would eventually ascend to power not because it smashed the KMT's official or elite nationalism with a popular or mass nationalism. Instead, the key to the CCP's success was its ability to mesh the two together, which the KMT was never able to accomplish.

Yet did the adoption of official Chinese nationalism by the CCP in the war years mean that it now joined the KMT on a path of alienating the non-Han groups of China? This is the question considered in the next chapter.

6

Borderization: Trans-Ethnic Reach

In the war years, the Chinese Communist Party (CCP) base in the northwest became officially known as the "Border Region" (*bianqu*). It is never clear why this name was chosen, or between what two domains it was a "border region." It is ironic that in 1937, when the Kuomintang (KMT, or National People's Party) government finally substituted its demarche of "internal pacification before external resistance" with cooperation with the CCP in a national war against Japan, this supposedly "external enemy" had "internalized" itself into China for several years. The Great Wall again proved useless in China's national defense, and all the important forts and passes of the Great Wall fell into the hand of the Japanese Army as of mid-1935.[1]

So the CCP's "border region," which lay between the Great Wall in the north and KMT-controlled areas in the south, indeed assumed the significance of a frontier zone between Japan's wartime empire and the KMT's official China. Replacing the more flamboyant "Chinese soviet republic," the new name certainly could provide a certain degree of comfort to the KMT regime. Nevertheless, the term also legalized the CCP's autonomy in northern China vis-à-vis the KMT's "central government" in the south. At the genesis of the Chinese history, the general region around the CCP base served as the "cradle of the Chinese civilization."

During the ensuing millenniums, however, the region gradually lost its centrality in China's cultural and political development to southern China.[2] Now, making this marginal region the cradle of its "Yan'an way" of revolution, the CCP assumed the historical role of reclaiming the north's pivotal position in China's national affairs. Years later, after achieving political power in China, the CCP would make the northwestern "Yan'an spirit" the most important moral pillar of the Communist "new China." However, there is one more (probably unintended) connotation of the "Border Region."

To those scholars of China who are attentive to the south–north dichotomy in China' national development, the "south" and the "north" represent different characters and effects of Chinese culture and politics. Yet these scholars' discussions have rarely gone beyond the ethnoculturally Chinese and geographically eastern matrix. They have paid little attention to the "northern" and "southern" models' varied relationships with the non-Han communities of Chinese Inner Asia in the west.[3] It appears that in Chinese history, dynasties established by northern "barbarians" (the Mongol Yuan and Manchu Qing Dynasties, among others) tended to be more deft in managing their relations with Inner Asia than those "Chinese" dynasties. Indeed, the Tang Dynasty is one of the most grandiose "Chinese" dynasties in Chinese history that had a successful record of dealing with Inner Asia. Li Shimin, the dynasty's founder, extended the domain of the Chinese empire in all directions and instituted a series of practices for managing China's imperial territories.

Although he was never hesitant in using military force, Li successfully applied the peaceful *jimi* (rein by appeasement, or loose control) scheme in dealing with China's ethnic peripheries in Inner Asia. He summarized his "ethnopolitics" in these words: "Ever since the ancient times everybody has valued the Chinese [*zhonghua*] and belittled the barbarians [*yidi*], but I alone love them as the same" (*zi gu jie gui zhonghua, jian yidi, zhen du ai zhi ru yi*).[4] This was not just a Confucian universalist acclamation. Li Shimin was able to cross the aged *yi xia zhi fang,* or the "barriers between the Chinese and the barbarians," largely because he was a northerner with a Turkic family background.[5]

In light of these historical precedents of trans-ethnicism and the overwhelmingly Han character of China's national affairs in the twentieth century, it is not only legitimate but also imperative to take account of China's *leading* policymakers' personal experiences in ethnic-frontier affairs when their policies and practices of interethnic significance are evaluated. Such experiences have historically proved to be a necessary basis for policy insights that can cross the interethnic barriers. The KMT leadership was deprived of such insights because none of its principals had the opportunity to foster a "frontier personality" in himself. The CCP had an advantage in this regard because the Long March reduced the physical distance between the Chinese Communist movement and China's ethnic frontiers.

To Mao Zedong and his associates, however, the interethnic barriers remained difficult to overcome. The leading core of the CCP and the Red Army consisted of mainly southern Han Chinese who had to make an effort to foster an emotional attachment to the Border Region as their adopted home. Physical contacts between the CCP and the Mongolian and the Hui peoples of the northwest might result in either a friendly or an antagonist relationship. The Red Army's frustrations with the Tibetans and the Hui during the Long March and the westward expedition from Yan'an certainly could not help make the CCP leaders follow Li Shimin's example of "loving them as the same." Yet during the war years, a collective "frontier personality" did manage to emerge within the CCP leadership. CCP leaders knew that to survive and thrive among an ethnically heterogeneous populace, their cadres and troops had to learn ways of life *and* thinking that were not Han. In a word, the CCP had to follow the precedents of the Tang, Yuan, and Qing rulers and "barbarize" itself to a certain degree.

Neighborly Behavior

A secret of the CCP's often successful "mass line" was that to win over the mass, one must first stand on the mass's side. This logic was behind the CCP's land revolution for winning over the Chinese peasantry. In the same vein, until it embraced the official Chinese nationalism at the onset of the Sino-Japanese War, the CCP professed its support for the minority peoples' right to national self-determination, presuming that this right was the top priority for every minority nationality's agenda. In so doing, the CCP—at least rhetorically—stood on the side of the non-Han peoples' ethnonationalism, in contradiction to Chinese nationalism. Its proclamations to the Tibetans, Inner Mongols, and Hui issued during and after the Long March were conspicuous examples of this orientation.

Although these proclamations identified foreign imperialism as the common enemy of Tibetans, Inner Mongols, and Hui as well as the Chinese peoples, the documents named the KMT government and Han oppressors as the culprits who had inflicted immediate harm on these peoples. During the anti-Japanese war, however, the "nationalization" of CCP programs resulted in the party's promotion of China's national unity with an inclusive ethnonym, *zhonghuan minzu* (Chinese nation). Now that Chinese nationalism superseded class struggles in the CCP's political strategy, the party switched to a stand opposing the non-Han, or anti-Han, ethnonationalism of the minority groups. The question for the CCP leadership now was what should be the new basis for a mass line in its "minority nationality work."

As a matter of fact, the CCP's reconsideration of its original stand on the minority peoples' right to national self-determination predated its second united front with the KMT. In the summer of 1936, when a Mongolian military government under Prince De was established with Japanese assistance, the CCP center was alarmed by Japan's "vicious conspiracy" to "enslave Inner Mongolia" and dismayed by the fact that the "banner of Inner Mongolia independence and autonomy" was effectively used by Japanese imperialists to harm China. Though continuing to blame the KMT regime's oppressive policies for alienating the Inner Mongols, the CCP warned the Mongolian elites that Japan would not give independence to them but would turn Inner Mongolia into a "second Korea or Manchuria." In the meantime, the CCP still adhered to its old formula and used "Outer Mongolia" as the model for the Inner Mongols' "liberation, construction, and national enhancement." A subtle change was nevertheless made by the CCP center in warning its apparatuses against organizing any independent Inner Mongolian government and army "prematurely."[6] The CCP did not hold for very long this delicate line of differentiating the "independence" pursued by the Inner Mongols in collaboration with Japan and that of the Outer Mongols under the Soviet aegis. Such a stand was no longer sustainable after the CCP adopted the official Chinese nationalism.

In the early months of 1937, the CCP center adopted a new Inner Mongolia orientation that also altered the party's general ethnopolitical strategy. In directives to its cadres in charge of Inner Mongolia work, the CCP center stressed the party's current "central mission" of fighting against Japan. Under the circumstances, therefore, "it is highly inappropriate to propagate the Mongols' independence or separation, or even their confrontation with the Han rulers." The party's Inner Mongol work should "dissipate the Han–Mongolian antagonism" and promote the two peoples' unified resistance against Japan.[7]

Along with this reorientation, the meanings of certain political labels in the CCP's political discourse also changed. During the long Chinese–Japanese conflict, a most serious national crime was collaboration with the Japanese. The collaborators were labeled as *hanjian,* or "traitors of the Han." "Han" in this term indicated both the ethnic identity of the perpetrators and the political entity that they betrayed. Clearly, by equating the betrayal of the Han with treason against the Chinese state, the label itself evidenced the surging Han-centric Chinese nationalism of the war years. The CCP also used *mengjian* (traitors of the Mongols) and *huijian* (traitors of the Hui) in its discussions of northwestern politics. Until 1936, however, these labels were used not only against perpetrators who collaborated with the Japanese but also against those who cooperated with the KMT regime. Thus, Prince De of Inner Mongolia and the four Muslim Mas became the most prominent *mengjian* and *huijian* in the CCP's list.[8] Since Prince De was collaborating with the Japanese but the Mas were not, their being similarly named as "traitors" of China and their own peoples made sense only in the CCP's prewar anti-KMT politics. Such denunciations had to be changed in the war years after the CCP modified its stand toward the KMT.

Because the Mas were on the Chinese side of the war against Japan, they could of course no longer be labeled as *huijian*. But because the Mas remained hostile neighbors to the Border Region, the CCP continued its effort to form a Hui popular organization as an alternative to the Hui warlord power in the northwest.[9] During the Sino-Japanese war, however, while cooperating with some local Hui military forces elsewhere, the CCP was never able to penetrate the Mas's power bases. Neither were the Japanese successful in this regard. In 1939, to facilitate its westward movement, the Japanese army in Suiyuan conceived a plan to create a "Hui state" in western Suiyuan and Ningxia. But in the next year, militarily frustrated by KMT troops under Fu Zuoyi and Ma Hongbin (one of the Mas), the Japanese plot went nowhere.[10] During the rest of the war, the ethnopolitics involving the Hui was largely stable and proved neither friendly toward the CCP nor separatist toward the Chinese state.

To the Chinese state, Prince De's politics in Inner Mongolia was indeed separatist, and the offense was further aggravated by his open collaboration with the Japanese. Yet surprisingly, after 1937 the CCP removed Prince De from its list of *mengjian*. A few days after the Marco Polo Bridge incident of July 7, 1937, which marked the beginning of an undeclared war between China and Japan, the CCP center set out to coordinate with the KMT regime in Mongolian affairs. Reversing its previous practice of using class and ethnic contradictions to incite revolution, the CCP now endeavored to "dissipate" quarrels among different Mongolian clans and to "mitigate" the antagonism between the Mongols and the KMT regime. To enlist as many Mongolian leaders as possible into the anti-Japanese camp, the CCP center decided to drop its slogan, "Down with *mengjian* Prince De," and to use an "upper-class united front" stratagem to turn Prince De around.[11]

Viewing Prince De as the trump card of the Japanese policies toward

Inner Mongolia, CCP leaders attached considerable significance to the work of winning him over. They refused to identify Prince De with Pu Yi, the puppet "emperor" of the "Manchukuo," believing that Prince De "used to represent the Mongolian nation's inspirations for independence and liberation" and still enjoyed a "broad trust" among the Inner Mongols. Thus, seeing Prince De as a leader of genuine nationalist conscience, the CCP construed his collaboration with Japan as a result forced by the KMT regime's suppressive policy.[12]

On this matter, the CCP's understanding of the Inner Mongolian question was very close to the conclusions of Owen Lattimore, arguably the most credible Western observer of Mongol affairs at the time. Lattimore published his opinions in the British *Journal of the Royal Central Asian Society* in mid-1936, and it was highly unlikely that the CCP leaders knew about him at this time. He did visit Yan'an in 1937 under the new cooperative atmosphere between the CCP and the KMT. There, he had a chance to quiz top CCP leaders about their policies toward the national minorities. He was "amazed" by many things he saw and heard in Yan'an, but his impression about the Chinese Communists was tarnished somewhat by their reluctance to allow him to talk to the Mongols there in their own language. The difference between the CCP's policy and Lattimore's opinion was that unlike Lattimore—who viewed Prince De's rally to the Japanese as a credibility disaster for Inner Mongolian elites and an end to any chance for a Chinese–Mongolian united front against Japan—the CCP still wanted to make an effort to correct the situation.[13] Yet aside from accordingly modifying its own propaganda toward the Inner Mongols, the CCP center did not have any concrete plan or means to play its self-assigned new role as a constructive corrector of the KMT's harmful policies.

When working among the Inner Mongols, CCP functionaries were often frustrated by the cultural and language barriers. One cadre reported how he had been maddened by his interpreter's inability to translate and explain the CCP's current political orientations to a Mongolian lama.[14] This, however, was by no means the most serious obstacle to the CCP's upper-class united front scheme regarding Prince De's group. For by this time, a significant portion of the Inner Mongolian ruling elites had achieved a remarkable knowledge of the Chinese language and culture. A more serious problem for the CCP policy was that at the time the CCP, the Comintern, and their agents in Inner Mongolia fell out of step with one another.

Until the beginning of the Sino-Japanese war in 1937, CCP underground organizations were scattered in Inner Mongolia, and most of them had no direct contact with the CCP center. Some received directives from Comintern agents based in the Mongolian People's Republic (MPR). A very active group around Yun Ze (a.k.a. Yun Shiyu and Ulanfu) could not make connection with the CCP center until 1938. In the CCP history, Yun Ze belonged to the "returned students" who received indoctrination and training in Moscow. But unlike those famous "returned Bolsheviks" such as Wang Ming and Bo Gu, who became involved in the leadership struggle in the CCP's top echelon in the early 1930s, Yun Ze returned to his home village in the Tumed Banner to "make revolution" from scratch.

In the summer of 1931, senior CCP cadre Wang Ruofei, as head of a "CCP special northwestern committee," arrived and made contact with Yun Ze. Wang came directly from Moscow via Outer Mongolia. Wang instructed Yun Ze to organize an Inner Mongolian Common People's Revolutionary Party as the CCP's front organization. This certainly was not an idea originated from the CCP center, which was still struggling for survival in the south. By instructing Yun Ze to set up a secret "international liaison station" for communication with the Comintern and the MPR, Wang probably wanted at once to strengthen the Comintern-guided work in Inner Mongolia and to establish a new channel between the CCP and Moscow. Wang was taken out of the maneuvering a few months later, when he was arrested by the local Chinese authorities.[15] Thus afterward, Yun Ze would have to continue his effort by following directives from the Comintern, without any contact with the CCP center. In the winter of 1933, following a directive from the Comintern, he began propagating anti-Japanese ideas among Inner Mongolian elites, with the special purpose of preventing Prince De's collusion with the Japanese.[16]

In March 1935, Yun Ze had a chance to talk with Prince De and tried in vain to dissuade the prince from approaching the Japanese for assistance. Realizing that he could not change Prince De's mind, Yun Ze allowed himself to be persuaded by some officers in the prince's security troops, including Yun Ze's relative Yun Jixian and secret CCP member Zhu Shifu, to support a military uprising in Bailingmiao (Bat-Khaalag). The uprising happened in late February 1936 and took about a thousand troops away from Prince De. The event, however, did not produce any lasting military or political effect.[17] Unaware of the CCP connection to the event, Prince De blamed Fu Zouyi, commander of the KMT troops in Inner Mongolia, for agitating the Bailingmiao uprising and was prompted by his Japanese advisers into launching a military offensive against Fu.[18] The uprising nevertheless had a negative consequence for the CCP as well: By taking the

CCP's secret members out of Prince De's organizations, it forestalled any chance for the party to work within the prince's camp when the CCP center decided to court the prince in 1937.[19]

Thus, despite its major policy readjustments after 1937, the CCP was unable to alter the basic ethnopolitical relationships in the northwest. In the war years, the CCP's nationality policy could only work to achieve a relatively stable relationship with its immediate non-Han neighbors. At the beginning, the Red Army's arrival in the northwest only intensified the region's already tense interethnic relations. The Red Army's relocation gave the KMT government a reason to enforce more vigorously than before its state-building measures in this previously secondary area. Both the Hui and the Mongolian communities had to suffer from the new pressure.

Between the two, however, the Mongolian banners were affected even more severely, because they were not shielded by their own strongmen. The Mongolian ruling elites were dismayed by the KMT's attempts to turn their banners into counties and to revoke their official seals issued during the Qing Dynasty or even earlier. The rich and the poor were similarly outraged by KMT troops' taking away from them thousands of horses. These developments in turn gave the CCP personnel an opportunity to present themselves with a new "Chinese" image to the Inner Mongols. By condemning the KMT regime for interfering with the Mongols' "internal affairs" (*menggu neizheng*) and violating their interests, the CCP found some new, concrete issues, other than the principle of national self-determination, to use to identify itself with the Inner Mongols.

Indeed, the CCP cadres' and troops' deeds concerning the Inner Mongols' daily life appeared more consequential than Mao's 1935 call for Inner Mongols' independence in the spirit of Genghis Khan. In mid-1936, after seizing from the local Han authorities a salt lake along the border between Shaanxi and Otog Banner of Yekejuu League, CCP cadres went out of their way to convince the Mongolian banner officials that the CCP sincerely wanted to restore the salt revenue to them. Events like this had been unheard of in previous Han–Mongol relations, in which the Han side had constantly acted as the exploiter. The action helped the CCP win the Mongols' trust and helped open more doors for political and commercial arrangements between the two sides.[20]

Yet, when regarding a region vital to the security of the CCP base, the CCP center would not hesitate to take the territory. Lying north to the Great Wall, the Hengshan Mountain range ran 155 miles along the border between Shaanxi and Yekejuu League. Historically, it was deemed by the Inner

Mongols to be part of their territory. In mid-1936, the Red Army occupied the area to set up a protective barrier for the CCP base and a gateway to the MPR. Afterward, a promise was made to the Mongols that the area would be returned to them after Japan and China's reactionary forces were defeated.[21] Although it cannot be documented to what extent the Mongols were offended by the occupation or placated by the promise, the CCP obviously intended to behave in a neighborly manner toward the Inner Mongols.

By siding with the Mongols against the KMT's practices concerning "salt revenue," "old official seals," and "horses," the CCP modified its erstwhile southern, agricultural, and Chinese character to accommodate the pastoral, Mongolian element of northwestern ethnopolitics. This marked the second stage of the CCP's cultural and political evolution after its changing from an urban-centered movement into a rurally based one. Its new posture might help the CCP to maintain a peaceful or even cooperative relationship with the neighboring Mongolian communities, but this was only the minimum objective of the CCP's wartime nationality policy. Its ultimate goal was to achieve a "great unity of all nationalities" in the war against Japan. Without the KMT government's cooperation, this goal could not be achieved. Yet, not surprisingly, this cooperation was not forthcoming.

General Fu Zuoyi was the KMT official that the CCP had to deal with in Inner Mongolia. Since August 1931, Fu had been governor of Suiyuan and in charge of KMT military affairs in the Inner Mongolia area. By the time the CCP consolidated its base in northern Shaanxi, Fu had already conducted several successful operations against the Japanese along the Great Wall. During the rest of the war, Fu endeavored to act as an effective administrator and implemented certain social and economic reforms in his area. Militarily, he was at least successful in achieving a stalemate with the Japanese Army in western Suiyuan. The CCP had every reason to maintain a working relationship with this relatively effective and firmly anti-Japanese KMT official. During the first two years of the war, Fu also welcomed CCP cadres to work in his region.[22]

Yet, insofar as his standing in northwestern ethnopolitics was concerned, Fu was a "frontier mandarin" who dutifully carried out the KMT's policies and was hated by the Inner Mongols. According to the CCP's standard, Fu Zuoyi's policy toward the Inner Mongols typically reflected the KMT's "Great Hanism."[23] But Fu had to be tolerated if he could not be changed. In early fall of 1938, the CCP center decided to create a guerrilla base in the Daqingshan Mountains of western Inner Mongolia and thereby to extend its influence to the front line between Fu's and the Japanese forces. Mao stressed to the CCP cadres responsible for the operation that "every aspect of the Suiyuan question must be considered in relation to [our] united front with Fu Zuoyi." He wanted the CCP's troops to "use our correct minority nationality policy to replace China's traditional wrong policy in the past, and to use our model to influence the KMT and, first of all, Fu Zuoyi to change." In practice, however, CCP leaders conceded that in Suiyuan "the work with the Mongols should be carried out uniformly under Fu Zuoyi."[24]

In the war years, no matter when the CCP and Fu Zuoyi were in cooperation before 1939 or in friction afterward, the CCP's "correct model" could neither change the KMT nor have much of an effect on the Mongolian population. The CCP's operation in the Daqingshan Mountains was a case in point. The area was contested by all the sides in the war because of its strategic location between China's border with the MPR in the north and the two largest cities of Suiyuan, Baotou and Guisui (today's Hohhot), in the south. In the region, the number of Mongols was rather small in certain counties (1 percent of Guyang County's population) but was substantive in some others (34 percent of Wuchuan County's population). From an ethnopolitical point of view, however, the small number of Mongols in comparison with the Han was not as significant as the fact that Mongol households existed in every village in the Daqingshan area.[25] Consequently, the CCP's operation there had to assume an ethnopolitical character.

To many Inner Mongols in Suiyuan, the Sino-Japanese war was an important event to their life not because a foreign force had invaded their land—which, in their view, had been taken away by the Han Chinese long time before—but because Japanese power provided an opportunity for them to get even with their Chinese oppressors. To the Han population, Japan's intrusion into the province had rearranged the world. At the time, a prevalent saying among the Han went: "The Mongols become puppet troops [of the Japanese], the Manchus run errands [for the Japanese], the Hui act as spies [for the Japanese], and the Han suffer." Li Jingquan, the CCP's leading official in the Daqingshan area, also observed that "today the Mongols think this is their world and therefore they can humiliate and revenge themselves on the Han."

Although the Japanese benefited from inflaming the Mongolian–Han hostility, the KMT troops' slogan, "Resistance against Japan must be preceded by extinction of the Mongols" (*kangri bi xian miemeng*), only added gasoline to the fire.[26] CCP operatives in Suiyuan admitted that the Japanese had effectively manipulated the Inner Mongols by simply reversing the KMT's negative policy toward the Mongols' aspiration for autonomy. Although accusing the Japanese for "deceiving and poisoning" the Inner Mongols with feigned support of their aspirations, the CCP could not "awake" the Inner Mongols to the Japanese plot with its own "genuine" support of Mongolian nationalism.[27]

This was the crux of the CCP's problem. To CCP cadres, who themselves were seasoned practitioners of counter-KMT tactics, the Japanese policy sounded just too familiar. Yet the CCP was supposedly on the KMT's side now and could not easily find an orientation appealing to the Mongols from its current ethnopolitical stand. Four years after the Daqingshan base was created, a CCP document admitted: "Our party and troops have some good political influence on a small number of Mongols, but [the influence] is not wide and deep enough. Our party has not achieved a solid basis within the mass and has not been able to mobilize and organize the masses in any large number."[28] From Yan'an in northern Shaanxi, the CCP center criticized the KMT regime for giving up on the Inner Mongols and viewing all the Inner Mongols in Japanese-occupied areas as *mengjian*. In the meantime, its own operatives in Suiyuan could not avoid viewing the Inner Mongols in the area as "under the Japanese aegis"; they called upon the "dear Mongolian compatriots" to "come over from the enemy's side" (*fanzheng*).[29]

There were several reasons for the ineffectiveness of the CCP's nationality policy in Suiyuan in general and in the Daqingshan area in particular. One was the CCP cadres' lack of knowledge about the Mongolian language and culture. Only in the Tumed Banner could the CCP organizations make some progress, mainly because they benefited from the banner's degree of sinicization. Tumed was in the close neighborhood of Guisui and had been subject to extensive cultural and economic sinicization since the Qing Dynasty; most of the banner's Mongolian residents did not speak the Mongolian language themselves.[30]

The "Great Hanism" among some CCP cadres was another obstacle to the CCP's ethnopolitical work. After facing initial frustrations, these cadres decided that the "people of Suiyuan were backward and could not be helped." Acting contrary to the CCP center's directive that CCP cadres must always use "reasoning and suasion" with the Mongolian mass, some cadres resorted to violence, bragging afterward that "three good words are not as effective as a *mabang*" (a rattan stick used by a rider to whip the horse). Within the party, such behavior was criticized as a "colonist policy."[31]

One more drawback of the CCP was its military weakness in the region. From the outset, the CCP center wanted the Daqingshan base to maintain a low profile. The strategic objective of the Daqingshan operation was to create a CCP foothold in the area that would give the CCP an easy access to the MPR in the event of a Soviet–Japanese war. "Long-term concealment for survival" and "avoidance of overly provoking the enemy" were the center's consistent policies to guide the operation. It was never in the CCP's plan to enlarge its military and political influence in the Daqingshan area, which would both have annoyed Fu Zuoyi and attracted attacks from the Japanese. Therefore, in the area, the CCP only used a cavalry detachment of 1,000 to keep the guerrilla warfare alive. Mao wanted it to be a "cavalry detachment of nomadic character." Consequently, the CCP's "governmental" establishments in Suiyuan were constantly on the run.[32] Militarily weaker than both the KMT and the Japanese in the region, politically the CCP could not be very persuasive to the Mongols.

In ethnopolitics, surely, power is not always the most persuasive factor. In the final analysis, in dealing with the Inner Mongols, the CCP was hindered by its wartime programs of Chinese nationalism. In Suiyuan and Chahar, the Japanese military authorities' success in manipulating the Inner Mongols should be attributed more to its ethnopolitical schemes than to its military power.[33] As an unflagging critic of the KMT's oppressive policies in Inner Mongolia, the CCP leadership was not blind to this fact. Unfortunately, because of its wartime alliance with the KMT and its fundamental stand of defending the Chinese Republic against Japan, the CCP could not deploy any strong ethnopolitical measures to counterbalance the Japanese.

One example was the issue of the "Mongolian land." In Mao's 1935 proclamation to the Inner Mongols, the CCP pledged to roll back the Han's encroachment on the Mongolian land, one of Mongols' basic grievances. But after 1937, as the CCP ceased working to gain the Inner Mongols' "support to the reds" (*qinhong*) and began to induce them to "resist Japan," its policy on the issue of the "Mongolian land" also changed. Now the CCP center's attitude was that "the Mongolian land should be returned to the Mongols, but this is not a formula and has to be decided according to circumstances." The slogan of "restoration of the Mongolian land" was still used by the party, but its new meaning was to regain the land from the Japanese, not from the Han Chinese.[34]

In the war years, the "circumstances" regarding the land issue in Suiyuan were that under the Japanese incitement, the Inner Mongols took action to roll back the Han Chinese's agricultural inroad into their areas. Reporting the development to Yan'an, CCP officials in the Daqingshan area suggested that the process might be stopped by "bribing" the Mongols. Thus the CCP center agreed to experiment with a policy stipulating that the Han occupants of the lands in dispute with the Mongols should pay compensations to the latter. In the field, however, different understandings of the policy occurred along ethnic lines. Some Mongolian members of the CCP, such as Liu Buyi (a.k.a. Kui Bi), who was in charge of the CCP's work in the Tumed Banner, believed that the policy confirmed the necessity to adjust the Han and Mongol landownership in Suiyuan. By contrast, their Han superiors in Suiyuan decided that landownership adjustment would not be conducive to the party's objective of assuaging the Han–Mongol quarrels and that the best approach for the moment was to maintain the status quo.[35] Obviously, over the issue of land there seemed little room for compromise between Chinese nationalism and Mongolian nationalism. The chasm between the two stands was as real within the CCP as in society at large.

A Time for "Incidents"

Clearly, the CCP's wartime ethnopolitical stand proved awkward not only because it had an uncooperative partner in the KMT but also because its own policy was wobbling between Chinese nationalism and a desire to appease the non-Han peoples' grievances. Despite Mao's intention to include "all domestic nationalities" in "our national united front against Japan," the CCP could not easily find a program acceptable to both the KMT government and the national minorities.[36]

When an interethnic united front was difficult to materialize, the CCP's interpartisan united front with the KMT went downhill. The convenient KMT–CCP marriage in the war years merely locked the two parties into a "cold war" peppered with bloody "incidents." The eruption of the relationship came sooner than most people expected. In December 1939, Hu Zongnan, one of Jiang Jieshi's trusted generals, moved into Xi'an with instructions from Jiang himself: "Resist Japan in the east, contain the Communist bandits in the north, guard against the Soviet Russia in the west, and deter the Moslem Mas from within."[37] In about a year, the shocking "New Fourth Army incident," in which Jiang Jieshi's troops severely damaged the CCP's military arm in southern China, removed any doubt in China and abroad that the wartime unity between the KMT and the CCP was just a sham.

In the meantime, the KMT regime's ethnopolitics did not even allow a mere facade of "internationality unity" to emerge in China. In the war years, ethnic conflicts in China intensified rather than abated. The best known of these was the anti-KMT and anti-Chinese Ili rebellion in Xinjiang in 1944.

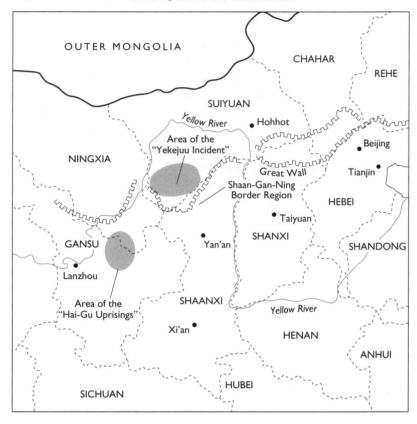

Map 3. The Border Region and the Uprisings of the Hui and Inner Mongols, 1937–45

Between 1937 and 1942, the CCP had an office in Dihua (today's Urumqi) to implement a "special united front" with Xinjiang warlord Sheng Shicai, who in these years maintained a pro-Soviet position. Yan'an's real purpose, however, was to keep Xinjiang open as a channel for its contact with Moscow. Under this orientation, the CCP office in Dihua did not have a mission to conduct revolutionary activities in Xinjiang. In 1942, Sheng Shicai rallied to Jiang Jieshi, and the CCP personnel in Xinjiang became the first group to be persecuted. Thus, when the Ili rebellion took place in 1944, CCP influence no longer existed in Xinjiang. The CCP was unable to establish a direct connection to the rebels until the postwar years.[38]

Two other less known ethnic conflicts are more relevant to this study because they took place in the immediate neighborhood of the CCP's Border Region and accentuated the CCP's impossible ethnopolitical position in the war years. One of these involved three waves of a Hui rebellion in the Haiyuan-Guyuan (Hai-Gu) region of southern Gansu (in today's Ningxia) between 1938 and 1941. In the winter of 1938, the rebellion started in the familiar pattern of the Han–Hui conflicts: Angered by the local KMT troops' and officials' derogatory behavior toward their religious and dietary practices, the Hui people first protested to the Chinese authorities; then the protest developed into an armed struggle. In a typical fashion, the KMT government greeted the protesting Hui with ruthless suppression; it deployed divisions of regular troops to "restore order," and before the rebellion was crushed, many collective executions were carried out.

As the rebellion was unfolding, it developed into a popular military struggle with considerably more participants than any armed Hui force organized by the CCP during the war. The last phase of the uprising lasted for more than six months and involved more than 20,000 insurgents. After 1939, the leaders of the struggle—trying to gain wider support from other ethnic and political groups—demonstrated political acumen in presenting their originally Hui uprising as an anti-KMT and anti-Japanese movement. They introduced such new slogans as "The Hui and the Han are the same family" and "Five-nation harmony; down with the Jiang [Jieshi] clique" as part of their mobilization effort.[39] Because of these characteristics, the Hai-Gu rebellion appeared as a windfall to Yan'an, which finally had its opportunity to foster a following within the Hui populace to counterbalance the anticommunist Hui warlords.

Yet there is no evidence that the CCP leadership made any serious effort to do so. In the spring of 1939, the organizers of the Hui rebellion contacted Yan'an, and the latter also despatched Yang Jingren, one of its Hui cadres, to the Hai-Gu area. These contacts, however, did not lead to further cooperation between the two sides. During the next two years, the Hui rebels had to continue to fight the KMT troops in isolation. In the end, Yan'an did just one thing for the rebels: After the rebellion was completely crashed by the KMT force, about 200 survivors were allowed to come to the Border Region for asylum.[40]

Yan'an's cautiousness could have been derived from purely military considerations. The Hui rebellion might endanger the CCP's strategic position in the northwest. The KMT regime was using several regular divisions in the northwest to suppress the Hui rebels. In view of Jiang Jieshi's practice in the past of using a military campaign continuously to deal with different adversaries, it was not unlikely that this time Jiang might want to expand the suppression campaign against the Hui into a thrust against the CCP's

Border Region. To Yan'an, another similarly dangerous scenario was that the Japanese force nearby would be tempted by the "civil" strife between the Hui and the KMT troops and intensify its pressure in the region.[41] In a word, the Hai-Gu rebellion might become a catalyst to tip the delicate balance of power in the northwest and cause the CCP to suffer. Therefore, not surprisingly, the CCP was reluctant to encourage the Hui rebels and to prolong the militarily hazardous development.

In addition, the Hai-Gu insurgents' anti-KMT and anti-Japanese orientation did not make them a natural ally of the CCP. As a matter of fact, there were disagreements among the participants in the rebellion on whether or not they should seek an alliance with the CCP. By May 1941, the rebels' force had declined from 20,000 to fewer than 7,000. But even then, only about 200 troops were willing to go to the CCP's Border Region. The rest chose to stay in their home area, and they would eventually be slaughtered by the KMT. Given the fact that the people of the Hai-Gu area had their first experience with the CCP in 1936 when the latter's western expedition passed through the area, the insurgents' reluctance to rally to Yan'an in 1941 demonstrated a general suspicion about the CCP among the Hui of the region.[42] The suspicion must have been reciprocal on Yan'an's side as well because of the CCP leaders' still fresh memory about their western expedition fiasco. Interestingly, the lack of cooperation between the CCP and the Hai-Gu insurgents between 1938 and 1941 would deprive the rebellion of a position in the CCP's official history on China's resistance against Japan. Until today, party historians in China still have not treated the Hai-Gu rebellion as a worthy topic before its 200 survivors arrived in the Border Region in 1941.[43]

Yet the fundamental reason for the CCP's torpid reaction to the Hai-Gu rebellion had to be its political truce with the KMT government during the war years. Yan'an's passiveness during the three years of the Hai-Gu rebellion constituted a sharp contrast to Mao's 1936 call for the Hui to organize their "independent Hui anti-Japanese army" and to strive for the "Hui nation's independence and freedom."[44] In the limited number of declassified wartime CCP documents bearing on the Hui question, one can see only occasional and passing references to the "Hai-Gu incident" as a consequence of the KMT's "Great Hanist" policy. In other words, Yan'an seemed to refrain intentionally from taking full advantage of the event's propaganda value.[45] Because the CCP never stopped criticizing the KMT government's policies toward the minorities, its mere murmuring about the Hai-Gu rebellion was highly unusual. There could be only one reason: The event did not fit the CCP's *wartime* standards for good propaganda material.

Since the beginning of the anti-Japanese war, as far as the relationship between the non-Han peoples and the KMT regime was concerned, the CCP had stopped inciting these peoples' antigovernment political actions. It now took a "loyal opponent's" position and criticized the KMT's policies that debased these peoples' legal status and exacerbated their socioeconomic plight *within* the Chinese state system. For instance, in the war years, CCP propaganda often quoted a Muslim journal entitled *Tujue* (Sudden Rise), which was a stern critic of the KMT government's policy toward the Hui and openly demanded that the government to recognize the Hui as a nationality.[46] Limiting itself to voicing statutory disagreements with the KMT, Yan'an had to regard the Hai-Gu insurgents' action as overly aggressive and therefore as insupportable. In the meantime, to the Hui rebels who were struggling for their lives, Yan'an's concern about their nationality status appeared academic.

Would Yan'an have reacted more positively to the Hai-Gu rebellion if the rebels had actively sought the CCP's support? The CCP center's attitude toward the "Yekejuu incident," the Inner Mongolian side of which did actively seek the CCP's support, may shed light on this question. Yekejuu, located in western Suiyuan, was the immediate northern neighbor of the Border Region. After the Japanese Army occupied Baotou and Guisui (Hohhot) in late 1937, Yekejuu became the only Inner Mongolian league that was not occupied by the Japanese. In the territory, the Mongols were small in number (37.2 percent of the 245,000 population) but dominant in local politics. This was reflected in the fact that the league had only one county but seven banners. Because Genghis Khan's tomb was located in Yekejuu, the territory had a symbolic significance to the Mongolian nation.

During the war years, Prince Sha (Shagdurjab), head of the league, used his tremendous political skill and courage to resist Japanese pressure and remained loyal to the Chinese government. Conversely, he also made efforts to fend off the KMT regime's county-building scheme in the territory. Inevitably, Yekejuu became an arena of intense and intricate contests involving not only the Japanese, the KMT, and the CCP but also such local influences as Fu Zuoyi and the Muslim Mas. Prince Sha's allegiance, naturally, became a high prize in these contests.[47]

In the war years, Owen Lattimore, the perceptive observer of Inner Mongolian politics, made a comparison between Inner Mongolian nationalism and warlord politics in Inner Mongolia: Although the former was always "anti-prince and anti-monastic," the latter tended to "exaggerate the power of princes and high lamas" in pursuing territorial and population control.[48] In light of this observation, the wartime Japanese–KMT–CCP competition for Mongolian princes' allegiance continued the old warlord politics. In early 1938, Zhang Wentian told his colleagues at a CCP politburo meeting: "The Mongols are a weak people and they are afraid that they cannot go home when the Japanese come. It would be nice to have a prince assume responsibilities, but the princes may not be willing to come over [to our side]. It should be alright if many of these princes should raise the Japanese color and deal with Prince De outwardly but resolutely favor us in their hearts. . . . The standard for the princes should not be overly high."[49] From such a perspective, Prince Sha was way above the "standard" and was the best asset that the Chinese side could have in the war years.

The KMT regime understood this as well and showered Prince Sha with various official titles. Aside from being the head of Yekejuu League, Prince Sha was also appointed as commander of the league's "peace preservation corps," chairman of the Suiyuan Mongolian Political Council, and councilor of both the Suiyuan and the national governments. Yet the KMT's courting of the Mongolian princes was accompanied by a haughty disregard for the Inner Mongols' collective will against sinicization. In March 1943, this fallacious approach at last caused the Yekejuu Mongols to rebel.

In 1941, Jiang Jeishi dispatched 20,000 troops to Yekejuu League to strengthen the KMT's military position there against both the Japanese and the CCP. But the effort to gain military benefits soon led to a serious political loss. A string of ethnic incidents began as Chen Changjie, commander of the newly arrived KMT troops, forcefully pushed forward a land cultivation policy. In December 1942, Chen's headquarters ordered the nonagricultural Mongolian banners of Yekejuu to supply 3,000 *dan* (82,491 bushels) of grain to his troops within ten days.

Then, in February 1943, with Jiang Jieshi's approval, Chen set up a "supervisory office of land cultivation" to implement a plan for opening up 300,000 *mu* (49,421 acres) of farmland. The actual implementation of the plan was even more menacing to the Mongols than the figure implied: A great number of Chinese peasants were brought into the region; the KMT troops at times forced the Mongols to give up their land at gunpoint; and even the land around Genghis Khan's tomb was earmarked for cultivation. In a petition letter to the KMT "central government," Prince Sha protested that the cultivation plan was intended to "confiscate our Mongolian land and to cut off us Mongols' life."[50]

In the beginning, Prince Sha and other Mongolian officials hoped to use peaceful petitions and negotiations to dissuade the KMT authorities from enforcing the planned land cultivation. But Chen Changjie's intransigence soon led to armed resistance by the rank and file of the Mongolian "peace preservation corps," which started in late March 1943. The rebellion was neither well planned nor coordinated. The KMT's far superior troops suppressed the insurgents banner by banner. In just a few days, the rebellion in Price Sha's home area, Jasag Banner, was suppressed. Prince Sha was forced to abandon his palace and go into temporary exile.[51] It was to Prince Sha's credit that he did not run into the arms of the Japanese but sought a Chinese alternative in the CCP. After being on a southward trail for two months, the prince and his followers reached a CCP base in Western Uushin Banner. A member of the prince's group wrote to an acquaintance in the CCP area, likening their anxiety to get help from the CCP with a "desire for rain after a severe drought." The prince also sent an envoy to the CCP to request its "assistance in counterattacking the KMT."[52]

The CCP leadership watched the crisis with mixed feelings. Until that time, the CCP's work with the Mongolian elites had made little progress. As early as 1937, the CCP began to conduct military propaganda in Yekejuu League, calling upon Mongolian princes to forge a anti-Japanese coalition with the CCP. At the time, Prince Sha was identified as a possible unifying figure for that purpose. The effort was interrupted in 1939 when the KMT government began to tighten its encirclement of the Border Region.[53] Now, in 1943, Prince Sha's voluntary offer of cooperation presented the party with a golden opportunity to advance its Mongolian work and allowed Yan'an to revive the idea of building a pro-CCP Mongolian movement with Prince Sha at the center. Yet Yan'an remained very cautious, lest its involvement in the KMT–Mongolian conflict endanger its already fragile truce with the KMT.

After receiving Prince Sha's plea for help, Yan'an offered some weapons to the prince's bodyguard squad and urged the prince to continue his resistance against the KMT until the latter agreed to rescind its current policy in Yekejuu. The CCP's local organizations were also directed to spread "simple and vivid slogans" to incite the Yekejuu Mongols to participate in a guerrilla struggle against the Japanese and the "diehards" in the KMT.[54]

These, however, fell short of what Prince Sha needed at the time. He hoped that Yan'an could offer him immediate and direct assistance with troops, or at least an open pledge of support to deter Chen Changjie's further military assaults on the Mongols.[55] Yan'an's reason for its restrained response to Prince Sha was secretly explained by the CCP's northwestern bureau to its local organizations. Actually, what might be behind Yan'an's aloofness toward the Hui rebellion between 1938 and 1941 was now clearly spelled out as its reasons not to meet Prince Sha's requests. According to the bureau, the Yekejuu crisis should not be viewed simply as an ethnic conflict. The CCP suspected that Chen Changjie's hidden agenda was to use the incident as a pretext to invade the Border Region.

In addition, not entirely trusting Prince Sha, the bureau asserted that the Japanese Army must have helped plot the Mongols' anti-KMT rebellion to advance its influence in Yekejuu League. The CCP leadership was determined not to fall into the presumed traps laid separately by Chen Changjie and the Japanese. To leaders in Yan'an, a guerrilla war waged by the Mongols and secretly backed by the CCP was the only acceptable form of cooperation with Prince Sha. Any CCP assistance to the Mongols therefore had to be limited and concealed; all anti-KMT slogans must be devised in such a way as if they came from the Mongols themselves. In the meantime, the Mongolian resistance must not be allowed to develop into an anti-Han upheaval because that would only benefit the Japanese.[56]

Disappointed and seeing no hope in further resisting the KMT, Prince Sha could only wait in the CCP area for an opportunity to reconcile with the KMT. Thus the purpose of the prince's southward journey to the CCP region changed from seeking the CCP's assistance to inducing the KMT's concessions. Unwilling to benefit the CCP politically, in October 1943 Jiang Jieshi ordered suspension of the land cultivation program in Yekejuu and also recalled Chen Changjie from his post. At this juncture, despite his CCP hosts' repeated suggestions that he continue to stay in the Border Region, Prince Sha decided to accept the KMT regime's conciliatory gesture and resumed his precrisis official positions in Yekejuu.[57]

The Yekejuu incident taught the KMT regime a lesson. To avoid ethnic friction, Dong Qiwu, Fu Zuoyi's successor in Suiyuan in the postwar years, would follow a policy summarized in a sentence, "The Mongols do not repossess the farm land and the Han do not open up the wasteland." This was similar to the CCP's status quo orientation toward the land problem in the war years.[58] The CCP had its own lessons to learn as well. The CCP's cautious approach toward the KMT–Mongolian conflict was indeed conducive to a quick settlement of the incident and thus to preserving the wartime anti-Japanese united front in the northwest. But the CCP failed to use the opportunity to advance its relationship with the Inner Mongols; its policy for "sparing no effort to win over Prince Sha" bore no result.[59]

Between the CCP's success and failure stood a controversial question of the party's "legitimacy." When the KMT regime allowed its troops to brutalize the loyal Yekejuu Mongols, its legitimacy was lost in the latter's eyes. As far as the Yekejuu Mongols were concerned, Prince Sha's travel to the Border Region implied a transition of the Chinese central authority from the KMT to the CCP. The Inner Mongols' "free unity" with the CCP, however, was declined by Yan'an because, at the time, the CCP wanted to maintain its own "legitimacy" within, but not in contradiction to, the KMT state.

During both the Hai-Gu rebellion and the Yekejuu incident, therefore, Yan'an behaved in the same pattern to diminish ethnic conflict in China and to preserve the CCP's strategic and political status quo within the KMT state. Although in the war years the CCP and the KMT frequently ran into friction with each other, their manifested united front against the Japanese and tacit compact vis-à-vis the non-Han peoples remained intact. In his 1935 proclamation to the Inner Mongols, Mao asserted that the "nation is supreme." Yet in practice, the CCP never granted every nation or nationality in China the same degree of loftiness. In 1935, what was really "supreme" to the CCP was its "class struggle" against the KMT. In China's war against Japan, a "nation" indeed became supreme to the CCP, but it was the Chinese nation only.

"Minorities" Close Up

Like other "loyal" Mongol princes, Prince Sha held to a strong loyalism and usually saw the KMT government as the proper authorities to deal with. His brief courting of the CCP should be understood as an act of desperation. Yet the episode did indicate that to a certain degree the CCP's effort to cultivate good feelings among the Inner Mongols bore results. In the spring of 1941, when the Border Region dispatched a "Mongolian cultural investigation corps" to Yekejuu League, the corps' members heard local Mongols singing a song, "Follow the Eighth Route Army for Ever," among their love songs and songs praising Mongol heroes.[60] So after a few years of habitation side by side, a certain degree of intimacy had been achieved between the northern ethnic group and the CCP movement from the south. In the process, members of the Chinese Communist movement of course neither changed their Han culture nor shifted their focus of attention from the Han population to the minority nationalities. What happened during these years was the addition of threads of the northern frontier and ethnic affairs to the fabric of the CCP movement. The process involved certain personnel, institutional, and perceptual developments.

In 1937, to meet the need of its "nationality work" in the northwest, the CCP center started a training program for cadres of non-Han background in its Central Party School. A more systematic effort was launched in September 1941, when a Yan'an Nationality School was opened. Before the school ceased to exist in 1948, it enrolled about 500 trainees for different durations. More than half of these were from six minority nationalities, and the rest were Han trainees. The two largest minority student groups were the Mongols (150) and the Hui (60). The school's curriculum was designed to "enhance the trainees' political consciousness" by teaching them the CCP version of Communism.[61] Most of the trainees were young, low-ranking cadres. After graduation, they would not advise the CCP center on policies but would be sent to the field to carry out the party's nationality work. Thus, from the point of view of interethnic communication, the training program in the Border Region was a one-way-street indoctrination well in keeping with China's tradition of cultural assimilation. The only difference was that the content of the training program was supposedly "supranational."

Indeed, during the Yan'an period, a small number of cadres of minority nationality began to participate in the CCP's deliberation of nationality policies. But in the process, their role was secondary, and they never functioned as spokespeople for their own nationalities. Five decades later, Ya Hanzhang, a Han cadre who participated in the CCP's top-level policy study regarding the minorities, would attest that not a single Hui cadre contributed to the party's study of the Hui question. As a result, the study had to be a one-sided, subjective exercise. Speaking for those Han contributors to the study, Ya admitted that "from personal experiences, we did not and could not possibly have any knowledge of the Hui people's national consciousness, national feelings, and religious belief." This evaluation may be applied to the CCP's wartime study of the Inner Mongolian question or any other minority nationality questions.[62] Clearly, the CCP leadership was unable to gain insight about the minority nationalities' "consciousness," "feelings," and "religious beliefs" because it did not find a way to reach the "other's" side ethnoculturally.

Before China's war against Japan ended, a cross-ethnic cadre named Yun Ze (a.k.a. Ulanfu) began to influence the CCP's policy toward the Inner Mongols. Yun Ze was from a Mongolian peasant family in Tumed Banner,

Suiyuan. In the early 1920s, when studying in the Mongolian and Tibetan School in Peiping (Beijing), Yun Ze came under Communist influence and became a member of the CCP in 1925.[63] Between 1926 and 1929, Yun Ze received training at the Moscow Zhongshan University (named after Sun Yat-sen) and worked for the Comintern. After returning to Suiyuan in September 1929, he engaged in underground activities under the Comintern's direction. Not until 1938 was Yun Ze able to establish a direct organizational contact with the CCP center. In the summer of 1941, Yun Ze concluded his military work in Yekejuu League and arrived in Yan'an.

During the next few years, Yun Ze first endured the CCP's "rectification movement" and then rapidly climbed the ladder of the CCP hierarchy. In the summer of 1945, during the CCP's Seventh Congress, Yun Ze was elected as an alternate member of the CCP's Central Committee.[64] Yun Ze's entrance into the CCP's upper echelon would prove a significant development in the CCP's relationship with the "national question." In the postwar years, Yun Ze would play a vital role in the CCP–KMT competition for Manchuria and Inner Mongolia by bringing the Inner Mongols to the CCP's side. During the Sino-Japanese War, however, Yun Ze was still waiting for his time to come, and the CCP center was still contemplating its nationality policy as a uni-ethnic operation.

In the war years, the official organ of the operation was the Nationality Affairs Committee under the Border Regions government. The committee was set up by the CCP in October 1941 as a counterpart to the KMT's Mongolian and Tibetan Affairs Committee. The name of the committee indicated that the CCP's recognized the non-Han peoples' "nationality" status and therefore set the CCP apart from the KMT. Yet the distinction was not as significant as it sounded. According to an organizational guideline of the Border Region government issued in 1937, "the minority nationalities (the Mongols and the Hui) have the right to organize their autonomous governments freely and to participate in or withdraw from the Border Region government freely."[65] Thus the two specified minorities would exercise their right to secession only in their relationship with the Border Region but not the Chinese state. Obviously, this clever qualification or narrowing of the national self-determination principle was made to reconcile the CCP's wartime goal for a unified Chinese state with its "Bolshevik" stand on the "national question."

The Nationality Affairs Committee was set up mainly as a public facade of the Border Region government. It included about twenty members and was headed by Zhao Tongru. Zhao was a *Beida* (Peiping University) graduate and an early participant in the soviet movement of northern Shaanxi.

He was also one of the few CCP cadres who had working experiences with the Mongols, but his middle-echelon status within the CCP hierarchy indicated the committee's secondary importance in the CCP's policymaking mechanism.[66]

Yet one aspect of the committee's work is worth mentioning because of a misunderstanding among some historical studies of this period. One of the Nationality Affairs Committee's responsibilities was to implement the minority nationalities' "autonomy" within the Border Region. The Border Region's practice in this regard has been identified by some commentators as the forerunner of the CCP's "autonomous region" practice after 1949.[67] As a matter of fact, before the Border Region's "autonomy" practice, the CCP had created about a dozen "nationality autonomous" regimes in different areas. These, including the Border Region's practice, were referred to as *quyu zizhi* (regional autonomy) in CCP documents of the time, a conception that would also be used for the CCP practice after 1949. Yet *quyu zizhi* practiced by the CCP during and before China's war with Japan bore no resemblance to the post-1949 institution, which (in theory at least) is "territorial autonomy" by a non-Han people. The first instance of the CCP's endorsement of "territorial autonomy" took place in 1947, when an Inner Mongolian autonomous government was established under the CCP's aegis.[68]

During the Yan'an period, although the CCP indeed used minorities' "regional autonomy" in the Border Region to glamorize its record of governance, the practice did not mark any significant development in the CCP's nationality policy. The Hui population in the Border Region totaled less than 1,300, and an even smaller number of Hui residents in certain townships were involved in "regional autonomy."[69] The scope of the "autonomy" was also limited. This can be seen from the mission of the Nationality Affairs Committee. On the one hand, the committee was responsible for implementing "the Hui and Mongol nationalities' regional autonomy within the Border Region." On the other, the committee was in charge of "the matters relevant to the political, defense, economic, cultural, educational, and public health constructions" of these supposedly "autonomous" regions.[70]

There is evidence that in the Border Region, "regional autonomy" was implemented not as a principle but according to circumstances. For instance, in May 1942 the Border Region government decided to combine two Hui villages in Dingbian and Yanchi Counties into a "Hui autonomous district." This was done in response to a resolution passed by the Border Region's political council. The reason for the proposed reorganization was that "[because of] the vast territory and complicated situation of nationalities of the northwest, the administration cannot reach all the places and laws cannot always be enforced." Therefore, the Hui district was organized for the purpose of "improving administrative efficiency."[71]

In comparison with the Border Region's Nationality Affairs Committee, a far more important development in the CCP's nationality policy involved the organization of a series of working committees specialized in the "national question." These involved high-ranking party officials and did contribute to the party's policymaking. In August 1935, while still in its long journey to northern Shaanxi, the standing committee of the CCP's politburo set up a "minority nationality committee" and put one of the politburo members, He Kaifeng (a.k.a. Kai Feng and He Kequan), in charge. This committee existed for less than a year and did not leave any memorable mark. After arriving in northern Shaanxi, the CCP leadership made a series of organizational adjustments to find a suitable structure that could both advise the party center's policymaking and facilitate the party's rapidly expanding nationality work at the local level.[72]

The search was consummated in early 1939. Soon after Mao made the nationality question one of the "urgent tasks for the whole nation" at a conference of the CCP's central committee, a Northwestern Working Committee was established. The committee was headed by Zhang Wentian, and all of its members were high-level CCP cadres. In the years to come, the committee would serve as a switchboard for the party's nationality work and secret activities in the so-called six northwestern provinces (Shaanxi, Gansu, Ningxia, Qinghai, Xinjiang, and Suiyuan). With the committee's help, for the first time in its history the CCP began to consider China's "national question" systematically.[73]

Just as Mao could not possibly have written his poem "Snow" amid Jiangxi's rice paddies, the CCP could carry out empirical studies of the frontier nationalities only in northern Shaanxi's cave dwellings. Still without its own "marvelous Georgian," the CCP's study of the "national question" in the Yan'an period was made collectively by a National Question Research Office under the Northwestern Working Committee. This inquiry differed from that in the 1920s, when the CCP leadership was mainly interested in learning about Marxist-Leninist doctrines on the subject. This was a time when Mao was achieving an indisputable leading position in the CCP and the party, in Zhang Wentian's words, was striving to "sinicize its organizational work" and to implement the "content of internationalism in national form."[74] In this context, the CCP's exploration of the "national question" shed much of its usual "Bolshevik" and "Soviet" clichés and came to terms with the ethnopolitical reality of the northwest.

From the outset, the Research Office pursued a pragmatic agenda. It focused on the concrete conditions of the Hui and the Mongols but not on any general theory. The office gathered a group of cadres knowledgeable about these ethnic groups. Some members, including its director, Liu Chun, had studied China's frontier affairs when they were university students. The rest were either Hui or Mongols themselves or had previous working experience among the northwestern nationalities.[75] Inevitably, the office's inquiry was conducted within the "theoretical" framework defined by the CCP's wartime stand on the "national question," but the process also involved fieldwork and the collection of printed information about the Hui and Mongolian communities. Because much of the research had to be done in KMT-controlled areas, the researchers often had to disguise themselves. On one occasion, the fieldwork in an area controlled by Ma Hongkui cost several investigators' lives.[76]

Eventually, the Research Office was able to produce several publications. By far the most important were two "outlines" done separately on the Hui and the Inner Mongolian questions. The Northwestern Working Committee discussed drafts of these documents before submitting them to the CCP center for approval. The Secretariat of the CCP Central Committee approved these documents in the spring and summer of 1940 and then circulated them within the party through an internal journal, *Gongchandangren* (Communists).[77] Thus these outlines served as the CCP's official guide to its work with the Hui and the Mongols and also manifested the Chinese Communists' newly achieved familiarity with northwestern ethnic affairs.

Because the CCP leadership had already decided its wartime orientation on the "national question," further deliberation on the matter by a group of party intellectuals would not change the established policies. Rather, these so-called guiding documents confirmed and justified the current party line and were used by the CCP's northwestern organizations as a criterion to evaluate their policy practices. In the meantime, the documents did add texture to the CCP's understanding and presentation of the "national question." In terms of their policy content, the outlines attempted to "put the spirit of the [CCP's] sixth plenum into concrete steps." Although they listed a series of political, economic, cultural, and religious measures to redress the Hui's and the Mongols' grievances and to improve their relationships with the Han, the documents' silence on the minority nationalities' right to self-determination was resounding. Now the minority nationalities could only "correctly" claim a "right of equality with the Han" within the Chinese republic.

In these documents, the CCP's "dialectical view" of the historical "Han–Barbarian" relationship also had come to an end. Now the CCP defined non-Han ethnonationalism with a pejorative conception, "parochial local nationalism" (*xia'ai difang minzuzhuyi*), which had been suggested by Mao himself. For the first time in the CCP's discussion of the "national question," non-Han ethnonationalism became completely negative, even when it involved non-Han peoples' emotional and political actions against the "Great Hanism" of the KMT government.[78] Having identified a negative pair of "parochial local nationalism" and "Great Hanism," in the years to come the CCP would no longer accept the legitimacy of any non-Han ethnonationalism. An unstated aphorism applied to this stand was "The minority nationalities' parochial ethnonationalism can be provoked only by the KMT's Great Hanism; under the CCP's just system there is no reason for such an ethnonationalism to exist." During the war years, however, the CCP demanded the minority nationalities to demolish their own ethnic nationalism not because a "just system" existed in China but because the Chinese nation's struggle against Japan was held as the highest priority.

The outlines were honest enough to admit that a tremendous distance existed between the CCP's desire and the Hui's and Mongols' political tendencies. In the outlines' words, these nationalities constituted a "very serious problem" in China's war against Japan because of their "wavering," "passive," and "wait-and-see" attitude toward the struggle. Aside from blaming the KMT's and Japanese policies for the situation, the outlines also engaged in detailed discussions of these nationalities' "characters" as reasons for their ambiguous position in the war.

These documents' central argument was that the Hui and the Mongols were both "backward nationalities." Three standards were used to established this backwardness. The first was the Marxist view of a linear development of human societies. Thus the alleged "feudal" relations of the Hui's agricultural economy and the Mongols' nomadic way of life and banner system were held as clear evidence of these peoples' backwardness.[79]

The second standard used to established their backwardness was the degree of these people's sinicization (*hanhua*). The Inner Mongols were deemed less sinicized than the Hui. Consequently, they were more backward and economically and politically less dynamic. The authors of the outlines endorsed "natural" but not "forced" sinicization in history, contending that the natural process had been beneficial but the forced assimilation had antagonized the non-Han peoples. Yet in their opinion, even forced assimilation had not been a completely negative process; at least in the case of the Hui nationality, the Chinese authorities' violent suppressions had allegedly helped foster in the Hui what the CCP valued most, a "fighting spirit."[80]

In contrast, during the past century, the central government of China had appeased the Mongols and had made the Mongolian nation a mere "appendage" to others' (the Manchu, KMT, and Japanese) imperialism. The CCP's disappointment with the Mongols' performance in the war was grave; the Inner Mongols were described in the documents as "demoralized and corrupt," and their wartime conditions as evidence of the Mongolian nation's "decadence, listlessness, and dependent tendency." In presenting such a saddening profile of the Inner Mongols, the CCP leadership decided that, worse than the Hui, the Inner Mongols lacked the ability of self-liberation and had to be incorporated into the Chinese revolution to get assistance.

The third determinant of these nationalities' backward characters was religion. Committed atheists themselves, the CCP leaders viewed both Lamaism of the Mongols and Islam of the Hui as "dark influences" in these peoples' path of progress. Yet in the war years, they were willing to make a pragmatic distinction between the two. Blaming Lamaism as a "poison" that spiritually castrated the Mongolian nation, the CCP's rejection of the religion was sweeping and absolute. In contrast, the CCP leadership adopted a dialectical view of Islam. On the one hand, the religion was seen as an obstacle that hindered the Hui people's "national and class awakening." On the other, it was valued as a "sacred banner" that unified the Hui people in their struggles against tyrannical oppression. Accordingly, although the outlines proposed that both Hui imams and Mongolian lamas receive political training to enhance their "cultural and political standards," CCP officials believed that in the war years only Islam could be promoted as an "anti-Japanese religion." Thus "freedom of religion" for the Hui people was explicitly spelled out as a measure to make Islam "a banner to unify the Hui nationality in the struggle against Japan." But no such recommendation was made about Lamaism.

The differentiated policies toward the Hui and the Inner Mongols indicated that the CCP's "nationality work" had become more sophisticated than before. In retreating from its prewar rhetoric, which had generally promoted the minority nationalities' right to self-determination, the CCP nevertheless waged propaganda campaigns tailored to gain sympathy among the Hui and the Mongols. Like such questions as the "old seals," landownership, and horses among the Inner Mongols, an outstanding issue regarding the Hui was its "status." The issue allowed the CCP to take a stand opposing the KMT government's practice.

During the Qing period, the Manchu government used *shenghui* (raw Hui) or *yihui* (barbarian Hui) to refer to the Muslims of Xinjiang and used *shuhui* (tamed Hui) or *minhui* (subject Hui) to name the Muslims in China proper. In the early years of the Chinese Republic, these names were respectively replaced with *chanhui* (turbaned Hui) and *Hanhui* (Chinese Hui). At the time, however, in their communications with the Chinese government, both princes of Xinjiang and representatives of the Hui in China proper identified themselves as *Huizu* (Hui nationality). A clear distinction between the two was made in China's official terminology in 1935, when Sheng Shicai in Xinjiang issued an ordinance to change the name of the province's principal ethnic group from *chanhui* to *Weiwuer* (Uigur).[81] Yet the KMT government continued to deny that the Hui in China proper were a nationality. Its most authoritative statement on this matter was made by Jiang Jieshi's book *China's Destiny,* first published in 1943, which asserted that the Hui people were "actually members of the Han clan who practice Islam."[82]

Although there was no consensus in Chinese society about the Hui's ethnic identity, the CCP's recognition of the Hui as a nationality was consistent. Since its establishment, the CCP had always regarded *huizu* (Hui nationality) as one of China's minority nationalities. Numerous CCP documents dated in the 1920s and 1930s indicated that in these years the CCP leadership and the Comintern also held the Hui in China proper to be part of *Huizu.*[83] Yet until 1940, the old conception, "Hui frontier" (*huijiang*), continued to influence the CCP's view that did not differentiate the Muslims in China proper from those in Xinjiang. For instance, the CCP's proclamation to the Hui people issued in Mao's name in 1936 treated the Muslims in Ningxia, Gansu, and Xinjiang as members of the same *Huizu.*[84] Therefore, due to the work of the Northwestern Working Committee, in 1940 the CCP for the first time treated the Hui in China proper as a nationality group distinct from the Muslim peoples of Xinjiang.

Interestingly, though after the Long March the CCP center demanded its organizations to use the Marxist-Leninist-Stalinist theories on the "national question" to guide their nationality work, the Northwestern Working Committee carried out its work in the spirit of the CCP's wartime pragmatism.[85] In 1940 Li Weihan, the secretary general of the Northwestern Working Committee, wrote an article to dispel any doubt within the party about the inconsistency between the CCP's view on the Hui question and Stalin's definitions on "nation" and "self-determination." Li argued that Stalin's four criteria for a "modern nation" would not deny the Hui and other minorities in China from being seen as nationalities in formation.

By the same token, Li maintained that the connection between a nation and its right to self-determination had to be suspended because of Japan's invasion of China. Thus the CCP's recognition of the Hui's nationality status must not be construed as recognition of the Hui's right to self-determination. As for the prospect of this right in the future, Li was reluctant to make a definite prediction. Nevertheless, he hoped that after China overcame Japan's aggression, it would not have to repeat the fragmenting experience of Eastern Europe after World War I.[86]

Frontier Personality

If the Northwestern Working Committee's outlines exposed the mentality of the CCP's "frontier personality," it was surely a China-centered one. As reflected in these documents, the CCP leadership never failed to defend China's political interests in the war years and to promote Chinese cultural values when non-Han cultures and political aspirations were the presumed counterparts. Despite CCP leaders' claim that their views of the "national question" were "scientific," the outlines' analyses of the Hui and the Mongol questions were often subjective and distorted certain vital facts. For instance, the CCP's equation of non-Han peoples' social progress with the degree of their sinicization could not be supported by the social reality of the northwest. To an unbiased observer, the differences between the Han and the Hui residents in Gansu and Ningxia were indeed readily recognizable: The Hui were usually physically healthy and vigorous and their residences clean and tidy; the Han were often to the opposite in these matters. A reason for the sharp contrast was that most Hui people rejected the opium-smoking habit then prevalent among the Han population of the region. The consequences of sinicization in this regard could be seen in the local Tibetan communities; many of them became so "Chinese" that they "fell helplessly into the same abyss" with the Han.[87]

Yet in the war years the CCP's disappointment about the Hui's and Mongols' social, economic, and cultural "backwardness" was mainly derived from an overriding political concern that these non-Han groups appeared indifferent to China's war of survival against Japan. Having defined these peoples' ethnonationalist aspirations against the Chinese authorities as "parochial local nationalism," the CCP could not see any "positive" political dynamism in these peoples. The CCP's wartime conclusion on the Inner Mongols' "political numbness" was especially self-deceiving. The party leadership would be surprised in the postwar years when a vigorous autonomous movement seemed to emerge in Inner Mongolia so "suddenly."[88]

Thus, as indicated by Ya Hanzhang's remark mentioned above, despite its efforts in the war years, the CCP never really understood the northwestern peoples' "national consciousness, national feelings, and religious beliefs." In a word, after residing in the northwest for a decade between 1935 and 1945, the CCP remained unable to overcome the ethnopolitical and ethnocultural barriers between the Han and the "other" groups. But this does not mean that the CCP failed to develop a peculiar, collective "frontier personality." According to Owen Lattimore, a "primary difference" between the frontiers in American history and in Eurasian history is that the former involved a contact between two previously unrelated societies (European and "Indian") whereas the latter was consisted of an "unending ebb and flow of the human tide."[89]

As part of this human tide, China's northern and northwestern frontiers involved a process of non-Han peoples' sinicization and a counterprocess of Han settlers' "barbarization." Having relocated to the northwest, the CCP became a unique splash in the historical human tide in the sense that it would not simply repeat these processes. Unlike previous Han settlers, who had made inroads culturally and economically in the frontiers and had willingly or unwittingly served the purpose of sinicization, the CCP became "borderized" in the northwest as a group of "political settlers" armed with a supposedly supra-ethnic ideology and a kind of sensitivity toward the non-Han peoples' cultural and economic misgivings.

During its ten-year sojourn along China's interethnic frontiers, the CCP's greatest achievement was to learn to base its understanding of the "national question" on empirical information and to formulate policies accordingly. Yet the CCP's wartime position in China's ethnopolitics was awkward: China's struggle against Japan prevented the CCP from using the Leninist strategy of capitalizing on the minorities' ethnonationalism; the KMT's control of power blocked the CCP in allaying the Hui's and the Inner Mongols' antagonism against the Chinese state. Thus, just as its wartime alliance with the KMT was shot through with conflicting goals, the CCP and the northwestern ethnic groups were in the same neighborhood but had few shared communal interests. Nevertheless, it is dictated by history that both the alliance and the neighborhood were destined to become vital steps in the CCP's road to power and its effort to bridge the cleft between the Han and the non-Han societies of China.

7

Epilogue: From the "Chinese Nation" to China of Nations?

The Chinese Communist Party's (CCP's) ethnopolitical journey certainly did not end with the conclusion of the Sino–Japanese war. Between 1945 and 1949, the CCP would bring its power struggle with the Kuomintang (KMT, or National People's Party) to a successful conclusion. The last phase of the CCP's road to power was especially characterized by intricate and intensified ethnic conflicts and negotiations that involved Chinese political parties, foreign influence, and ethnic groups seeking autonomy or sovereignty in China's northern and western borderlands. The dynamics of this process are crucial for our understanding of the emergence of a multiethnic system in the People's Republic of China (PRC); therefore, they need to be considered in a separate study. This examination of the CCP's ethnopolitics from 1921 to 1945 should be able to make a sufficient case that the Marxist interpretation of the phenomenon is based on a too narrow an approach of investigation. The Marxist paradigm gives preeminence to the Soviet-originated dogmas and practices over other variables that had roots in China's history, culture, and twentieth-century political conditions.

In such inquiries, quite often the reading of Marxist pronouncements on the "national question" replaces empirical analyses of the CCP's behavior in China's particular ethnopolitical environment. Their leading question is usually *how,* but rarely *whether or not,* the CCP applied Marxism to China's "national question." The reality is that at the outset the CCP's knowledge of Marxism and Leninism was as poor as its understanding of China's "national question." In later years, when the CCP became increasingly knowledgeable about China's ethnopolitical conditions, it also began to "de-Bolshevize" and "sinicize" its nationality policy. The cliché about the CCP's "creative" application of Marxism to China needs to be balanced by an unstated aspect: The CCP also creatively continued China's age-old practices in the name of Marxism. Just as Mao Zedong's rural guerrilla strategy had precursors in the countless peasants' rebellions throughout Chinese history, so the CCP's nationality policy did not break away from China's ethnopolitical culture. It had precedents in Chinese authorities' frontier management from the time of China's first emperor to the Republic of China.

There is indeed a cultural variant of the Marxist interpretation that is mainly interested in the "national question" as part of the CCP's political strategy. In comparing the Chinese Communists' ethnic practices with those historical precedents implemented in the spirit of Confucianism and Christianity, Stevan Harrell views the CCP's nationality policy as but part of a long historical process consisting of a series of "civilizing projects." By functioning as "civilization centers," these Confucian, Christian, and Communist projects sought to objectify those groups in China that need to be "civilized." They respectively used "culture," "race," and "political economy" as their criteria to differentiate the "civilization centers" and the "peripheral peoples."

With this approach, the examination of the Chinese Communists' ethnopolitics can be extended beyond the Marxist-Leninist strategy and connected to China's long interethnic history. Harrell's civilizational trilogy, however, has the same drawback as its Marxist political science companions. In admitting that the three civilizing projects were not as distinct from one another in practice as they were in theory and that there was especially much to share between the Confucian and the Communist projects, Harrell nevertheless assigns the CCP's practices to the Marxist category and falls short of identifying Chinese nationalism as an independent stage of the "civilizing" process.[1]

In light of the present study, two questions may be raised about Harrell's abstention from Chinese nationalism. First, can the CCP be viewed as a civilization center between 1921 and 1945, when it itself was on China's political and cultural peripheries? Second, because more clearly than anywhere else Communism in China took a national form, and because certain key elements of Confucianism survived China's transition from a ethnocultural empire to a nation-state, would not it be more useful to investigate the *national* civilizational project in twenty-century China, "hybrid" though it may be, than to study the "pure" forms of the "Confucian," "Christian," and "Communist" projects?

A Matter of "Maturity"

History does provide evidence that during the twentieth century a *national* civilizational project unfolded in China and had the Chinese Nationalists and the Chinese Communists as its most vigorous agents. This national project developed under strong Confucian, Western, and Communist influence but had some distinct features of its own. Evolving from the Confucian ethnopolitical tradition, the national project upheld the Han as the center vis-à-vis the frontier peoples as the peripheries. In the meantime, the discourse of the project deployed a set of Western as well as Communist conceptions, such as "nation," "progress," "modernity," "autonomy," "equality," and "national minority."

In other words, the project redefined the content of Chinese civilization with modern terminology and repositioned the Han at the "leading position" among China's ethnic groups from a socioeconomic, developmental point of view. In launching their ethnopolitical enterprises under Moscow's aegis in the early 1920s, the KMT and particularly the CCP had to absorb and digest Marxist-Leninist conceptions on the "national question." Yet neither copied the Soviet practices. In the end, the most lasting Soviet influence on China's official ethnopolitics in both the Republican and the People's Republican periods was limited to the notion of equality in social, political, and ethnic terms.

Harrell correctly identifies his trilogy as "civilizing" projects because in theory Confucianism, Christianity, and Communism are all supranational. By contrast, both the KMT's and the CCP's ethnopolitical enterprises were highly nationalistic, fiercely state oriented, and constantly wary of foreign interference. Therefore, they must be categorized as "nationalizing" projects designed to transform China from a traditional polyethnic empire into a modern multinationality "nation-state."[2]

As such, the CCP's ethnopolitical experience between 1921 and 1945 was no longer a process in which the CCP gradually achieved a "mature" understanding of China's "national question" according to Marxist doctrines. Rather, during the period, through acquiring an incomplete knowledge of the Soviet theories and practices regarding the "national question," making a forced physical movement in China's cultural-ethnic landscape, reconnecting to Chinese nationalism, and contacting directly certain frontier non-Han groups, the CCP adopted a set of objectives, ideas, and practices for its particular "nationalizing" project. Irrespective of the Communist jargon used by the CCP leaders in their policy deliberations or statements, Marxism and Soviet precedents were far less influential on the CCP's ethnopolitical behavior than is usually presumed. In the meantime, traditional Han-centric ethnoculturalism, China's ethnodemographic and ethnogeographical conditions, foreign encroachments along China's ethnic frontiers, the anti-Japanese war, and the CCP's constant marginalization in China's political life all played significant roles in shaping the CCP's ethnopolitics.

Because of these conditions, the CCP could not possibly view and deal with China's "national question" in the same vein as did the Russian Bolsheviks. As far as the CCP's relationship with the Bolshevik "solution" of the "national question" was concerned, from 1921 to 1945 the tendency was just the opposite of the conventional wisdom that the CCP constantly followed the Leninist strategy and matured increasingly in applying Marxist doctrines to China's reality. In this regard, the more "mature" the CCP grew, the less "Marxist-Leninist" it became. Not surprisingly, because the CCP and the KMT shared most of the conditions listed above, by the end of China's war against Japan, the two parties' objectives in China's ethnopolitics were essentially identical, though they continued to disagree on the means.

Of course, before the PRC period, the CCP was not just a "civilizing" or "nationalizing" agent. It was first and foremost a revolutionary movement. Marxism, Leninism, and the Bolsheviks' revolutionary experiences constituted the frame of reference for the CCP's political strategy. But the CCP's ethnopolitical strategy was a far cry from the Bolshevik precedent that, as ably summarized by Richard Pipes, was to "exploit" but not to "solve" the "national question" before the Bolsheviks took power.[3]

During the CCP's first decade, its "nationality policy" was not even about ethnopolitics. Rather, when the CCP adopted the Comintern formula on the "national question" in the early 1920s and proclaimed the Chinese Soviet nationality program in the early 1930s, the party's principal concerns were respectively to establish its credentials with the Comintern and to challenge the KMT regime with its own "incipient state." During the Long March, the CCP for the first time prioritized the "national question" in policymaking because of its frequent contact with certain "minority" groups. But as the policy dispute between Zhang Guotao and Mao indicates, the CCP's own marginalization from China's "civilization center" caused a serious doubt among the party principals about the Bolshevik presumption that the anti-center tendency of the "minorities" could be beneficially exploited by the revolution.

Clearly, either as a "nationalizing" agent or as a revolutionary party, the

CCP would have to maintain a solid connection with its own social and ethnocultural basis, which was the Han populace. The revolutionary party's "center" position was an absolute precondition for the Leninist nationality strategy, but this position eluded the CCP during its first sixteen years. During China's eight-year war against Japan, the CCP managed to gain such a position by taking a ride with "peasant nationalism" in China. Yet its simultaneous embracing of the KMT's official nationalism dictated that the CCP take the KMT "central government's" side in "solving" China's "national question," which was exacerbated by Japan's aggression, but not "exploit" the question in opposition to the KMT regime.

A fallacy in previous studies of the CCP's nationality policy is their focus on the CCP's doctrinal relationship with the Leninist formula on "national self-determination." In the first place, over the years, the CCP documents' reference to the principle was never consistent. Furthermore, at most the relationship could serve as an index to but did not provide clues about the reasons and conditions that compelled the CCP to readjust its ethnopolitical strategy. The Chinese Communists encountered their ethnopolitical issues under conditions and from positions rather different from those of the Russian Bolsheviks.

Although the CCP did not produce a distinct set of theories on China's ethnopolitical affairs, in this area its practices were as heretical from Moscow's point of view as was Mao's rural revolution. The Bolsheviks' pre-power strategy was revolutionary, using non-Russian peoples' nationalisms as a destructive "yeast" to undermine Russia's old regime. In contrast, the CCP's nationality policy, which had evolved to the time of China's war against Japan, was based on coordination. Its method was to use political criticism and suasion to keep the non-Han groups within the Chinese state and to use cultural, economic, and ethnopolitical reforms to win these groups' loyalty not only to the CCP but also to the official Chinese state.

After Japan surrendered in August 1945, the CCP and the KMT again openly stood at the opposite ends of China's political spectrum, waging respectively a "war of liberation" (*jiefang zhanzheng*) and a war of "rebellion suppression" (*kanluan*) against each other. Although the Chinese Civil War between 1945 and 1949 appeared to be a struggle between Communism and Nationalism, it was actually a military competition between two Chinese "nationalizing" projects.

In other words, although the renewed civil war in China and the intensifying Cold War between the United States and the Soviet Union dictated that the CCP continue to readjust its ethnopolitical tactics, the thematic drive of the CCP's ethnopolitics, however, would remain unchanged. In maintaining a political edge over the KMT by implementing social and economic reforms among the minorities, the CCP nevertheless insisted that all nationalities' "liberation" must be achieved as part of the Chinese revolution. During the next few years, the CCP succeeded not only in ousting the KMT regime to Taiwan but also in effectively incorporating China's estranged ethnic borderlands into the PRC, a task that the KMT had never been able to accomplish during its twenty years in power.[4]

"Historic Self-Determination"

The foundation of the PRC in October 1949 marked the beginning of Communist power in China. The CCP's programs thereby became China's state policies. The official literature in the PRC has defined the development as the "historic self-determination by the Chinese nation," meaning the Chinese nation's decisive choice of the CCP as its leading force *and* the conclusive choice of the PRC by the "minority nationalities" as their motherland.[5] If one accepts the "Mandate of Heaven" rendering of Chinese political history, the CCP's ascendance to power in 1949 can indeed be construed as the Chinese people's "choice." Yet the facts have to be stretched to assert that in 1949 the right to "national self-determination" was also exercised by every politically self-conscious ethnic group in China.

In early September 1949, in a speech to the new People's Political Consultative Council, Zhou Enlai conceded that "without question, any nationality must have the right to self-determination." But, he added, because foreign imperialists were plotting to separate Tibet, Taiwan, and Xinjiang from China, the CCP decided to establish a unitary republic but not a pluralistic federation, lest the minority nationalities be confused by imperialists' instigation.[6] A month later, the CCP center issued a directive to its regional apparatuses to explicate the party's decision:

The question of the minority nationalities' "right to self-determination" should no longer be stressed under today's circumstances. During the civil war periods in the past, the slogan was emphasized to oppose theKMT's reactionary rule. At that time the policy was correct. Today the new China has already come into being. To accomplish the great cause of state unification, and to oppose the imperialists and their running dogs' conspiracy to split the nationality unity of China, the slogan should no longer be stressed in relation to the domestic nationality question. What should be stressed is the friendly cooperation, mutual assistance, and unity among the various nationalities of China.[7]

Zhou's speech and the CCP center's directive were straightforward and did not try to hide the party's intention behind any corrupted interpretation of the national self-determination principle. In other words, the CCP fully exercised its newly achieved leading role in China's nation building and made a "determination" for all the nationalities of the land. Among Western commentators, there is a view that the Soviet Union ended the "facts" but not the "fiction" of the nationalities' right to self-determination.[8] The PRC obviously found no use in either the "facts" or the "fiction" and kept its distance from the Soviet model.

In 1949, the CCP's explicit rejection of the Soviet model of a multi-national-republic union and the Leninist thesis on national self-determination indicated its self-confidence as the new ruling party of China as well as its genuine apprehension about the PRC's seemingly perilous international environment.[9] But except for the explicitness, the CCP's nationality policy after 1949 did not constitute a departure from the ethnopolitical stance that it had established during the anti-Japanese war. As this study has indicated, as a subject in the CCP's nationality policy, national self-determination was put aside by the party leadership as early as in the late 1930s. After nationalizing its programs for the sake of the war against Japan, the CCP leadership would never want to put down the politically powerful "national banner." In other words, after 1949, a supranational, "Communist civilizational project," as defined by Harrell, never took place in China. The CCP, now as the power-holding party, simply continued its "nationalizing" mission.

Thus, to the nationality policies and practices of the PRC period, the most important legacy of the CCP's earlier experiences is the Han-centric Chinese nationalism, or patriotism, as the CCP leadership prefers to call it. After 1949, the CCP de-northernized and de-borderized by moving from the northwest to its new capital in Beijing. The resultant "urbanization" and "centralization" would nevertheless not re-Bolshevize or re-sovietize its nationality policy. Han-centric nationalization would remain the core objective of the policy.

During the Mao era of the PRC, the Marxist class-struggle doctrine was indeed embedded in the CCP's thinking. Yet even Mao's successive "class struggles" between 1949 and 1976 cannot support an argument that the CCP's nationality policy in this period was supranational or supraethnic.

Amid Mao's "continuous revolution," ethnic conflicts and party-made "class struggles" meshed together. When the CCP launched an "anti-rightist campaign" in 1957 to silence its intellectual critics, those non-Han critics were persecuted similarly yet labeled differently as "local nationalists."

After 1966, when Mao began to purge his own party with the horrendous Great Proletarian Cultural Revolution, Mongolian cadres in Inner Mongolia suffered from an ethnic-specific campaign for "digging out and eradicating the Inner Mongolian People's Revolutionary Party."[10] Predictably, these were presented by the party as proletarians' revolutionary actions against bourgeois nationalist tendencies. But a few years after Mao's death, Ulanfu, who himself was then a rehabilitated victim of the "cultural revolution" in Inner Mongolia, made a different interpretation:

Certain comrades still harbor ideas of Great Hanism, a spiritual legacy of feudal despotism. Traditional perceptions of the feudal ages valued the Huaxia [the Han] and demeaned the Yidi [the non-Hans], and these have by no means disappeared from the minds of some of our comrades. What is flabbergasting is that these rotten perceptions should chime in so readily with [these comrades'] fallacious "leftist" ideas. These comrades have never really trusted the cadres and masses of the minority nationalities or respected their autonomous rights. They talk about the nationalities' regional autonomy, but quite often they just make an empty gesture or take over and monopolize everything [*baoban daiti*].[11]

In the 1980s and 1990s, "leftism" was a general diagnosis for the excesses of the Mao era. Ulanfu's attack on Han officials' "monopoly" tendency was right on target. What Ulanfu failed or was unwilling to admit is that as part of China's "nationalizing" project, the CCP's nationality policy could not avoid the Han-centric tendency. The tendency certainly has connections to China's traditional ethnoculturalism, but it is also determined by China's political course at home and on the international scene during the twentieth century.

As a matter of fact, the CCP has never opposed Han-centrism per se. The pre-1949 contention that the minority nationalities' "liberation" had to be achieved as part of the Chinese revolution and the post-Mao theme that all the minority nationalities need to "catch up with or reduce their distance from the level of the Han nationality's development" are unquestionably Han-centric.[12] In the early 1980s, a new start seemed to be made by the CCP center, then with Hu Yaobang as the secretary general. By concentrating on improving the interethnic relationship in Tibet, the Chinese government adopted a new orientation that "all policies and measures [in Tibet] first must surely have the wholehearted agreement and support from the Tibetan cadres and the Tibetan people; otherwise these policies have to wait or to be changed." Under this orientation, a series of favorable policies for Tibet were implemented, and a large number of Han cadres were withdrawn from the region.[13]

This trend did not last long. In the wake of the Tiananmen Square massacre of 1989, Chinese premier Li Peng made a speech at the Nationalities Affairs Commission to warn against an alleged plot by a "tiny minority of separatists" to split the "grand unity of the Chinese nation." He stressed that "our country has several tens of nationalities, but the Han accounts for the vast majority and generally speaking its level of development is higher [than the others]; therefore, as far as national equality and unity are concerned, the Han comrades must assume more important responsibility in the country."[14] Clearly, in today's China the "Han comrades'" predominance in the national enterprise cannot be questioned.

A "New Era"

During the final two decades of the twentieth century, the CCP shifted its focus from making revolutions to reforming and developing the economy. As the subject of class struggle became obsolete, inevitably the CCP also repudiated the Maoist thesis that the "national question is essentially a class-struggle question."[15] Since the 1980s, in the PRC the "interclass character" of the "national question" has been replaced by an "interpeople relationship" among different ethnic groups.

This is a "new era," in which any ethnic disharmony in China can presumably be caused only by an alleged "actual inequality" between *the* advanced (Han) nationality and the other nationalities whose "backward conditions" are rooted in history. On the basis of this reasoning, the CCP currently holds economic development in the non-Han communities and regions as the key to maintaining the stability of China's multiethnic structure. Yet, although at present soft socioeconomic measures take precedence over hard political suppressions, the latter are still deemed necessary for annihilating any separatist activity "in embryo."[16]

Undoubtedly, as in the time of China's war against Japan, the current overwhelming concern of the CCP's nationality policy is to preserve the unity of the "Chinese nation," or *zhonghua minzu*. During that war, the KMT and the CCP—wielding respectively the "one nation of many clans" creed and the "various nationalities of China" formula—followed different paths to support the same politics centered on the "Chinese nation." At the beginning of 1947, the KMT government adopted a revised constitution for the Republic of China. The new version stipulated the "equality among all the nationalities of the Chinese nation."[17] After that, even the rhetorical difference between the two parties disappeared.

Actually, the conceptual roots of the Chinese nation can be traced further back. At the beginning of the twentieth century, to roll back foreign encroachments on China, Chinese nationalists superimposed a "Chinese nation-state" conception on the domain of the Qing Empire. Here lies an innate contradiction of Chinese nationalism: Chinese nationalists from the KMT to the CCP have been convinced that China cannot be fully rehabilitated from foreign humiliations and encroachments without claiming the entire domain of the bygone Qing Empire. For China's national humiliations and loss of territories began with the Qing Dynasty.

To claim the areas of the Qing Empire within the modern world order, however, a modern political stance had to be invented. The KMT once tried the "five-race harmony" creed and the CCP used the "free union of all nationalities" formula, but eventually neither felt able to work within a pluralistic system. Consequently, through a succession of political maneuverings and rhetorical adjustments, by the time of China's anti-Japanese war, the Chinese Nationalists and the Chinese Communists cooperated in amplifying *zhonghua minzu* from a "generic ethnonym" for the Han Chinese into an inclusive political identity for all ethnic groups within the Chinese state.[18]

The fact that the term *zhonghua* has never been translated into Western languages indicates the term's basically introspective significance. During World War II, sensitive to the derogatory implication of "China" (*zhina*) in the Japanese language, Jiang Jieshi asked the Ministry of Foreign Affairs to consider changing the customary English translation of *zhonghua minguo*, which was the "Republic of China." After some deliberation, the ministry's recommendation was against modification of the then-current translation, for three reasons. First, it argued, if *zhonghua minguo* was translated into "Central Glorious Republic," this "somewhat pretentious" name could easily cause the Western allies' suspicions about China's expansionist intentions.

Second, the English term "China" had ancient roots in the Sanskrit, Greek, and Latin languages, and these did not have any derogatory implications. Third, Jiang was advised that in the Japanese language, "China" meant a "territorial domain during our country's most glorious time, including both the Northeast and Mongolia." As a matter of fact, it was the Japanese who since the 1920s had substituted "China" with *zhonghua* or *zhongguo* (middle state) in their propaganda so as to exclude Manchuria and Mongolia from the political conception of "Republic of China."

Jiang was not satisfied by these arguments, and he instructed the Ministry of Foreign Affairs to prepare to use "Republic of Zhonghua" in its foreign communications in due course.[19] But Jiang's preferred English rendering of the Chinese state's name would never be adopted. Thus, until today, there is no English term that can convey the ascendency of the *zhonghua* conception in China's political life since its war against Japan.

The most recent definition of *zhonghua minzu* in China was made by Fei Xiaotong, the renowned sociologist. Fei defines the "Chinese nation" as a "plural unitary body" (*duoyuan yiti*). Yet this seemingly novel representation carries the same old message: The "plurality" exists only in a cultural sense, and the political unity remains Han-centered.[20] As awkward and disingenuous as it is in delineating the polyethnic situation of China, *zhonghua minzu* has nevertheless proven a powerful political tool to rally the vast Han population of China.

In the past two decades, the economic reforms in China have transformed the country into a "quasi-capitalist" society. The Communist ideology is fading away. These trends have only enhanced the importance of the "Chinese nation" theme in the Chinese government's propaganda. The most recent official invocation of the conception was made after the eleven-day standoff between China and the United States over twenty-four U.S. crew members of a spy airplane detained by the Chinese government. After releasing the Americans, the Chinese government declared a moral victory through the *People's Daily*, asserting that the "Chinese nation" had been fair and fearless in confronting the sole superpower. The *People's Daily* also praised all the member nationalities of the "Chinese nation" for their "strong patriotism and high morale" during the standoff.[21]

"From the Forefathers' Footsteps"

In his "macro" study of Chinese history, the historian Ray Huang remarks: "What freedom of choice we are entitled to starts from where we stand, in the footsteps left by our forefathers."[22] In this sense, the CCP's choice of the Han ethnopolitical approach and rejection of the Soviet model in dealing with China's ethnic issues is logical. Whereas the Russian Bolsheviks were dealing with the tsarist imperialist legacy of a few centuries in length, the CCP has had to wrestle with China's "grand unity" ideology of two millenniums. This difference can give us a starting point in speculating on the near future and asking questions about the prospects of China's current ethnopolitical system. If the collapse of the USSR can provide any clue to this speculation, it is the irrelevance of the Soviet precedent to the Chinese case.

The seemingly lighter historical burden that Lenin and his associates had to carry does not diminish in any way their revolutionary creativity in dealing with Russia's "national question." The lasting significance of the Bolsheviks' practices in this regard is incisively considered in Rogers Brubaker's study of post–Cold War nationalisms in Europe. According to Brubaker, on the ruins of the Romanov dynasty, the Bolsheviks constructed a Soviet multinationality based on a federation of clearly defined "sub-state ethnonational groups." The theoretical equality among these groups was reflected in their constitutional right to secession from the USSR and in the Soviet citizenry that neither claimed any "nationhood" prerogative nor gave centrality to any particular group. In the heyday of the Soviet Empire, the "federation" and "right to secession" indeed appeared to be only fictional.

But as Brubaker points out, these institutionalized structures and rights always had the potential to translate the "fiction" into a fact. Eventually, they did decide the way in which the USSR met its demise. In the early 1990s, when Moscow loosened its grip on the country, the ethnonational republics had their opportunity to exercise their right to self-determination, and they decided to secede from the USSR. Thus, since the disintegration of the multinational structures of the USSR, Yugoslavia, and Czechoslovakia, Europe has entered not a postnational but a "post-multinational" era. Europe has been repeating its post–World War I experience, in which many "successor states" reconfigured their political space by "nationalizing" themselves.[23]

This is a European cycle that China has never entered. By rejecting the Leninist formulas on nationalities' "federation" and "right to secession," the CCP has never intended to make the PRC a supranational structure that can "solve" the "national question." Instead, by adhering to the conception of *zhonghua minzu* and by organizing a unitary ethnopolitical system, the CCP has closely followed its "forefathers' footsteps." The CCP's "nationalities identification work" and "nationality autonomous regions" after 1949 seem indeed novel enough in Chinese history. In China, the standard party literature has cited these as examples of the CCP's creative application of Marxism-Leninism to China's "national question."

Nevertheless, once the Han ethnopolitical gist of the CCP's nationality policy is recognized, it is easy to see that these practices have not broken away from the patterns of Chinese history. The current Chinese government certainly does not want to claim any novelty on behalf of the PRC. On the PRC's fiftieth anniversary, its State Council issued a white paper titled "National Minorities Policy and Its Practice in China." The document described the PRC as a "united multiethnic country"; but, as such, China was "created by the Qin Dynasty and consolidated and developed by the Han Dynasty," not by the CCP in 1949.[24]

Metaphors such as "melting pot" and "salad bowl" for racial and ethnic relationships in the United States and "layered cake" for the multinational system of the former Soviet Union are not necessarily scientific, but they carry vivid images that can be easily grasped. Similarly, China's multiethnic system can be related to the image of a popular Chinese food, the Chinese dumpling (*jiaozi*), with the official *zhonghua minzu* identity as its wrapper and the nationality groups as its assorted stuffings. If the Constitution of the former Soviet Union still left room for the layers of the Soviet cake to be separated, the founders of the PRC certainly did not expect that the Chinese dumpling would break once it was wrapped up in 1949.

China, however, has its own historical cycles marked by unified and divisive "dynasties." After the collapse of the Qing Dynasty, China lapsed into a divisive chaos. Since then, it has been on its way to pursuing a perfect "grand unity" for some time. To borrow Brubaker's scale for European countries, China today may be viewed as an "unrealized nation-state," but of much larger magnitude and complexity than the European cases.[25] China's hypersensitivity toward national sovereignty, constant apprehension about troubles in its ethnic borderlands, and assertive aspiration for Taiwan's return to its fold all underline the paradox of this overcultured yet immature "nation-state" colossus.

But "immaturity" is probably not the right word for the quarter of humankind that has forged one of the world's richest and longest-lasting civilizations. China has been industrializing, democratizing, and "nationalizing" itself in the past century. In so doing, this ancient yet new state has been searching for compatibility with the modern world, not for "maturity" according to either the Communist or the Western standard. China's behavior has a frame of reference in its own long history and civilization. A perception of China resting on the passé Communism of its recent past or on the modernization-cum-Westernization of its near future would be too narrow or misdirected.

In terms of Chinese experience, the historical transformation from the Chinese world to China of the world by the end of the nineteenth century was reluctant, confused, frustrating, and other directed. In the next stage, the twentieth century, China's vigorous, positive, and self-conscious struggle for a proper position in the world successfully led it to invent the "Chinese nation." But in a sense, the Chinese nation has renewed the Chinese world in maintaining Han-centrism within a unitary and bordered ethnopolitical realm.

Will the "Chinese nation" be succeeded by a China of nations in the future? An answer to this question is beyond the disciplinary responsibility of a historical inquiry. It seems clear, however, that as long as the status quo of the "Chinese nation" continues, Sun Yat-sen's proclamation, "All under heaven is for all," will remain a mere ideal.

Notes

Chapter 1—Prologue: From the World of China to China of the World

1. The peaceful separation between the Czechs and Slovaks is an exception to the violent aftermath of these systems.

2. Liu Baoming, *Minzu Wenti yu Guoqing Jiaoyu Duben* (Study materials on the nationality question and the state of the country) (Beijing: Zhongyang Minzu Xueyuan Chubanshe, 1992), 2.

3. Nadia Diuk and Adrian Karatnycky, *The Hidden Nations: The People Challenge the Soviet Union* (New York: William Morrow, 1990), 25.

4. For different opinions on this issue, see A. Doak Barnett, *China's Far West: Four Decades of Change* (Boulder, Colo.: Westview Press, 1993), 592, 611–14; Melvyn C. Goldstein, *The Snow Lion and the Dragon: China, Tibet, and the Dalai Lama* (Berkeley: University of California Press, 1997), 100–31; Justin Jon Rudelson, *Oasis Identities: Uyghur Nationalism along China's Silk Road* (New York: Columbia University Press, 1997), 167–75; John Anderson, *The International Politics of Central Asia* (Manchester: Manchester University Press, 1997), 196–97; and Graham E. Fuller, "The New Geopolitical Order," in *The New Geopolitics of Central Asia and Its Borderlands,* ed. Ali Banuazizi and Myron Weiner (London: I. B. Tauris, 1994), 41.

5. Although multiethnicity has always been a reality of China, the official line in the People's Republic defines China as a country of fifty-six "nationalities." In 1954, there were several hundred self-identified ethnic groups in China. Two years later, the number was reduced to fifty-one as a result of an official "nationality identification" enterprise. In 1983, the State Council finally set the number of "minority nationalities" at fifty-five. According to the first census of the PRC in 1953, ten of these minorities had more than a million population. They were the Mongolian, Hui, Tibetan, Uigur, Miao, Yi, Zhuang, Buyi, Korean, and Manchu. See Luo Guangwu, *Xin Zhongguo Minzu Gongzuo Dashi Gailan, 1949–1999* (A survey of the important events in the nationality work of the new China, 1949–1999) (Beijing: Huawen Chubanshe, 2001), 154–55, 197.

6. June T. Dreyer, *China's Forty Millions: Minority Nationalities and National Integration in the People's Republic of China* (Cambridge, Mass.: Harvard University

Press, 1976), and Walker Connor, *The National Question in Marxist-Leninist Theory and Strategy* (Princeton, N.J.: Princeton University Press, 1984) are two pioneer studies that discuss the CCP's pre-1949 "nationality policies" and implications for the years to come. Their influence is easily discernible in more recent studies, e.g., Dru Gladney, *Muslim Chinese: Ethnic Nationalism in People's Republic* (Cambridge, Mass.: Council on East Asian Studies, Harvard University, 1996), and Colin Mackerras, *China's Minorities: Integration and Modernization in the Twentieth Century* (Hong Kong: Oxford University Press, 1994).

7. Dreyer, *China's Forty Millions,* 60.

8. Dreyer, *China's Forty Millions,* 91.

9. Connor, *National Question,* 38. This conclusion is adopted by Gladney, *Muslim Chinese,* 90.

10. W. J. F. Jenner, *The Tyranny of History: The Roots of China's Crisis* (New York: Penguin Press, 1992), 210–11.

11. Benjamin I. Schwartz, "The Maoist Image of World Order," in *Image and Reality in World Politics,* ed. John C. Farrell and Asa P. Smith (New York: Columbia University Press, 1967), 92, 98.

12. Anthony D. Smith, *The Ethnic Origins of Nations* (Oxford: Basil Blackwell, 1999), 16. Smith excludes "ethnocide" and "genocide" from "normal vicissitudes."

13. Smith, *Ethnic Origins of Nations,* 32.

14. Hu Shi, "A Tentative Commentary on 'Cultural Construction Based on Chinese Essence,'" originally published in *Duli Pinglun,* no. 145 (March 31, 1935), and reprinted in Luo Rongqu, ed., *Cong "Xihua" dao Xiandaihua: Wusi Yilai Youguan Zhongguo de Wenhua Quxiang he Fazhan Daolu Lunzheng Wenxuan* (From Westernization to modernization: selected post-May fourth essays on China's cultural tendencies and road of development) (Beijing: Beijing Daxue Chubanshe, 1990), 417–21.

15. Connor, *National Question,* 29–30, 96, points out that among the 132 states of today's world, only twelve (9.1 percent) can meet the test of ethic homogeneity and the vast majority are not "nation-states" but multinational-states. China cannot pass such a strict ethnic test. It today is and in any given historical time was consisted of more than one *ethnie* or "nation." Nor can China pass the Western democratic test for a "nation." China as a nation-state can therefore be understood only in two senses: (1) since the beginning of the nineteenth century, China has been gradually incorporated into the Europe-originated nation-state system, and (2) since the beginning of the twentieth century, the principal political forces in China have been nationalistic in their orientation. It might be preferable to classify China as a national state. But as Charles Tilly shows, "national states" typically represented a political tendency in the sixteenth-century Europe against any attempt to organize the continent into a universal body. In contrast, China is a case of a universalist civilization that did not break up but was transformed into a member of the modern state system. See Charles Tilly, "Europe and the International State System," in *Nationalism,* ed. John Hutchinson and Anthony D. Smith (Oxford: Oxford University Press, 1994), 251–54.

16. Smith, *Ethnic Origins of Nations,* 50–53, 55.

17. Zhang Chuanxi, "The Historical Characteristics of the Ancient Chinese State," in *Zhongwai Lishi Wenti Ba Ren Tan* (Eight scholars on questions in Chinese and foreign histories), Research Center on Social Sciences Development in Universities, the State Committee on Education, compiler (Beijing: Zhonggong Zhongyang Dangxiao Chubanshe, 1998), 395.

18. Ezra F. Vogel, ed., *Living with China: U.S.–China Relations in the Twenty-First Century* (New York: W. W. Norton, 1997), 19.

19. Dai Yi, "A Study of the History of China's Ethnic Frontiers," in *Zhongwai Lishi Wenti Ba Ren Tan,* 210, 221, 225–29. Dai suggests five reasons to explain China's lasting "grand unity": (1) economic interdependence, (2) peaceful and armed intercourse of the ethnic groups, (3) the inclusiveness of the Chinese culture, (4) the geographical features of China, and (5) the Western pressure since the Opium War. The idea that China has been a unified country during the better part of the past two millenniums is challenged in a thoughtful study by Ge Jianxiong, *Tongyi yu Fenlie: Zhongguo Lishi de Qishi* (Unification and division: revelation of Chinese history) (Beijing: Sanlian Shudian, 1994). According to Ge's calculation, if "unification" means a central dynasty's control of the broadest territorial reach in Chinese history, it existed only for 81 years during the Qing (1759–1840). If unification means restoration of the previous dynasty's domain and orderly rule in China proper, the accumulative length of such periods in Chinese history is 950 years, or 35 percent of recorded Chinese history starting with West Zhou.

20. R. Bin Wong, *China Transformed: Historical Change and the Limits of European Experience* (Ithaca, N.Y.: Cornell University Press, 1997), 76–77.

21. Morris Rossabi, ed., *China among Equals: The Middle Kingdom and Its Neighbors, 10th–14th Centuries* (Berkeley: University of California Press, 1983) includes eleven highly instructive essays on this point.

22. Such discussions can be found in such Confucian classics as *Li Ji; Da Xue* (The book of rites: the great learning) and *Mengzi* (The book of Mencius).

23. Chen Liankai, "Middle Kingdom, *Hua-Yi, Fan-Han, Zhonghua,* and the Chinese Nation: An Understood Process with Internal Connections and Development," in *Zhonghua Minzu Duoyuan Yiti Geju* (The plural unitary structure of the Chinese Nation), ed. Fei Xiaotong et al. (Beijing: Zhongyang Minzu Xueyuan Chubanshe, 1989), 72–113; Liu Zaifu and Lin Gang, *Chuantong yu Zhongguoren* (Tradition and the Chinese) (Hefei: Anhui Wenyi Chubanshe, 1999), 354–72.

24. This is part of *Shang Shu* (book of documents), compiled during the time of the Warring States between the fifth and third centuries B.C.

25. Fan Xiuchuan, ed., *Zhongguo Bianjiang Guji Tijie* (Annotated bibliography of ancient works on China's frontiers) (Urumqi: Xinjiang Renmin Chubanshe, 1995), 182–83; Chen Liankai, "Middle Kingdom," 83; Liu Zaifu and Lin Gang, *Chuantong yu Zhongguoren,* 360–61.

26. Prasenjit Duara, "Historicizing National Identity, or Who Imagines What and When," in *Becoming National,* ed. Geoff Eley and Ronald G. Suny (Oxford: Oxford University Press, 1996), 155.

27. When S. A. M. Adshead published the first edition of his *China in World History* (New York: Saint Martin's Press, 1988), he noted that there were no other similar studies in the field. But when the third edition was published in 2000, at least three excellent studies become its companions. These are Warren I. Cohen, *East Asia at the Center: Four Thousand Years of Engagement with the World* (New York: Columbia University Press, 2000); Joanna Waley-Cohen, *The Sextants of Beijing: Global Currents in Chinese History* (New York: W. W. Norton, 1999); and Valerie Hansen, *The Open Empire: A History of China to 1600* (New York: W. W. Norton, 2000).

28. Adshead, *China in World History,* 172.

29. Wong, *China Transformed,* 88–89.

30. Zhao Yuntian, *Zhongguo Bianjiang Minzu Guanli Jigou Yange Shi* (History of

the changing structures of China's administration of frontiers and nationalities) (Beijing: Zhongguo Shehui Kexue Chubanshe, 1993), 3–4, 14, 69.

31. John King Fairbank, *China: A New History* (Cambridge, Mass.: Belknap Press of Harvard University Press, 1992), 25; Smith, *Ethnic Origins of Nations,* 22–31.

32. David Arkush, "Orthodoxy and Heterodoxy in Twentieth Century Chinese Proverbs," in *Orthodoxy in Late Imperial China,* ed. K. C. Liu (Berkeley: University of California Press, 1990), 311–35, points out the fundamental differences between the values and dogmas of the Chinese gentry and the "orthodoxy" upheld by Chinese peasants. For a comprehensive treatment the various aspects of Chinese popular ideologies, see David Arkush, *Zhongguo Minzhong Sixiang Shilun* (North Chinese folk materials and popular mentality) (Beijing: Zhongyang Minzu Daxue Chubanshe, 1995).

33. Malcolm Anderson, *Frontiers: Territory and State Formation in the Modern World* (Oxford: Polity Press, 1996), 4.

34. *Si Yi* is a commonly used conception in Chinese historical classics. However, the meaning is not "four barbarians" but numerous "barbarous tribes" in the four directions.

35. Owen Lattimore, *Inner Asian Frontiers of China* (London: Oxford University Press, 1940), 276–78.

36. See Lattimore, *Inner Asian Frontiers,* 324–26, 341–46, on the difference between the "un-Chinese" or "not-yet-Chinese" in the course of China's agricultural expansion and the "non-Chinese" in the steppe who blocked the Chinese expansion. Magnus Fiskesjo, "On the 'Raw' and 'Cooked' Barbarians of Imperial China," *Inner Asia,* 1(2) (1999): 139–68, contends that these categories were basically Chinese representations to justify China's "civilizing mission" but did not necessarily reflect the reality of the peoples named.

37. Wong, *China Transformed,* 89, 90.

38. Zhao Yuntian, *Zhongguo Bianjiang Minzu Guanli Jigou Yange Shi,* 134–36. At one time, the number of such administrative units was more than 850.

39. Shen Youliang, *Zhongguo Beifang Minzu jiqi Zhengquan Yanjiu* (A study of the ethnic groups in northern China and their states) (Beijing: Zhongyang Minzu Daxue Chubanshe, 1998), 333–34. The so-called state system obviously predated these non-Han dynasties' control of large Han areas.

40. E.g., the Chinese government holds an argument that Tibet has always been part of China since ancient times. By contrast, the Dalai Lama's contention is that Tibet has been a "distinct and separate entity for over two thousand years."

41. Lattimore, *Inner Asian Frontiers,* 246.

42. Thomas J. Barfield, *The Perilous Frontier: Nomadic Empires and China* (Cambridge: Basil Blackwell, 1989), 49, 63.

43. Duara, "Historicizing National Identity," 154–56.

44. Zhang Chuanxi, "Historical Characteristics" 363; Chen Liankai, "Middle Kingdom," 80–81.

45. Fairbank, *China,* 77; Zhao Yuntian, *Zhongguo Bianjiang Minzu Guanli Jigou Yange Shi,* 4–5. The Li family of the Tang Dynasty had Turkic ancestors.

46. Zhang Chuanxi, "Historical Characteristics," 403; Fan Xiuchuan, *Zhongguo Bianjiang Guji Tijie,* 145–46.

47. Cited in Yu Xilai, "The Growing Course of a New World Power," *Zhanlue yu Guanli* (Strategy and management), no. 6, December 1999 (electronic edition).

48. Mao Zhenfa and Zeng Yan, *Bianfang Lun* (On frontier defense) (Beijing: Junshi Kexue Chubanshe, 1996), 105.

49. Zhou Enlai, *Zhou Enlai Xuanji* (Selected works of Zhou Enlai) (Beijing: Renmin Chubanshe, 1984), 2: 262.

50. Anderson, *Frontiers,* 34.

51. Anderson, *Frontiers,* 2.

52. Fan Xiuchuan, *Zhongguo Bianjiang Guji Tijie,* 3–4, 10–14, 40–41, discusses some of the important geographic works made from the Song to the Qing Dynasties. A recent publication in China, Cao Wanru, ed., *Zhongguo Gudai Ditu Ji* (Ancient atlas of China), 3 vols. (Beijing: Wenwu Chubanshe, 1990–97), includes many interesting images. Richard J. Smith, *Chinese Maps: Images of "All under Heaven"* (Hong Kong: Oxford University Press, 1996), is a valuable little book on this subject. Some of the ancient maps and images can also be viewed at a website based in Hong Kong, http://geog.hkbu.edu.hk/geog1150/chinese/index.html.

53. According to Lattimore, *Inner Asian Frontiers,* 238, the Great Wall was Chinese rulers' abortive effort to erect a liner boundary to separate the Chinese *orbis terrarum* from the barbarian "outer darkness." Arthur Waldron, *The Great Wall of China: From History to Myth* (Cambridge: Cambridge University Press, 1990), chaps. 5 and 6, argues that the Great Wall was part of a "static defense" strategy used by a weak central dynasty to guard the "inner" limits of its domain when the outer posts could no longer be held. These views do not disagree with my point here on the unilateral character of the "borderlines" in Chinese history. There are indeed exceptions. Tao Jing-shen, "Barbarians or Northerners: Northern Sung Images of the Khitans," in Rossabi, *China among Equals,* 71, mentions an episode in the early eleventh century in which the Song government negotiated with the Liao in the north to settle a border dispute. Pamela Kyle Crossley, *A Translucent Mirror: History and Identity in Qing Imperial Ideology* (Berkeley: University of California Press, 1999), 169, also mentions a border agreement between the Ming and the Jurchens (later Manchus) concluded in 1608, whereby the latter continued to pay tributes to the former. These lines were bilateral, but they were nevertheless "inner" from the perspective of the Chinese courts concerned.

54. Crossley, *Translucent Mirror,* 30, 118–19.

55. Indeed, when the Manchus entered China, the old Chinese conceptions of "internal" and "external" switched places; the Chinese populace became "outer," and the Manchus and their followers became "inner." See Crossley, *Translucent Mirror,* 108.

56. Mao Zhenfa and Zeng Yan, *Bianfang Lun* (On frontier defense) (Beijing: Junshi Kexue Chubanshe, 1996), 104, 130.

57. Laura Hostetler, *Qing Colonial Enterprise: Ethnography and Cartography in Early Modern China* (Chicago: University of Chicago Press, 2001), 75–76, 79, 208–9.

58. Benedict Anderson, *Imagined Communities: Reflections on the Origin and Spread of Nationalism* (London: Verso, 1991), 173.

59. Dai Yi, "A Study of the History of China's Ethnic Frontiers," in *Zhongwai Lishi Wenti Ba Ren Tan,* 240–51. Sinica Historica, *Zhonghua Minguo Shi Dilizhi (Chugao)* (Geographic gazetteer of the history of the Republic of China; preliminary edition) (Taipei: Guoshiguan, 1980), 40–52, summarizes the process of boundary demarcation during the late Qing Dynasty.

60. The conception of "bordered land" is borrowed from Jeremy Adelman and Stephen Aron, "From Borderlands to Borders: Empires, Nation-States, and the Peoples in Between in North American History," *American Historical Review* 104(3) (1999): 815–16. It should, however, be pointed out that despite the mapping and border-making exercises during the last century of the Qing Dynasty, Western observers were very slow

to develop a view of the Chinese Empire as a unitary political-territorial body. E.g., from John F. Davis's *The Chinese: A General Description of the Empire of China and Its Inhabitant* (New York: Harper & Brothers, 1836) to L. Richard's *Comprehensive Geography of the Chinese Empire and Dependencies* (Shanghai: T'usewei Press, 1908; English trans. by M. Kennelly from the same publisher's 1905 French edition), the practice was to describe the fifteen or eighteen provinces of China as "China proper" but to classify Manchuria, Mongolia, Xinjiang, Tibet, and some other territories as China's "dependencies."

61. Fang Weigui, "The Conceptions of 'Civilization' and 'Culture' in Modern China," East Asian Department, Göttingen University of Göttingen, China Group TU Berlin, www.gwdg.de/~oas/wsc/wenming.htm.

62. Mao and Zeng, *Bianfang Lun*, 88–89.

63. Chen Liankai, "Middle Kingdom," 86.

64. Zhao Yuntian, *Zhongguo Bianjiang Minzu Guanli Jigou Yange Shi*, 299–308.

65. Fan Xiuchuan, *Zhongguo Bianjiang Guji Tijie*, 216–18. E.g., France, Holland, and the United States were listed together with Korea, Japan, and Liuqiu as *dong yi*, or "eastern barbarians."

66. Mao Haijian, *Tianchao de Bengkui* (The disintegration of the celestial dynasty) (Beijing: Sanlian Shudian, 1995), 28 n. 15.

67. Wu Fuhuan, *Qi Ji Zongli Yamen Yanjiu* (A study of the Zongli Yamen of the Qing) (Urumqi: Xinjiang Daxue Chubanshe, 1995), 2–3, 11.

68. Iwo Amelung and Joachim Kurtz, "Researching Modern Chinese Technical Terminologies: Methodological Considerations and Practical Problems," paper presented at an international workshop at the University of Göttingen, Göttingen, October 24–25 1997, www.gwdg.de/~oas/wsc/ttreport.htm. Earl Swisher, *China's Management of American Barbarians: A Study of Sino–American Relations, 1841–1861, with Documents* (New Haven, Conn.: Far Eastern Publications, 1951), 468–69, contains an interesting memorial dated 1858 that reveals the Qing officials' purposeful choice between the terms of "barbarian" and "foreign" affairs for different occasions.

69. Zhao Yuntian, *Zhongguo Bianjiang Minzu Guanli Jigou Yange Shi*, 383–84. After the 1860s, Russia was no longer part of the Lifan Yuan's responsibility.

70. Ma Ruheng and Ma Dazheng, *Qingdai de Bianjiang Zhengce* (Frontier policies of the Qing Dynasty) (Beijing: Zhongguo Shehui Kexue Chubanshe, 1994), 85–91, 431–32.

71. Ge Jianxiong et al., *Jianming Zhongguo Yimin Shi* (A brief history of migration in China) (Fuzhou: Fujian Renmin Chubanshe, 1993), 474–78; Ma Ruheng and Ma Dazheng, *Qingdai de Bianjiang Zhengce*, 97–101, 110–23, 445–46. Xinjiang was organized into a province in 1882, three provinces were planned for Inner Mongolia in 1902, and the issue of a Tibetan province was debated in the Qing government but was then shelved in 1907.

72. Ma Ruheng and Ma Dazheng, *Qingdai de Bianjiang Zhengce*, 445.

73. This phrase was originally from the Confucian classic, *Li Ji Zheng Yi* (Book of rites with orthodox interpretations), and was followed in general by rulers of the Qing Dynasty. See Ma Ruheng and Ma Dazheng, *Qingdai de Bianjiang Zhengce*, 61–62.

74. Pamela Kyle Crossley, *Orphan Warriors: Three Manchu Generations and the End of the Qing World* (Princeton, N.J.: Princeton University Press, 1990), 223–24.

75. John Breuilly, *Nationalism and the State* (Chicago: University of Chicago Press, 1994), 234.

76. Mark C. Elliott, *The Manchu Way: The Eight Banners and Ethnic Identity in Late Imperial China* (Stanford, Calif.: Stanford University Press, 2001), 2–13.

77. The Qing's "taxonomic ideology" and practices are the subject matter of Crossley's *Translucent Mirror.*

78. Crossley, *Translucent Mirror,* 338–39. See also Frank Dikotter, *The Discourse of Race in Modern China* (Stanford, Calif.: Stanford University Press, 1992).

79. For Sun Yat-sen's extensive claim on China's "original territories," see his *San Min Chu I: The Three Principles of the People* (Chungking: Ministry of Information of the Republic of China, 1943), 33–35. Chiang Kai-shek, *China's Destiny* (New York: Roy Publishers, 1947), 36–39, makes a relatively moderate claim but still demands no less than the domain of the Qing Empire.

80. Anderson, *Imagined Communities,* 86.

81. Crossley, *Translucent Mirror,* 337–38.

82. For the Republic of China's diplomatic activism, see Bruce A. Elleman, *Diplomacy and Deception: The Secret History of Sino–Soviet Diplomatic Relations, 1917–1927* (Armonk, N.Y.: M. E. Sharpe, 1997), John W. Garver, *Chinese–Soviet Relations, 1937–1945* (New York: Oxford University Press, 1988), William Kirby, *Germany and Republican China* (Stanford, Calif.: Stanford University Press, 1984), Xiaoyuan Liu, *A Partnership for Disorder: China, the United States, and Their Policies for the Postwar Disposition of the Japanese Empire, 1941–1945* (Cambridge: Cambridge University Press, 1996).

83. Crossley, *Translucent Mirror,* 262.

84. John Fitzgerald, *Awakening China: Politics, Culture, and Class in the Nationalist Revolution* (Stanford, Calif.: Stanford University Press, 1996), 122.

85. Ernest Gellner, *Nations and Nationalism* (Ithaca, N.Y.: Cornell University Press, 1983), 24–25.

86. Chen Liankai in Fei Xiaotong et al., *Zhonghua Minzu Duoyuan Yiti Geju,* 104–11.

87. E. J. Hobsbawm, *Nations and Nationalism since 1780* (Cambridge: Cambridge University Press, 1991), 66.

88. In 1913, a dozen Inner Mongolian banners' officials held a conference to reject Outer Mongolia's call for the establishment of an independent state. Chen Liankai in Fei Xiaotong et al., *Zhonghua Minzu Duoyuan Yiti Geju,* 112, cites the final document of the conference as an example of a non-Han people's voluntary admission of being part of the Chinese nation. According to Cai Huidong, a Chinese official responsible for organizing the conference, at the meeting the Mongol princes were under constant "moral suasion by responsible officials." Therefore, the conference is not really a case of the Inner Mongols' "intransitive awakening" to Chinese patriotism but one of the Chinese government's "transitive" action to enlist the Inner Mongols' support. For a Chinese record of the conference, see Guest House for the Western League Princes' Conference, compiler, *Ximeng Huiyi Shimo Chi* (A record of the western league princes' conference) (Tianjin: Shangwu Yinshuguan, 1913?).

89. I have discussed in some detail the KMT government's ethnopolitics in two articles, "Cold War and China's Borderlands: A Study of the Secret Archives of China, Britain, and the United States," *Jindai Zhongguoshi Yanjiu Tongxun* (Newsletter for modern Chinese historical research) (Institute of Modern History, Sinica Academia, Taipei), no. 27 (March 1999): 88–107, and "The Kuomintang and the 'Mongolian Question' in the Chinese Civil War, 1945–1949," *Inner Asia* 1(2) (1999): 169–94.

Chapter 2—Bolshevization: Limitations of Conversion

1. Documentary Research Office of the CCP Central Committee, *Mao Zedong Nianpu* (Chronicle of Mao Zedong's life), 3 vols. (Beijing: Zhongyang Wenxian Chubanshe, 1993), 1: 24. In January, 1915, the Japanese government broached its Twenty-One Demands to the Chinese government secretly and demanded a series of political and economic privileges. These demands became known to the public after the Chinese government "leaked" the information.

2. Documentary Research Office of the CCP Central Committee, *Mao Zedong Zaoqi Wengao* (Early writings of Mao Zedong) (Changsha: Hunan Chubanshe, 1995), 503–8, 530–33.

3. Documentary Research Office, *Mao Zedong Zaoqi Wengao,* 571–72, 553–55.

4. Arif Dirlik, *The Origins of Chinese Communism* (Oxford: Oxford University Press, 1989), 12–14.

5. Walker Connor, *National Question in Marxist-Leninist Theory and Strategy* (Princeton, N.J.: Princeton University Press, 1984), xiii; Hugh Seton-Watson, "Russian Nationalism in Historical Perspective," in *The Last Empire: Nationality and the Soviet Future,* ed. Robert Conquest (Stanford, Calif.: Hoover Institution Press, 1986), 23–24.

6. Alexander Pantsov, *The Bosheviks and the Chinese Revolution, 1919–1927* (Honolulu: University of Hawaii Press, 2000), 29–31, discusses the gradual appearance of Marxist works in China between 1919 and 1927.

7. Michael Y. L. Luk, *The Origins of Chinese Bolshevism: An Ideology in the Making, 1920–1928* (Hong Kong: Oxford University Press, 1990), 5–6.

8. Hélène Carrère d'Encausse, *The Great Challenge: Nationalities and the Bolshevik State, 1917–1930* (New York: Holmes & Meier, 1992), 2.

9. d'Encausse, *Great Challenge,* discusses the theoretical and practical processes that formed the Soviet empire. The quotations are from contemporary Soviet documents in *Marxism and Asia,* ed. Hélène Carrère d'Encausse and Stuart R. Schram (London: Allen Lane The Penguin Press, 1969), 182–83, 32, 174–75.

10. Documentary Research Office, *Mao Zedong Nianpu,* 1: 184.

11. Dirlik, *Origins of Chinese Communism,* 270.

12. The first resolution of the Chinese Communist Party, no date, *Zhonggong Zhongyang Wenjian Xuanji* (Selected documents of the CCP Central Committee; hereafter *ZZWX*), 1: 6–9.

13. For an analysis of the debate from the time of the Second International to the Russian Bolshevik revolution, see d'Encausse, *Great Challenge,* chaps. 1 and 2.

14. Chen Yongfa, *Zhongguo Gongchan Geming Qishi Nian* (Seventy years of the Chinese communist revolution) (Taipei: Lianjing, 1998), 1: 48.

15. Deng Enming was the only "minority" (Shui) participant of the First National Congress of the CCP. He, of course, did not attend the congress as a representative of the minorities. There is no question that some early CCP activities in eastern and southern provinces involved local non-Han ethnic groups, but these were just part of the CCP agitations among the "peasants." Although the official literature in China implies the contrary, the CCP did not launch any "minority nationality work" in its formative years. See, e.g., Jiang Ping, ed., *Zhongguo Minzu Wenti de Lilun yu Shijian* (The theories and practices regarding China's nationality question) (Beijing: Zhonggong Zhongyang Dangxiao Chubanshe, 1994), 102–3.

16. Zhang Guotao, *Wo de Huiyi* (My memoirs) (Beijing: Xiandai Shiliao Congcan

Chubanshe, 1980), 1: 138, 184, 196, 235–36; *Minzu Wenti Wenxian Huibian* (Collection of documents on the national question; hereafter *MWWH*), 62 n. 2; Zhou Wenqi and Chu Liangru, *Teshu er Fuza de Keti—Gongchan Guoji, Sulian he Zhongguo Gongchandang Guanxi Biannian Shih 1919–1991* (Unique and complex subject: a chronicle of the relationship among the Comintern, the Soviet Union, and the Chinese Communist Party, 1919–1991) (Wuhan: Hubei Renmin Chubanshe, 1993), 22–23, 33–34; Allen S. Whiting, *Soviet Policies in China, 1917–1924* (Stanford, Calif.: Stanford University Press, 1968), 78–86. Zhang Tailei was then the head of the China Office of the Comintern's Secretariat for the Far East, and he may also have contributed to the CCP's new awareness of the "national question."

17. "Resolution of the CCP to join the Third Communist International, July 1922," *ZZWX*, 1: 67–72. There were altogether twenty-one conditions to qualify for the Comintern membership. The "national question" was covered by condition number eight. A Chinese version of the condition was attached to the resolution. According to an editorial note of *ZZWX*, the Chinese version contains several translation mistakes. The translation here is based on the Chinese version, and it should be compared with another English version in Robert V. Daniels, *A Documentary History of Communism, Volume 2: Communism and the World* (London: I. B. Tauris, 1985), 45.

18. Yang Kuisong, *Mao Zedong he Mosike de En En Yuan Yuan* (Benefactions and disaffections between Mao Zedong and Moscow) (Nanchang: Jiangxi Renmin Chubanshe, 1999), 9.

19. "Resolution on International Imperialism and China and the Chinese Communist Party, July 1922," *MWWH*, 8; "Proclamation of the Second National Congress of the CCP, July 1922," *MWWH*, 17; Shen Changyou, *Mao Zedong yu Gongchan Guoji* (Mao Zedong and the Comintern) (Beijing: Dangjian Duwu Chubanshe, 1994), 45. At the time, Mao Zedong was in Shanghai but did not participate in the meeting because, surprisingly, he could not remember the location of the conference.

20. John Fitzgerald, *Awakening China: Politics, Culture, and Class in the Nationalist Revolution* (Stanford, Calif.: Stanford University Press, 1996), 160–61.

21. Lenin's definition included recognition of "possible" secession by territorially definable minorities living in peripheral regions. See d'Encausse, *Great Challenge*, 67–68.

22. Yang Kuisong, *Mao Zedong*, 5–6; O. Edmund Clubb, *China and Russia: The "Great Game"* (New York: Columbia University Press, 1971), 228–40.

23. "Opinion of the CCP and the central bureau of the Chinese socialist youth league on the KMT national congress, December 1923," *MWWH*, 23.

24. For two recent and superbly documented studies of the Sino–Russian diplomatic relationship from the late nineteenth to the early twentieth century, see Bruce A. Elleman, *Diplomacy and Deception: The Secret History of Sino–Soviet Diplomatic Relations, 1917–1927* (Armonk, N.Y.: M. E. Sharpe, 1997), and S. C. M. Paine, *Imperial Rivals: China, Russia, and Their Disputed Frontier* (Armonk, N.Y.: M. E. Sharpe, 1996).

25. "Declaration to the Chinese people and the southern and northern governments of China by the government of the socialist republic of the Russian soviet federation, 25 July 1919," *Zhong Su Guojia Guanxi Shi Ziliao Huibian* (Collected documents on the history of the Chinese–Soviet state relationship *1917–1924;* hereafter *ZSGG*), 58–60; "Minutes number 24 of the meeting of the Russian Communist Party (Bolshevik) Central Politburo, 31 August 1922," *Gongchanguoji, Liangong (Bu) yu Zhongguo Geming Wenxian Ziliao Xuanji* (Selected documentary materials on the Comintern, Soviet Communist Party and the Chinese revolution; hereafter *GLZGWZ*), 1: 114–15.

26. "Telegram from people's commissar for foreign affairs Chicherin to the ministry of foreign affairs of China, 10 November 1920," ZSGG, 432–33; "Soviet Russian government's declaration to the Mongolian people and the Mongolian autonomous government, 3 August 1919," ZSGG, 458–59; "Russian–Mongolian treaty of friendship, 5November 1921," ZSGG, 462–63; "Xinjiang provincial and military governor Yang Zengxin's directive to commander Yang Feixia and mayor Xu Guozhen of Yili, 7 October 1919," ZSGG, 485; "Xinjiang provincial and military governor Yang Zengxin to mayor Zhang Jian of Tacheng, 24 May 1921," ZSGG, 504–5; "Agreement on the entry into the territory of the Republic of China by the red army of the socialist republic of the Russian soviet federation for the purpose of suppressing the white bandits in the Altai district, 12 September 1921," ZSGG, 516–17; "Tibetan Kashag officials' memorial to the Dalai Lama on the processing of a letter from Soviet Russian deputy people's commissar for foreign affairs Karakhan to the 13th Dalai Lama, winter 1920," ZSGG, 684–85; "Letter to Dalai Lama (from Karakhan), November 1922," ZSGG, 685–86; "Letter from deputy people's commissar for foreign affairs Karakhan to the 13th Dalai Lama, 9 June 1923," ZSGG, 687–88.

27. "Liu Jiang's report to the Russian Communist Party (Bolshevik) committee of the Amur district, 5 October 1920," GLZGWZ, 1: 44; "Borodin's notes on the situation of southern China, 10 December 1923," GLZGWZ, 1: 366; "Letter from Sun Yat-sen to the ministry of foreign affairs of the Russian soviet socialist republic, 28 August 1921," ZSGG, 673–74.

28. Yang Kuisong, "Sun Yat-sen's northwestern military plan and its demise: the Kuomintang's first attempt to receive military assistance from Soviet Russia," in Huang Xiurong, ed., Sulian, Gongchan Guoji yu Zhongguo Geming de Guanxi Xintan (New studies of the relationship between the Soviet Union, the Comintern, and the Chinese revolution) (Beijing: Zhonggong Dangshi Chubanshe, 1995), 200–23.

29. "Joffe's telegram to Chicherin, 7 and 8 November 1922," GLZGWZ, 1: 147–50; "Letter from Joffe to the leaders of the Russian Communist Party (Bolshevik), Soviet government, and Comintern, 13 January 1923," GLZGWZ, 1: 197; "Letter from Joffe to the leaders of the Russian Communist Party (Bolshevik), Soviet government, and Comintern, 26 January 1923," GLZGWZ, 1: 213–15; "Joffe's opinion on the prospect and possible consequences of cooperation with Sun Yat-sen, 26 January 1923," GLZGWZ, 1: 218–22.

30. "Report to the executive committee of the Comintern on the organization and work of the department of Oriental nations of the Siberian bureau of the Russian Communist Party (Bolshevik), 21 December 1920," GLZGWZ, 1: 49–57; "Report from the Oriental department of the Comintern's executive committee to the presidium of the Comintern's executive committee, 16 May 1925," GLZGWZ, 1: 617–22; "Minutes number 24 of the meeting of the Russian Communist Party (Bolshevik) central politburo, 31 August 1922," GLZGWZ, 1: 114–15; "Minutes number 53 of the meeting of the Russian Communist Party (Bolshevik) central politburo, 8 March 1923," GLZGWZ, 1: 225–26.

31. Second Historical Archives of China, Jiang Jieshi Nianpu Chugao (Preliminary draft of the chronicle of Jiang Jieshi's life) (Beijing: Dang'an Chubanshe, 1992), 137–38, 140; "Balanovskii's report on the meeting between the KMT delegation and Sklianskii and Kamenev, 13 November 1923," GLZGWZ, 1: 309–13; "Shorthand minutes of the meeting of the Comintern executive committee participated by the KMT delegation,

26 November 1923," *GLZGWZ,* 1: 330–38; "Balanovskii's report on the KMT delegation's visit of Trotsky, 27 November 1923," *GLZGWZ,* 1: 339–41.

32. On the relationship between the Comintern and the Inner Mongols, Christopher
P. Atwood wrote a fascinating article, "A Buriat Agent in Inner Mongolian: A. I. Oshirov (c. 1901–1931)," in *Opuscula Altacia,* ed. Edward H. Kaplan and Donald W.
Whisenhunt (Bellingham: Western Washington University Press, 1994). Andrew D. W.
Forbes's *Warlords and Muslims in Chinese Central Asia: A Political History of Republican Sinkiang, 1911–1949* (Cambridge: Cambridge University Press, 1986) is a useful
survey that sheds light on the Soviet position in Xinjiang.

33. "Presidium of the Comintern executive committee's resolution on the Chinese
national liberation movement and the KMT question, 28 November 1923," *GLZGWZ,*
1: 342–45.

34. "Proclamation of the KMT's first national congress, 23 January 1924," *MWWH,*
26–28.

35. "Borodin's notes and reports, after 16 February 1924," *GLZGWZ,* 1: 433, 448–
49, 463–68. For Borodin's role in forging the KMT–CCP alliance in 1924, see Allen
Whiting, *Soviet Policy in China, 1917–1924* (Stanford, Calif.: Stanford University Press,
1968), 244–47. According to "Borodin's notes" cited above, the first version of the KMT
proclamation was prepared in Russian by Borodin and the CCP's central bureau in
Shanghai. Some KMT members participated in the discussion for revision. From the
beginning to the end, Qu Qiubai played an important role in drafting and translating
the document.

36. Yang Kuisong, "Sun Yat-sen's northwestern military plan and its demise," 205;
"Minutes of the Borodin–Qu Qiubai conversation, 16 December 1923," *GLZGWZ,* 1:
382–85.

37. Second Historical Archives of China, *Jiang Jieshi Nianpu Chugao,* 167.

38. Elleman, *Diplomacy and Deception,* 213–20, points out that after Sun's death
the Comintern "intensified" revolution in China in the next two years, and the resultant
policies increased the distrust between the KMT and Moscow and should share the responsibility for the collapse of the CCP–KMT united front in 1927. But insofar as Jiang's
psychological change regarding the Soviets is concerned, his 1923 mission constituted
a decisive turning point.

39. "Balanovskii's report on the meeting between the KMT delegation and Sklian-
skii and Kamenev, 13 November 1923," *GLZGWZ,* 1: 312; "Minutes of the Borodin–Qu
Qiubai conversation, 16 December 1923," *GLZGWZ,* 1: 382–84. In addition to Jiang and
Zhang, Shen Dingyi and Wang Dengyun were the other two members of the delegation.
Shen was a former CCP member, and he took Zhang's side in Moscow and criticized
Jiang's and Wang's attitudes toward the Mongolian question.

40. Elleman, *Diplomacy and Deception,* 88–90.

41. "Report to the Comintern by Chen Duxiu, secretary of the CCP executive committee, 30 June 1922," *MWWH,* 6.

42. Chen Duxiu, "Our answer," 17 September 1924, *MWWH,* 60–61; Xiao Chunu,
"The 'waking lion faction' under the microscope," October 1925, *MWWH,* 65.

43. Gu Weijun, *Gu Weijun Huiyilu* (Memoir of Gu Weijun) (Beijing: Zhonghua
Shuju, 1983–1992), 1: 340.

44. For the Chinese–Soviet agreement on Mongolia, see Elleman, *Diplomacy and
Deception,* 106–9 and Peter S. H. Tang, *Russian and Soviet Policy in Manchuria and*

Mongolia, 1911–1931 (Durham, N.C.: Duke University Press, 1959), 380–84. In this period, the CCP's writings and statements relevant to the Mongolia issue were Li Shouchang (Dazhao), "Mongol Nation's Liberation Movement," 1925, *MWWH,* 69–70; Qu Qiubai, "Lenin and China's People's Revolution," 21 January 1926, *MWWH,* 71–71; Chen Duxiu, "KMT's Rightist Conference," 23 April 1926, *MWWH,* 73; "The CCP central committee's open letter to the members of the KMT on the first anniversary of Mr. [Sun] Zhongshan's [Yat-sen] passing away, 12 March 1926," *MWWH,* 43–44; "Resolution on national revolutionary movements adopted by the fourth national conference of the CCP," February 1925, *ZZWX,* 1: 329–41.

45. Zhou Wenqi and Chu Liangru, *Teshu er Fuza de Keti,* 102–3.

46. See Li Shouchang (Dazhao), "Populism," January 1923, *MWWH,* 55–59; Li Shouchang (Dazhao), "The liberation movement of the Mongolian nation," 1925, *MWWH,* 69–70.

47. "Borodin's notes and reports, after 16 February 1924," *GLZGWZ,* 1: 469.

48. Fitzgerald, *Awakening China,* 136–37.

49. Zhao Yuntian, *Zhongguo Bianjiang Minzu Guanli Jigou Yange Shi* (History of the changing structures of China's administration of frontiers and nationalities) (Beijing: Zhongguo Shehui Kexue Chubanshe, 1993), 299, 384; Li Dazhao, "Populism," 55–59.

50. Frank Dikotter, *The Discourse of Race in Modern China* (Stanford, Calif.: Stanford University Press, 1992), traces a historical Chinese "racial" prejudice based mainly on a physical premise.

51. A pioneer study of the history of China's ethnology is Wang Jianmin, *Zhongguo Minzuxue Shi* (History of ethnic studies in China), 2 vols. (Kunming: Yunnan Jiaoyu Chubanshe, 1997 and 1998). For the beginning of China's ethnology see 1: 73–122.

52. Qu Qiubai, *Qu Qiubai Wenji* (Essays by Qu Qiubai) (Beijing: Remin Chubanshe, 1989), 3: 79–82, 387–88, 409–10, 474–76, 488–534. In the mid-1920s, Qu delivered a series of lectures on the "question of modern nations" at Shanghai University.

53. "Resolution on the liberation of the Miao and the Yao by the first assembly of Hunan peasant representatives, December 1926," *MWWH,* 52. For the historical conditions of the "minorities" in southern China and their encounters with the Han and the outside world, see the essays by Charles F. McKhann, Stevan Harrell, Norma Diamond, Ralph A. Litzinger, Margaret Byrne Swain, Siu-woo Cheung, and Shih-chung Hsieh in *Cultural Encounters on China's Ethnic Frontiers,* ed. Stevan Harrell (Seattle: University of Washington Press, 1995).

54. This school was created by Yuan Shikai's government in 1914 to train Mongolian and Tibetan youths. But until the mid-1920s, only students were from Inner Mongolia attended it. Zhao Yuntian, *Zhongguo Bianjiang Minzu Guanli Jigou Yange Shi,* 426; Ulanfu, *Wulanfu Huiyilu* (Ulanfu's memoirs) (Beijing: Zhonggong Dangshi Ziliao Chubanshe, 1989), 44.

55. Wang Shusheng and Hao Yufeng, *Wulanfu Nianpu* (Chronicle of Ulanfu's life) (Beijing: Zhonggong Dangshi Chubanshe, 1989), 1: 31.

56. "Documents of the enlarged executive committee of the CCP central committee, October 1925": "Resolution on current political situation of China and the CCP's responsibilities," "Resolution on organizational questions," and "Resolution on the Mongolian question," *ZZWX,* 1: 459–60, 472–76, 492–93; Party History Office of the Inner Mongolian CCP Committee, *Neimenggu Dang de Lishi he Dang de Gongzuo* (History and works of the [Chinese Communist] party in Inner Mongolia) (Hohhot: Neimenggu Renming Chubanshe, 1994), 26.

57. Owen Lattimore, *Inner Asian Frontiers of China* (London: Oxford University Press, 1940), 246–51.

58. For an informative discussion of the Qing's immigration policy, see Huang Shijian, "On the Qing government's 'immigration and frontier substantiation' policy in Inner Mongolia in the late Qing period," *Neimenggu Jindaishi Luncong* (Essays on the modern history of Inner Mongolia), compiled by Chinese Communist Party's Research Institute of the Inner Mongolian Regional Party History (Huhhot: Neimenggu Renmin Chubanshe, 1982), 1: 106–27. According to Zhang Zhihua, "A survey of Inner Mongolia's Mongolian population from the Qing to the Republic of China," *Neimenggu Jindaishi Luncong* 2 (1983): 221–51, at the Qing's end, the Mongolian population of Inner Mongolia was about 1.1 million. Ge Jiangxiong et al., *Jianming Zhongguo Yimin Shi* (A brief history of migration in China) (Fuzhou: Fujian Renmin Chubanshe, 1993), 478, indicate that by 1908 about 1.6 million Han migrants had moved into Inner Mongolia. The latter study's estimate on the Mongolian population is even lower, at 830,000.

59. Lattimore, *Inner Asian Frontiers of China,* 246.

60. Baabar, *Twentieth Century Mongolia* (Cambridge: White Horse Press, 1999), 137–41, 252–57. Ulanfu, a leading Inner Mongolian member of the CCP, recalled in later years how, in 1924, a report on Outer Mongolia's "socialist revolution and construction" inspired a "wave of idealism" among the radical Inner Mongolian students in the Peking Mongolian and Tibetan School. See Ulanfu, *Wulanfu Huiyilu,* 56.

61. For this issue see Bruce A. Elleman, "The Final Consolidation of the USSR's Sphere of Interest in Outer Mongolia," in *Mongolia in the Twentieth Century: Landlocked Cosmopolitan,* ed. Stephen Kotkin and Bruce A. Elleman (Armonk, N.Y.: M. E. Sharpe, 1999), 123–36.

62. "Voitinsky's report in writing, 28 September 1925," *GLZGWZ,* 1: 693–94. According to Christopher Atwood, "A. I. Oshirov (c. 1901–1931): A Buriat Agent in Inner Mongolia," the original idea about an Inner Mongolian party was proposed by Serengdonrub, a Kharachin Mongol, in April 1924. The standard historical literature in China attributes the idea to Li Dazhao, who allegedly proposed the party organization to the Comintern and the CCP's central committee at the end of 1924. See, e.g., Hao Weimin, "The Inner Mongolian people's revolutionary party during the first and second domestic revolutionary wars," in *Zhongguo Menggushi Xuehui Chengli Dahui Jinian Jikan* (The proceedings of the founding conference of the Chinese Society of the Mongolian Studies, comp. by the Chinese Society of the Mongolian Studies, 1979), 583, and the Party History Office of the Inner Mongolian Committee of the CCP, *Neimenggu Dang de Lishi he Dang de Gongzuo* (The party's history and work in Inner Mongolia) (Hohhot: Neimenggu Renmin Chubanshe, 1994), 20.

63. Hao Weimin, "Inner Mongolian People's Revolutionary Party," 585.

64. In October 1924, in collaboration with some other warlords, Feng Yuxiang conducted a military coup in Peking. Afterward, he took his army to Zhangjiakou and showed a willingness to cooperate with the KMT and Soviet Russia. In September 1926, Feng formally declared his cooperation with the KMT's Northern Expedition. "Minutes No. 1 of the Meeting of the China Committee of the Russian Communist Party's (Bolshevik) Central Politburo, 17 April 1925," *GLZGWZ,* 1: 602–4, adopted the policy of providing military assistance to Feng Yuxiang.

65. Luo Hong and Sun Zhongyao, "Our party's assistance to Feng Yuxiang and facilitation of the military effort from Wuyuan," *Neimenggu Dangshi Ziliao* (Materials on the party history in Inner Mongolia) 1 (1988): 248.

66. The CCP decided to gain complete control of the IMPRP only in early 1928, after the latter also disintegrated into factions. See Hao Weimin, "Inner Mongolian People's Revolutionary Party," 595.

67. "Special meeting of the CCP Central Committee, 21–24 February 1926," *MWWH*, 42, stipulated that after the dissolution of the "grand alliance," its former Mongolian members should join the IMPRP or the KMT, and that the KMT's work in Inner Mongolia needed to be greatly expanded to maintain a friendly relationship with the IMPRP.

68. "Voitinsky's report in writing, 28 September 1925," *GLZGWZ*, 1: 693–94.

69. "Qijia's [code name for the CCP center] opinion on the work of the Inner Mongolian KMT, December 1926," *MWWH*, 50; "Letter from the Inner Mongolian KMT to the center of the Chinese KMT, 8 November 1926," *MWWH*, 51. At the time the Inner Mongolian people's revolutionary party was also called the Inner Mongolian Kuomintang, obviously for the sake of cooperation with the Chinese KMT. At the time, the KMT had four party departments in Inner Mongolia, all established by CCP members in the capacity of KMT members.

70. Liu Jinren, "Reminiscence on the revolutionary struggle in Suiyuan during the period of the great revolution," *Neimenggu Dangshi Ziliao* (Materials on the party history of Inner Mongolia) 2 (1989): 174–91; "Report on the investigation of the history of the CCP special branch in Suiyuan," *Neimenggu Dangshi Ziliao* 2 (1989): 270–75; Hao Weimin, "Inner Mongolian People's Revolutionary Party," 595.

Chapter 3—Sovietization: A Rebellious Option

1. Lucian W. Pye, *Warlord Politics: Conflict and Coalition in the Modernization of Republican China* (New York: Praeger Publishers, 1971), 8.

2. "On the Shanghai Armed Uprising, 3 March 1927," Zhou Enlai, *Zhou Enlai Junshi Wenxuan* (Selected military works of Zhou Enlai) (Beijing: Renmin Chubanshe, 1997), 1: 22–23.

3. John K. Fairbank, *China: A New History* (Cambridge: Belknap Press of Harvard University Press, 1992), 191.

4. According to Wang Huichang, *Zhongguo Wenhua Dili* (China's cultural geography) (Wuchang: Huazhong Shifan Daxue Chubanshe, 1992), 181–82, during the Song Dynasty, southern China began to supply more than half of China's intelligentsia, and between the Ming Dynasty and the present, more than 80 percent of China's intelligentsia have been southerners.

5. Edward Friedman, *National Identity and Democratic Prospects in Socialist China* (Armonk, N.Y.: M.E. Sharpe, 1995), especially 77–86, is an example of using the south–north theme to analyze China's conditions today.

6. Xu Shishen, ed., *Guomin Zhengfu Jianzhi Zhiminglu* (Guide to the structure and official titles of the Nationalist Government) (Taipei: Guoshiguan, 1984), 32, 50. In 1928, declaring itself the central government of China, the KMT government took over the Mongolian and Tibetan affairs management approach from the Beijing government and set up a commission.

7. Vol. 1 of *Zhonggong Zhongyang Wenjian Xuanji* (Selected documents of the CCP Central Committee; hereafter *ZZWX*) covers the period from 1921 to 1925, and

includes twelve documents focusing on developments in North China. Vol. 2 covers 1926 and contains sixteen documents on North China, all related to the northern expedition.

8. "Report by the central bureau, 5 December 1926," *ZZWX*, 2: 502–3, 507.

9. "Meeting minutes number 2 of the China committee of the Russian Communist Party (Bolshevik) central politburo, 29 May 1925," *Gongchanguoji, Liangong (Bu) yu Zhongguo Geming Wenxian Ziliao Xuanji* (Selected documentary materials on the Comintern, Soviet Communist Party and the Chinese revolution; hereafter *GLZGWZ*), 1: 623–27.

10. Vols. 3–6 of *ZZWX* separately cover 1927 to 1930, but only the volume on 1928 contains four documents on Japanese and warlord activities in North China.

11. "CCP's fifth national congress, 27 April–9 May 1927": "Resolution on the political situation and the party's tasks," *ZZWX*, 3: 54–55; Zhou Wenqi and Chu Liangru, *Techu er Fuza de Keti—Gongchan Guoji, Sulian, he Zhongguo Gongchadang Biannianshi, 1919–1991* (Unique and complicated subject: a chronological history of the relationship between the Comintern, the Soviet Union, and the CCP) (Wuhan: Hubei Renmin Chubanshe, 1993), 156. Mao first uttered the sentence at a CCP conference in August 1927.

12. "Center's circular number 68: on the calling of a national conference of the soviet areas, 4 February 1930," *ZZWX*, 6: 15–20; "New revolutionary upsurge and victory at first in one or several provinces: the resolution on current political tasks by the meeting of the politburo on 11 June 1930," *ZZWX*, 6: 115–35.

13. "Resolution on the China question by the political secretariate of the Comintern executive committee, 23 July 1930," *ZZWX*, 6: 583–95; "Letter from the Comintern executive committee to the CCP central committee on the 'Lisan line,' 16 November 1930," *ZZWX*, 6: 644–55; Zhou Wenqi and Chu Liangru, *Techu er Fuza de Keti*, 191–202.

14. "Center's resolution on the question of the Hebei party, January 1931," *ZZWX*, 7: 94–98.

15. The *ZZWX* volumes on 1931–33 contain nineteen documents relevant to North China. After the Long March of 1934–35, the CCP's headquarters would be relocated to the border region of Shaanxi, Gansu, and Ningxia in the northwest.

16. Zhou Wenqi and Chu Liangru, *Techu er Fuza de Keti*, 223; "Center's resolution on the guerilla work and the establishment of new soviet areas in the Shaan[xi]-Gan[su] border, 20 April 1932," *ZZWX*, 8: 203–8; "Central bureau of the soviet region's resolution on striving to gain victory first in Jiangxi and neighboring provinces, 17 June 1932," *ZZWX*, 8: 240–61; "Letter from the center to Hebei provincial committee on implementation of the spirit of the northern province representative conference, 22 July 1932," *ZZWX*, 8: 316–33; "Central propaganda department's discussion outline on the northern province representative conference, 30 July 1932," *ZZWX*, 8: 335–45.

17. "Telegram from Chicherin to Yanson, 31 October 1921," *GLZGWZ*, 1: 65.

18. "Letter 36: To Molotov and Bukharin, 9 July 1927," in *Stalin's Letters to Molotov*, ed. Lars T. Lih et al. (New Haven, Conn.: Yale University Press, 1995), 140. About the same time, the Comintern directed the CCP to "deprive those of responsible positions in the center who have not obeyed the Comintern instructions." As a result, Chen Duxiu and some others were removed from the CCP Central Committee. See Zhou Wenqi and Chu Liangru, *Techu er Fuza de Keti*, 148.

19. *Stalin's Letters*, 141.

20. Zhou Wenqi and Chu Liangru, *Techu er Fuza de Keti*, 150–51. Stalin's first two

phases were separately "national united front" and "bourgeois democratic" revolutions for previous periods when the KMT and the CCP had been cooperating.

21. Stalin to Politburo members, 13 August 1927, *GLZGWZ,* 7: 21; Stalin's speech at the joint conference of the Comintern Executive Committee and the Supervising Committee, 27 September 1927, *GLZGWZ,* 7: 92–93; Zhou Enlai's record of the conversation between Stalin and Qu Qiubai and other CCP leaders, 9 June 1928, *GLZGWZ,* 7: 477–82.

22. Documentary Research Office of the CCP Central Committee, *Mao Zedong Nianpu* (The chronicle of Mao Zedong's life), 3 vols. (Beijing: Zhongyang Wenxian Chubanshe, 1993), 1: 194–205; Documentary Research Office of the CCP Central Committee, *Zhou Enlai Nianpu, 1898–1949* (Chronicle of Mao Zedong's life) (Beijing: Zhongyang Wenxian Chubanshe, 1993), 124–25.

23. Documentary Research Office, *Mao Zedong Nianpu,* 1: 208–9.

24. Documentary Research Office, *Mao Zedong Nianpu,* 1: 211–13.

25. "Letter from Hunan to the center, 20 August 1927," *ZZWX,* 3: 354–55.

26. "Letter from the center to the provincial committee of Hunan—a reply on the questions of uprising plans, form of government, and land, 23 August 1927," *ZZWX,* 3: 350–54; "Resolution on the questions of the 'left-wing KMT' and the soviet slogan, 19 September 1927," *ZZWX,* 3: 369–71; Zhou Wenqi and Chu Liangru, *Techu er Fuza de Keti,* 152; Documentary Research Office, *Mao Zedong Nianpu,* 1: 219.

27. Documentary Research Office, *Zhou Enlai Nianpu,* 141, 130; Zhou Enlai, *Zhou Enlai Junshi Wenxuan* (Selected military works of Zhou Enlai) (Beijing: Renmin Chubanshe, 1997), 1: 93.

28. Documentary Research Office, *Mao Zedong Nianpu,* 1: 246, 248–49, 255.

29. Documentary Research Office, *Mao Zedong Nianpu,* 1: 255, 264–65; Zhou Enlai, *Zhou Enlai Junshi Wenxuan,* 1: 68.

30. Documentary Research Office, *Mao Zedong Nianpu,* 1: 269, 271, 294–95, 299; Zhou Enlai, *Zhou Enlai Junshi Wenxuan,* 1: 81–83, 114–30; Documentary Research Office, *Zhou Enlai Nianpu,* 170; Bo Yibo, *Qishinian Fendou yu Sikao* (Seventy years' struggles and deliberations) (Beijing: Zhonggong Dangshi Chubanshe, 1996), 1: 84.

31. [Zhou] Enlai, "Report on the transmitting of the Comintern resolution, 24 September 1930," *ZZWX,* 6: 364; Yang Kuisong, *Mao Zedong he Mosike de En En Yuan Yuan* (Benefactions and Disaffections between Mao Zedong and Moscow) (Nanchang: Jiangxi Renmin Chubanshe, 1999), 16–17; Zhou Wenqi and Chu Liangru, *Techu er Fuza de Keti,* 216, 223–24.

32. "Draft constitution of the Chinese soviet republic, November 1931," Jiangxi Provincial Archives, *Zhongyang Keming Genjudi Shiliao Xuanbian* (Selected historical materials on the central revolutionary base) (Nanchang: Jiangxi Remin Chubanshe, 1982), 121–32; "Provisional articles on the administrative division of the Chinese soviet republic, November 1931," *Zhongyang Keming Genjudi Shiliao Xuanbian,,* 192–93. The soviet constitution announced fifteen people's commissar positions, but actually only nine of these were manned, with Zhu De as the commissar for military affairs (not "naval, ground, and air forces" as pretentiously announced in the constitution) and Wang Jiaxiang as that for foreign affairs.

33. "Public notice number one of the central executive committee of the Chinese soviet republic, 1 December 1931," *Zhongyang Keming Genjudi Shiliao Xuanbian,* 201–2.

34. Zhou Wenqi and Chu Liangru, *Techu er Fuza de Keti,* 202, 217, 229, 231. After

the KMT turned against the CCP and the Soviet Union in 1927 and established a new central government of China in 1928, the Soviet–Chinese diplomatic relationship continued until the summer of 1929, when the two sides came into conflict over Soviet interests in Manchuria. For Moscow's view about its relationship with the KMT government in 1929 and 1932, see "Note from Karakhan, vice-commissar for foreign affairs, to the Chinese chargé d'affaires in Moscow on the withdrawal of Soviet representatives from China, 17 July 1929," and "Press statement by Litvinov on the resumption of relations with China 12 December 1932," in *Soviet Documents on Foreign Relations,* ed. Jane Degras (New York: Octagon Books, 1978), 2: 387–89, 550–51.

35. "Chinese Communist Party's letter to the Chinese workers in Mongolia, October 1929," *Minzu Wenti Wenxian Huibian* (Collection of documents on the national question; hereafter *MWWH*), 113–14.

36. Hélène Carrère d'Encausse, *The Great Challenge: Nationalities and the Bolshevik State, 1917–1930* (New York: Holmes & Meier, 1992), 35.

37. The Bolsheviks created a Commissariat of Nationalities under Stalin in late October 1917. See d'Encausse, *Great Challenge,* 101–2.

38. Wen-hsin Yeh, *Provincial Passages: Culture, Space, and the Origins of Chinese Communism* (Berkeley: University of California Press, 1996), 5–6.

39. Mary Clabaugh Wright, *The Last Stand of Chinese Conservatism: The Tung-Chih Restoration, 1862–1874* (Stanford, Calif.: Stanford University Press, 1957), 73–75; Jack Gray, *Rebellions and Revolutions: China from the 1800s to the 1980s* (Oxford: Oxford University Press, 1990), 135.

40. Li Rui, *Zaonian Mao Zedong* (Young Mao Zedong) (Shenyang: Liaoning Renmin Chubanshe, 1993), 294.

41. Documentary Research Office, *Mao Zedong Nianpu,* 1: 78–79.

42. Li Rui, *Zaonian Mao Zedong,* 294–97; Documentary Research Office, *Mao Zedong Nianpu,* 1: 57, n. 1; Yang Kuisong, *Mao Zedong,* 118–19.

43. This judgment is based on a close reading of Documentary Research Office of the CCP Central Committee, *Mao Zedong Zaoqi Wengao* (Early writings of Mao Zedong) (Changsha: Hunan Chubanshe, 1995) that contains Mao's pre-1921 writings and Mao Zedong, *Mao Zedong Wenji, 1921–1937* (Manuscripts of Mao Zedong, 1921–1937) (Beijing: Renmin Chubanshe, 1993).

44. Li Rui, *Zaonian Mao Zedong,* 42–43, 144; "Classroom Notes: Self-Cultivation, 15 November 1913," *Mao Zedong Zaoqi Wengao,* 590–91.

45. "Such a National Self-Determination, 14 July 1919," *Mao Zedong Zaoqi Wengao,* 316.

46. "Program of the Problem Study Society, 1 September 1919," *Mao Zedong Zaoqi Wengao,* 396–402; "Hunan Republic—the Fundamental Question of Hunan's Reconstruction, 3 September 1920," *Mao Zedong Zaoqi Wengao,* 503–5; "To Cai Hesen and others, 1 December 1920," Mao Zedong, *Mao Zedong Shuxin Xuanji* (Selected correspondence of Mao Zedong) (Beijing: Renmin Chubanshe, 1983), 3.

47. Li Dazhao's attention to the issue of ethnicity was reflected in his writings such as "Popularism, January 1923," *MWWH,* 55–59, and "The Liberation Movement of the Mongolian Nation, 1925," *MWWH,* 69–70. In contrast, Mao's early discussion of "The Grand Union of the People," which was published as a series in the *Xiangjiang Pinglun* (Xiang River Review) in 1919, was concerned only with how inter- and intraclass unities could result in a "grand union of the Chinese nation" (*Mao Zedong Zaoqi Wengao,*

338–41, 373–78, 389–94). In the 1920s and 1930s, Mao's numerous meticulous investigations of the sociopolitical conditions in the countryside of southern China also completely ignored the issue of ethnicity.

48. Documentary Research Office, *Mao Zedong Nianpu*, 1: 165–66; Jane L. Price, *Cadres, Commanders, and Commissars: The Training of the Chinese Communist Leadership, 1920–45* (Boulder, Colo.: Westview Press, 1976), 80–81, 86 n. 17. Office to Collect Sources on Party History, the CCP Committee of Huhhot Municipality, "Report on the Investigation of the Conditions of the Suiyuan Peasant Movement during the Great Revolution Period," *Neimonggu Dangshi Ziliao* (Inner Mongolian materials on the party history), 2: 256–59. These Inner Mongols were Jia Ligeng (a.k.a. Kang Fucheng), Gaobuzebu (a.k.a. Li Baohua), Yun Jizhen, Ren Dianbang, Lin Xiang, Li Chunrong, and Zhao Wenhan. Among these, only the first two would later continue to be part of the CCP movement.

49. Documentary Research Office, *Mao Zedong Nianpu*, 1: 173, 175; "Resolution on the Liberation of the Miao and Yao; adopted by the first congress of the Hunan peasant representatives, December 1926," *MWWH*, 52.

50. "Xunwu Investigation, May 1930," Mao Zedong, *Mao Zedong Wenji*, 1: 131.

51. Mao's pragmatism, ironically, may be an offspring of John Dewey's via Dewey's student Hu Shi. Li Rui, *Zaonian Mao Zedong*, 286–87, points out that in the summer of 1919—when Li Dazhao and Hu Shi were debating the merit between studying "problems" and supporting "isms"—Mao Zedong planned to organize a "problem study society" along Hu Shi's line of thinking. According to Edgar Snow, *Red Star Over China* (New York: Grove Press, 1968), 148, 154, and Stuart Schram, *Mao Tse-tung* (Baltimore: Pelican Books, 1974), 48, in later years Mao admitted that Hu was one of his early idols, though the personal relationship between the two was far from cordial. Hu Shi's influence on Mao's early writings can be seen in "Program of the Problem Study Society, 1 September 1919," *Mao Zedong Zaoqi Wengao*, 396–402, and "Objection to Unification, 10 October 1920," *Mao Zedong Zaoqi Wengao*, 530–33.

52. "'Communist Manifesto' by the party department of the CCP in the worker–peasant red fourth army, January 1929," *MWWH*, 96–97; "Public notice by the command of the worker–peasant red fourth army, January 1929," *MWWH*, 98–99.

53. This statement is based on an examination of *ZZWX*, vol. 3, on 1927, and vol. 4 on 1928. In the period the only reference by the CCP leadership to the "national question" appeared in a draft land program of November 1927, which pointed out that the land question might assume some particular forms in areas inhabited by non-Han nationalities; see *MWWH*, 3: 83.

54. "Resolution on the National Question, 9 July 1928," *ZZWX*, 4: 388.

55. "Resolution on the National Question, 9 July 1928," *ZZWX*, 4: 388.

56. d'Encausse, *Great Challenge*, 104. See Ted Robert Gurr, *Minorities at Risk: A Global View of Ethnopolitical Conflicts* (Washington, D.C.: United States Institute of Peace Press, 1993), 15, for definitions of "national peoples" and "minority peoples."

57. Ren Yinong et al., *Minzu Zongjiao Zhishi Shouce* (Manual of common knowledge on nationalities and religions) (Beijing: Zhonggong Zhongyang Dangxiao Chubanshe, 1994), 192.

58. "Conclusion on the discussion of the organizational question at the second plenum of the CCP's sixth central committee, 25 June 1929," *MWWH*, 109.

59. "Political secretariat of the Comintern executive committee's Resolution on the China Question, 23 July 1930," *ZZWX*, 6: 589.

60. Stalin to Molotov, 7 October 1929, *GLZGWZ*, 8: 187; CCP Politburo to the CCP delegation to the Comintern, 21 August 1929, *GLZGWZ*, 11: 558; Liu Shaoqi to Huang Ping, 11 January 1930, *GLZGWZ*, 9: 24–26; Manchurian Committee of the CCP to the Far Eastern Frontier Committee of the Soviet Communist Party, 11 January 1930, *GLZGWZ*, 9: 27–28. For the Sino-Soviet dispute over the C.E.R. in 1929, see Peter S. H. Tang, *Russian and Soviet Policy in Manchuria and Outer Mongolia, 1911–1931* (Durham, N.C.: Duke University Press, 1959), 199–241.

61. "CCP Central Politburo's Report to the Comintern, 28 November 1928," *ZZWX*, 4: 714–722; "CCP Center's Directive No. 20, November 1928," *ZZWX*, 4: 723–40; "Political Resolution: Current Revolutionary Conditions and the CCP's Task, June 1929," *ZZWX*, 5: 179–221; "CCP Center's Directive No. 60: Practical Tactics for Implementing Armed Defense of the Soviet Union, 8 December 1929," *ZZWX*, 5: 561–74.

62. "CCP Center's Directive Letter to the Inner Mongolia Special Branch, 23 October 1928," *MWWH*, 91; "CCP Center's Letter to the Mongolia Committee, 30 February 1929," *MWWH*, 100–7; "CCP Center's Outline Plan on the Work in Inner Mongolia, 5 November 1930," *MWWH*, 136–41.

63. "CCP Center's letter to the Manchurian Committee (of the CCP), 6 November 1928," *MWWH*, 92; "CCP Center's letter to the Manchurian Committee (of the CCP), 6 November 1929," *MWWH.*, 115; meeting minutes no. 124 and no. 132 of the Politburo of the Soviet Communist Party Central Committee, 15 September and 27 October 1927, *GLZGWZ*, 7: 71, 135.

64. "CCP Manchurian Committee's Open Letter to Korean Peasants in Manchuria, 1928," *MWWH*, 94–95; "CCP Center's letter to the Yunnan Provincial Committee, 20 March 1930," *MWWH*, 117.

65. "Report [by Zhou Enlai] on the Comintern Resolution at the Third Enlarged Plenum of the CCP Sixth Congress, 24 September 1930," *MWWH*, 131.

66. Yang Kuisong, *Zhonggong yu Mosike de Guanxi, 1920–1960* (Relationship between the CCP and Moscow) (Taipei: Dongda Tushu Gufen Youxian Gongsi, 1997), 403 nn. 21 and 23, identifies Ren Bishi, Gu Zuolin, Wang Jiaxiang, Zhou Enlai, Zhang Wentian, and Bo Gu and others as these "Messrs."

67. Documentary Research Office, *Mao Zedong Nianpu*, 1: 358–59; Documentary Research Office, *Zhou Enlai Nianpu*, 212-214; Yang Kuisong, *Mao Zedong*, 17. As early as November 1930, in a letter to the CCP center, the Far Eastern Bureau of the Comintern Executive Committee suggested that "Mao Zedong should not only be responsible for the army's conditions and operations, he should also be put into the government and assume some responsibilities. He should be appointed as a member of the government (chairman of the revolutionary military committee). The benefits of such an arrangement would be so obvious and there is no need to say any more." See *GLZGWZ*, 9: 452. Mao's official title in 1931 was "chairman of the central executive committee of the Chinese soviet republic."

68. "Letter from the presidium of the Comintern executive committee to the CCP, July 1931," *ZZWX*, 7: 761.

69. Documentary Research Office, *Zhou Enlai Nianpu*, 183–84, 214; Zhou Wenqi and Chu Liangru, *Techu er Fuza de Keti*, 223–24.

70. Walker Connor, *National Question in Marxist-Leninist Theory and Strategy* (Princeton, N.J.: Princeton University Press, 1984), 67–74, suggests that in 1931 the "Chinese soviet republic" made the minorities' right to national self-determination an "essential element" in the CCP's pre-1949 political strategy and thus changed the CCP's

"unexplained slighting" of the matter during its first ten years. By contrast, recognizing the discrepancy between the 1931 policy and the CCP's practices after 1949, China's scholars either choose to omit the 1931 formula from their discussion or to stress only the "correct" portions of the formula. See Jiang Ping, ed., *Zhongguo Minzu Wenti de Lilun yu Shijian* (The theories and practices regarding China's nationality question) (Beijing: Zhonggong Zhongyang Dangxiao Chubanshe, 1994), 98–102, and Zhang Erju, *Zhongguo Minzu Quyu Zizhi Shigang* (Outline history of China's [minority] nationalities' regional autonomy) (Beijing: Minzu Chubanshe, 1995), 14–16.

71. Documentary Research Office, *Zhou Enlai Nianpu,* 210–11.

72. "CCP Center's Resolution on the Incident of Japanese Imperialist Occupation of Manchuria, 22 September 1931," *MWWH,* 158–60; "CCP Center's Proclamation to the Country's Workers, Peasants, and Laboring Masses on the First National Soviet Congress, 20 October 1931," *MWWH,* 161–62; "Provisional Government of the Chinese Soviet Republic's Proclamation to the World, 7 November 1931," *MWWH,* 167–68.

73. Meeting minutes of the Politburo of the CCP Central Committee, 6 December 1929, *GLZGWZ,* 8: 242–48; minutes of the joint conference of the Far Eastern Bureau of the Comintern Executive Committee and the Politburo of the CCP Central Committee, 10 and 13 December 1929, *GLZGWZ,* 8: 249–67; Stalin to Molotov, 13 August 1930, *GLZGWZ,* 9: 300; meeting minutes no. 5 of the Politburo of the Soviet Communist Party Central Committee, 25 August 1930, *GLZGWZ,* 9: 330–32; Far Eastern Bureau of the Comintern Executive Committee to Zhou Enlai and Qu Qiubai, 16 September 1930, *GLZGWZ,* 9: 348–50.

74. "CCP center's No. 1 Directive after the Fourth Plenum of the Sixth Congress, January 1931," *MWWH,* 146–47; Chen Shaoyu, "Struggle for a More Bolshevized CCP, February 1931," *MWWH,* 148.

75. "Telegram No. 7 of the CCP Center to the Central Bureau of the Soviet Region—on Important Principles of the Constitution, 5 November 1931," *ZZWX,* 7: 492–93; "Outline Constitution of the Chinese Soviet Republic, 7 November 1931," *ZZWX,* 7: 772–76; "Resolution on the Question of the Minority Nationalities in the Chinese Territory, November 1931," *MWWH,* 169–71.

76. Ren Yinong et al., *Minzu Zongjiao Zhishi Shouce,* 213, 219, 387–388; Jiang Ping, *Zhongguo Minzu Wenti,* 493–94.

77. "CCP Central Committee's letter to the CCP frontal committee of the Seventh Army, 16 June 1930," *MWWH,* 127; "CCP Central Committee's letter to the CCP Guangdong provincial committee, 4 January 1932," *MWWH,* 176; "CCP Central Committee's letter to the CCP Sichuan provincial committee, 14 February 1932," *MWWH,* 177–80; "CCP Central Committee's letter to the CCP Shaanxi provincial committee, 1 August 1932," *MWWH,* 172; "CCP Central Committee's letter to all the CCP organizations and members in Manchuria, 26 January 1933," *MWWH,* 193–95; Zhou Enlai, "Report on the Comintern resolutions, 24 September 1930," *ZZWX,* 6: 375–80; "Resolution on current situation and the party's tasks, 18 January 1934," *ZZWX,* 10: 43–46.

78. Stalin's definition of the right of self-determination is discussed in Connor, *National Question,* 33.

79. See June T. Dreyer, *China's Forty Millions: Minority Nationalities and National Integration in the People's Republic of China* (Cambridge: Harvard University Press, 1976), 63–64; and Colin Mackerras *China's Minorities: Integration and Modernization in the Twentieth Century* (Hong Kong: Oxford University Press, 1994), 72. Mackerras,

based on Walker Connor, *The National Question in Marxist-Leninist Theory and Strategy* (Princeton, N.J.: Princeton University Press, 1984), 68–73, is mistaken in suggesting that until the soviet republic was established, the "idea of self-determination for minorities was notably absent" from the CCP's policies.

80. The fact that Mao did not view this as the CCP's *internationalist* obligation indicates a lingering confusion within the CCP at the time about who made up the "minority nationalities" of China. A CCP Central Committee's document dated 1929 included all foreign nationals in China as part of the "minority nationality question." See "Conclusion on the organizational question discussed by the Second Plenum of the CCP's Sixth Congress, 25 June 1929," *MWWH,* 109.

81. Mao Zedong, "Report to the Second National Soviet Assembly [on behalf of] the Central Executive Committee and the People's Commissariat of the Chinese Soviet Republic, January 1934," *MWWH,* 210–11.

Chapter 4—Northernization: The Search for a Peripheral Strategy

1. Cited in Mei Jian, ed., *Yan'an Mishi* (Inside history of Yan'an) (Beijing: Hongqi Chubanshe, 1996), 1.

2. Mark Selden's *The Yenan Way in Revolutionary China* (Cambridge, Mass.: Harvard University Press, 1971) is a classic study of the subject.

3. Kong Xiandong and Gu Peng, "'*Hongxing Bao*' during the Long March," *Zhonggong Dangshi Ziliao,* 60 (December 1996): 197–98.

4. Instruction on the winning over of minority nationalities, issued by the general political department of the Chinese Workers' and Peasants' Red Army, 19 June 1935, *Minzu Wenti Wenxian Huibian* (Collection of documents on the national question; hereafter *MWWH*), 339–40; "Destroy the Enemy in Large Numbers with Offensive and Create New Chuan-Shaan-Gan [Sichuan, Shaanxi, and Gansu] Soviet Regions," 10 July 1935, *MWWH,* 296–97.

5. Although the CCP was ideologically adherent to the Marxist class-struggle doctrine, it usually meant class distinctions when using such concepts as lower and upper "strata." These terms, as the discussion below will show, would assume a peculiar meaning during the CCP's Long March for the sake of a smooth interethnic relationships.

6. The CCP Central Committee's letter to the Sichuan provincial committee of the CCP, 19 February 1932, *MWWH,* 177–80; decision of the Sichuan provincial committee of the CCP on the acceptance of the outline of the thirteenth conference of the Comintern and the resolution of the CCP Central Committee's fifth plenum, 11 June 1934, *MWWH,* 220–23.

7. Instruction on the principles of the work within the Miao and Yao nationalities, issued by the political department of [the First Front Army of] the Chinese Workers' and Peasants' Red Army, 29 November 1934, *MWWH,* 244–46; Documentary Research Office of the CCP Central Committee, *Mao Zedong Nianpu* (Chronicle of Mao Zedong's life), 3 vols. (Beijing: Zhongyang Wenxian Chubanshe, 1993), 1: 438–39.

8. Documentary Research Office, *Mao Zedong Nianpu,* 1: 456–57. According to Ye Xinyu, "'Alliance at Yi Lake and the Party's Nationality Policy,' *Zhonggong Dangshi Ziliao,* 58 (June 1996): 191, the CCP's policy to win over ordinary Yi people included five items: (1) every soldier must give a gift to the Yi people, (2) to enlist the Yi into the

Red Army and establish Yi guerrilla units, (3) no struggle against Yi "local tyrants" (*tuhao*), (4) strict observation of the Red Army's discipline, and (5) every company should hold get-together with the Yi people.

9. A good discussion of situational effects of interethnic contact and theories concerned is H. D. Forbes, *Ethnic Conflict: Commerce, Culture, and the Contact Hypothesis* (New Haven, Conn.: Yale University Press, 1997).

10. "Zhang Guotao's report at the meeting of government activists on the development and prospect of the Chinese soviet movement and our current tasks, 1 April 1936," *Zhongguo Gongnong Hongjun Disi Fangmianjun Zhanshi Ziliao Xuanbian, Changzheng Shiqi* (Selected materials on the combat history of the fourth front army of the Chinese workers' and peasants' red army, the long march period; hereafter *DFZZ*), 419, 425.

11. "Excerpts from Chen Bojun's diaries, June 1935–July 1936," *DFZZ*, 160, 177; "Plan for the Xia [River]–Tao [River] battle, 3 August 1935," *DFZZ*, 95.

12. Actually, at the conference Mao was just promoted into the standing committee of the politburo. The conference confirmed Zhou Enlai as the final authority to decide military policies, and Mao exerted his influence as Zhou's assistant. In a following conference in early February 1935, Luo Fu (Zhang Wentian) was elected to the position in charge of the CCP's general works. See Zhang Peisen et al., *Zhang Wentian zai 1935–1938* (Zhang Wentian from 1935 to 1938) (Beijing: Zhonggong Dangshi Chubanshe, 1997), 1–2.

13. Documentary Research Office, *Mao Zedong Nianpu,* 1: 443–44, 448, 449, 454, 458, 460–61; Zhang Peisen, *Zhang Wentian,* 16–18; "[CCP] center to the Fourth Front Army on the establishment of soviet governments in Sichuan, Shaanxi, and Gansu provinces and the current plan, 16 June 1935," *DFZZ*, 58.

14. Documentary Research Office, *Mao Zedong Nianpu,* 1: 479. The English translation is from *Poems of Mao Tse-tung,* translated and annotated by Wong Man (Hong Kong: Eastern Horizon Press, 1966), 38.

15. Yang Kuisong, "An Attempt by the Soviet Union to Offer Large-scale Assistance to the Chinese Red Army," in *Sulian, Gongchan Guoji yu Zhongguo Geming de Guanxi Xintan* (New studies of the relationship between the Soviet Union, the Comintern, and the Chinese revolution), ed. Huang Xiurong (Beijing: Zhonggong Dangshi Chubanshe, 1995), 306–7; Cai Hesen, "On Chen Duxiuism," in *Bao Luo Ting zai Zhongguo de Youguan Ziliao* (Materials on Borodin in China) (Beijing: Zhongguo Shehui Kexue Chubanshe, 1983), 228.

16. Bai Zhensheng, et al., *Xinjiang Xiandai Zhengzhi Shehui Shilue, 1912–1949* (Brief political and social history of modern Xinjiang, 1912–1949) (Beijing: Zhongguo Shehui Kexue Chubanshe, 1992), 141–80.

17. Oriental Secretariat of the Comintern Executive Committee to the Political Secretariat of the Comintern Executive Committee, 23 April 1931, *Gongchanguoji, Liangong (Bu) yu Zhongguo Geming Wenxian Ziliao Xuanji* (Selected documentary materials on the Comintern, Soviet Communist Party and the Chinese revolution; hereafter *GLZGWZ*), 10: 251–56. According to this document, at the time the Soviet Union's shares in Xinjiang's export and import trade were respectively 90 and 80 percent.

18. Osip A. Pyatnitsky to Lazar M. Kaganovich, 10 September 1931, *GLZGWZ,* 10: 345–46.

19. Yang Kuisong, "An Attempt by the Soviet Union"; Institute of Historical Studies of the Xinjiang Academy of Social Science, *Xinjiang Jianshi* (A brief history of Xinjiang) (Urumqi: Xinjiang Renmin Chubanshe, 1987), 145–65; Andrew D. W. Forbes, *War-*

lords and Muslims in Chinese Central Asia: A Political History of Republican Sinkiang, 1911–1949 (Cambridge: Cambridge University Press, 1986), 97–116; Bai Zhensheng et al., *Xinjiang Xiandai Zhengzhi Shehui Shilue,* 193.

20. Letter from the Central Committee of the CCP to the Red Fourth Front Army, 25 August 1933, *Zhonggong Zhongyang Wenjian Xuanji* (Selected documents of the CCP Central Committee; hereafter *ZZWX*), 9: 313–22; directive letter from the Central Bureau of the CCP on conducting a self-arming movement, 25 July 1934, *ZZWX,* 10: 370.

21. Zhou Wenqi and Chu Liangru, *Teshu er Fuza de Keti—Gongchan Guoji, Sulian he Zhongguo Gongchandang Guanxi Biannian Shih 1919–1991* (Unique and complex subject: a chronicle of the relationship among the Comintern, the Soviet Union, and the Chinese Communist Party, 1919–1991) (Wuhan: Hubei Renmin Chubanshe, 1993), 254, 255, 263, 275; Documentary Research Office, *Mao Zedong Nianpu,* 1: 476, 489. Several attempts were made during the period by the CCP and Moscow to restore their communications, but these were successful only when Lin Yuying (a.k.a. Zhang Hao) brought a cipher code to the CCP center in northern Shaanxi in mid-November 1935. Even after that, technical problems continued to create difficulties for the communications between the two sides. According to a telegram from the CCP center to Zhu De et al., dated July 22, 1936 (*DFZZ,* 580), communications with the Comintern had become "unimpeded" only two weeks before.

22. The whole episode is treated in detail by Yang Kuisong, *Xi'an Shibian Xintan: Zhang Xueliang yu Zhonggong Guanxi zhi Yanjiu* (A new examination of the Xi'an incident: a study of the relationship between Zhang Xueliang and the CCP) (Taipei: Dongda Tushu Gongsi, 1995). This is a careful study of the CCP during the Long March based on new Chinese and Russian archival materials. Also valuable is Benjamin Yang, *From Revolution to Politics: Chinese Communists on the Long March* (Boulder, Colo.: Westview Press, 1990).

23. "Declaration on the establishment of the government of the northwestern federation of the Chinese soviet republic, 30 May 1935," *MWWH,* 268–70; "Congratulatory message from the CCP committee of the northwestern special region to the government of the northwestern federation of the Chinese soviet republic, 1935," *MWWH,* 273–74; Military Museum of China, *Mao Zedong Junshi Huodong Jishi* (Record of Mao Zedong's military activities) (Beijing: Jiefangjun Chubanshe, 1994), 158–59, 162; Zhang Guotao, *Wo de Huiyi* (My memoirs) (Beijing: Xiandai Shiliao Congcan Chubanshe, 1980), 3: 213–33; "[CCP] center's decision on the strategic orientation after the meeting between the First and Fourth Front Armies, 28 June 1935," *DFZZ,* 74.

24. Documentary Research Office, *Mao Zedong Nianpu,* 1: 471, 482–83, 599; Zhang Guotao, *Wo de Huiyi,* 3: 287; "Lin Yuying to Zhang Guotao and Zhu De on the Comintern's complete agreement with the policy of the CCP center, 24 January 1936," *DFZZ,* 328; "Lin Yuying and Zhang Wentian to Zhu De and Zhang Guotao on the strategic orientation of the Fourth Front Army, 14 February 1936," *DFZZ,* 371–72; "Lin Yuying, Zhang Wentian, Mao Zedong, and Zhou Enlai to Chu De, Zhang Guotao, Liu Bocheng, and Xu Xiangqian on the political conditions at home and abroad, 20 May 1936," *DFZZ,* 519–20.

25. "[CCP] center's supplementary decision on the current strategic orientation, 20 August 1935," *DFZZ,* 127–28; "Mao Zedong's report and conclusion at the Ejie conference, 12 September 1935," *DFZZ,* 152; "Central politburo's decision on comrade Zhang Guotao's mistakes, 12 September 1935," *DFZZ,* 153–54; "Zhang Guotao to

Comintern representative Lin Yuying in the name of the 'second center,' 6 January 1936," *DFZZ*, 311; "Zhang Guotao's report at a cadres' meeting on the prospect of the development of the Chinese soviet movement, 15 March 1936," *DFZZ*, 393–400.

26. "The significance of advancing toward the Song-Li-Mao area and our current battle tasks, 23 May 1935," *DFZZ*, 4.

27. "[CCP] center's supplementary decision on the current strategic orientation, 20 August 1935," *DFZZ*, 126–27.

28. "Zhang Guotao to the [CCP] center via Xu Xiangqian and Chen Changhao on the southward orientation, 9 September 1935," *DFZZ*, 144; "Zhou Enlai, Luo Fu, et al. to Zhu De, Zhang Guotao, and Liu Bocheng on the Red Army's movement at present, 8 September 1935," *DFZZ*, 142.

29. "[CCP] center's letter to comrades for the implementation of the northward orientation, 10 September 1935," *DFZZ*, 146.

30. "Mao Zedong's report and conclusion at the Ejie conference, 12 September 1935," *DFZZ*, 151; Zhang Guotao, *Wo de Huiyi*, 3: 279, 287, 300; "Ren Bishi to the [CCP] center on the second and sixth army groups' meeting with the fourth front army on July 1 and current northward movement, 6 July 1936," *DFZZ*, 572; Fu Zhong, "Glorious mission of the northwestern bureau," *DFZZ*, 744. The First, Second, and Fourth Front Armies were the three main forces of the Red Army. According to a CCP report to the Comintern dated August 1936, cited in Yang Kuisong, *Xi'an Shibian Xintan*, 133–34, the First Front Army in northern Shaanxi was 21,000 strong. Ren Bishi's report cited above indicated that the Second Front Army had 14,500 troops. The Fourth Front Army was at least 45,000 strong.

31. "Records of the Chinese–Tibetan Exchanges of Opinions," in Second Historical Archives of China and Chinese Institute of Tibetan Studies, *Huang Musong, Wu Zhongxin, Zhao Shouyu, Dai Chuanxian Fengshi Banli Zangshi Baogaoshu* (Reports by Huang Musong, Wu Zhongxin, Zhao Shouyu, and Dai Chuanxian on their missions to Tibet) (Beijing: Zhongguo Zangxue Chubanshe, 1993), 31–46.

32. Jiang Zhiyu to Jiang Jieshi, 16 June 1935. Jiang Zhongzheng zongtong dangan: "tejiao wenjian," di 58 juan (zhengzhi): Xizang wenti (Archives of President Jiang Zhongzheng [Jieshi]: "specially submitted documents," volume 58 [political]: Tibetan question).

33. Reting Hutuktu to Jiang Jieshi and Huang Musong, 19 June 1935. Jiang Zhongzheng zongtong dangan: "tejiao wenjian," di 58 juan (zhengzhi): Xizang wenti (Archives of President Jiang Zhongzheng [Jieshi]: "specially submitted documents," volume 58 [political]: Tibetan question).

34. Jiang Jieshi to Liu Wenhui, 12 August 1935. Jiang Zhongzheng zongtong dangan: "tejiao wenjian," di 58 juan (zhengzhi): Xizang wenti (Archives of President Jiang Zhongzheng [Jieshi]: "specially submitted documents," volume 58 [political]: Tibetan question).

35. Zhang Guotao, *Wo de Huiyi*, 3: 287.

36. "Central politburo to Zhang Guotao on the supplementary decision on the current strategic orientation, 24 August 1935," *DFZZ*, 132–33; "Peng Dehuai to Zhu De and Zhang Guotao on continuous northward advance for gaining the masses and creating a Shan-Gan-Ning soviet region, 18 September 1935," *DFZZ*, 156.

37. "Central politburo's decision on comrade Zhang Guotao's mistakes, 12 September 1935," *DFZZ*, 153; "Zhang Guotao's report and conclusion at a meeting of

official activists on the development and prospect of the Chinese soviet movement and our current task, 1 April 1936," *DFZZ*, 415.

38. Qu Qiubai, "Sun Yat-sen and the Chinese revolutionary movement, February 1925," in *Qu Qiubai Wenji* (Collected essays of Qu Qiubai) (Beijing: Renmin Chubanshe, 1989), 3: 79–80, 82.

39. "The opinion of the CCP and the central bureau of the Chinese socialist youth league on the KMT national congress, December 1923," *MWWH*, 23; "Proclamation of the first national congress of the KMT, 23 January 1924," *MWWH*, 26; "Resolution of the fourth national congress of the CCP on the nationalist revolutionary movement, January 1925," *MWWH*, 32.

40. "CCP center's letter to the members of the KMT on the anniversary of Mr. [Sun] Yat-sen's passing away, 12 March 1926," *MWWH*, 43; Li Shouchang (Dazhao), "Popularism, January 1923," *MWWH*, 56.

41. "CCP center's outline plan for work in Inner Mongolia, 5 November 1930," *MWWH*, 141.

42. "Resolution of the minority nationality question within the Chinese territory, November 1931," *MWWH*, 169.

43. Chen Shaoyu (Wang Ming), "Strive to make the CCP still more Bolshevized, February 1931," *MWWH*, 148.

44. "CCP center's letter to the Sichuan provincial committee on the questions of anti-imperialism, minority nationalities, and party, 19 February 1932," *MWWH*, 178–79; "Resolution by the CCP Sichuan provincial committee on the minority nationality work in the border regions of western, southern, and northern Sichuan, 24 June 1932," *MWWH*, 189.

45. "CCP center's representative in the north to Inner Mongolian party committee, 7 July 1934," *MWWH*, 232–33; "Political department of the Chinese workers' and peasants' red army's directive on the principles for the work within the Miao and Yao nationalities, 29 November 1934," *MWWH*, 245.

46. Jiang Ping, 404; Qu Qiubai, "Controversial questions in the Chinese revolution, February 1927," *MWWH*, 79.

47. "Zhang Guotao to Comintern representative Lin Yuying in the name of the 'second center', 6 January 1936," *DFZZ*, 311; "Zhang Guotao's report at a meeting of official activists on the prospect of the development of the Chinese soviet movement and our current tasks, 1 April 1936," *DFZZ*, 414–20; "Zhang Guotao's report at a meeting of the central column's activists to abolish reluctantly the 'second center,' 6 June 1936," *DFZZ*, 534–35.

48. Zhang Peisen, 18; "[CCP] center's decision on strategic orientation after the meeting between the first and fourth front armies, 28 June 1935," *DFZZ*, 74; "CCP Central Committee's open letter to the *Fan* people of Xikang, Tibet, and western [Sichuan]— a fighting program for the Tibetan national revolutionary movement, June [*sic*] 1935," *MWWH*, 285–91. Some earlier references to Tibet include "CCP center's letter to the Sichuan provincial committee, 19 February 1932," *MWWH*, 177; "Proclamation by the provisional government of the Chinese soviet republic and the revolutionary military committee of the workers' and peasants' red army, 15 April 1933," *ZZWX*, 9: 470.

49. E.g., as Zhang Guotao recalled later (Zhang Guotao, *Wo de Huiyi*, 3: 286), cadres of the Red Army could not find a Tibetan word to translate the Chinese word, *tuanti* (organization, association), and finally used a Tibetan phrase meaning "one mind."

50. "Mao Zedong's report and conclusion at the Ejie conference, 12 September 1935," *DFZZ*, 151. "*Fan* people" (*fan min*) was a term used loosely in CCP documents for the non-Han nationalities in western Sichuan and Xikiang. Sometimes it was used exclusively to refer to the Tibetan, but sometimes the Qiang and the Yi were also included.

51. "[CCP] northwestern special committee's resolution on the work within the Tibetan people, 5 June 1935," *DFZZ*, 36; "Declaration of the first national congress of the Pod-pa people, May 1936," *DFZZ*, 473–75; "Zhang Guotao's report at the central bureau meeting on the policy orientation toward the minority nationalities, 29 April 1936," *DFZZ*, 468.

52. "Outline for the organization of the political examination department of the Bod-pa people's republic, 20 April 1936," *DFZZ*, 466; "Zhang Guotao's report at the central bureau meeting on the policy orientation toward the minority nationalities, 29 April 1936," *DFZZ*, 469; "Outline for the organization of the Bod-pa independent government, May 1936," *DFZZ*, 475–76; "Draft provisional regulations on the national political examination department of the Bod-pa people's republic, May 1936," *DFZZ*, 477; "Discussions of the work in Jinchuan, May 1936," *DFZZ*, 489; Zhang Guotao, *Wo de Huiyi*, 3: 286.

53. "Directive letter from the political department of the northwestern military district to political departments and offices of all levels, 23 May 1935," *DFZZ*, 26-27; "Fu Zhong's report to Zhang Guotao on the operations and road conditions in the Matang and Kangmaosi area, 27 June 1935," *DFZZ*, 71; "Resolution of the first CCP provincial congress in Jinchuan on current political situation and the party's tasks, 7 February 1936," *DFZZ*, 451–52; "Constitution of the Bod-pa revolutionary party, 18 April 1936," *DFZZ*, 465; "Zhang Guotao's report at the central bureau meeting on the policy orientation toward the minority nationalities, 29 April 1936," *DFZZ*, 469–70; "Discussions of the work in Jinchuan, May 1936," *DFZZ*, 484–85, 487–88.

54. "Directive on the minority nationality work, March 1936," *DFZZ*, 455.

55. "Northwestern special region's regulations on the minority nationality work, 5 May 1935," *DFZZ*, 20; "Constitution of the Bod-pa people's revolutionary party, 18 April 1936," *DFZZ*, 465; "Zhang Guotao's report at the central bureau meeting on policy orientations toward the minority nationalities, 29 April 1936," *DFZZ*, 467, 471; "A few regulations passed by the first congress of Bod-pa people's representatives in Daofu, 15 April 1936," *DFZZ*, 464. The Red Army levied four types of taxes separately on grains, livestock, slaughter, and commerce. Under the old "exorbitant" system, six *sheng* of grain was levied for every *dou* of seed (a *dou* equals ten *sheng* and about 2.2 gallons); two *yuan* money tax was collected for slaughtering a cattle or a pig. The Red Army reduced the grain tax to five *sheng,* and the slaughter tax on the pig was reduced to one *yuan* but did not change on the cattle.

56. "Report by Dong Zhentang, Huang Chao et al. on the enemy situation and the conditions of the troops, 8 January 1936," *DFZZ*, 313–14; "Directive on the minority nationality work, March 1936," *DFZZ*, 456; "A few regulations passed by the first congress of the Bod-pa people's representatives of Daofu, 15 April 1936," *DFZZ*, 462.

57. Zhang Guotao, *Wo de Huiyi*, 3: 212–14, 276–78, 286–87. Liu Wenhui was the warlord who controlled Sichuan and Xikang.

58. Liu Ruilong, "Unforgettable Journey," in *Hongjun Changzheng Huiyi Shiliao* (Reminiscences of the Red Army's Long March), ed. Compiling Committee of the Historical Materials Series on the People's Liberation Army (Beijing: Jiefangjun Chubanshe,

1992), 1: 105–17; Tianbao, "Red Army's Long March Going through the Tibetan Areas," in *Hongjun Changzheng Huiyi Shiliao,* 89–96; Guan Xianen, "For the Victory of the Long March," in *Hongjun Changzheng Huiyi Shiliao,* 436–39; Ji Shibai, "Red Army's Tibetan Independent Division Remembered," in *Hongjun Changzheng Huiyi Shiliao,* 83–88; and Li Zhongquan, "Unforgettable Minority Nationalities in Sichuan and Xikang," in *Hongjun Changzheng Huiyi Shiliao,* 434. The commander of the Tibetan division had a Chinese name, Ma Zun. His Tibetan name is not known to this author.

59. Conclusive report on the Second and Sixth Army Groups' political works during the Long March, by the political department of the Second Front Army of the Chinese Workers' and Peasants' Red Army, 19 December 1936, *MWWH,* 436–40.

60. Roman Smal-Stocki, *The Nationality Problem of the Soviet Union and Russian Communist Imperialism* (Milwaukee: Bruce Publishing Company, 1952), 36.

61. In 1944, an "Eastern Turkestan Republic" rebelled in Xinjiang with Moscow's support. But the CCP could not even have a contact with the rebels until the late 1940s. After Japan's surrender, an independent Inner Mongolian autonomous movement took place in Manchuria and Inner Mongolia. The CCP did develop a close relationship with the movement. But by that time the CCP's ethnopolitical stance had already been well established in China's "one-revolution" environment.

Chapter 5—Nationalization: In Lieu of Internationalization

1. "Snow," *Poems of Mao Tse-tung* (translated and annotated by Wong Man. Hong Kong: Eastern Horizon Press, 1966), 40–43.

2. Yang Kuisong, *Xi'an Shibian Xintan: Zhang Xueliang yu Zhonggong Guanxi zhi Yanjiu* (A new examination of the Xi'an incident: a study of the relationship between Zhang Xueliang and the CCP) (Taipei: Dongda Tushu Gongsi, 1995), 17–18, 133–34, 142.

3. Zhou Wenqi and Chu Liangru, *Techu er Fuza de Keti—Gongchan Guoji, Sulian, he Zhongguo Gongchadang Biannianshi, 1919–1991* (Unique and complicated subject: a chronological history of the relationship between the Comintern, the Soviet Union, and the CCP) (Wuhan: Hubei Renmin Chubanshe, 1993), 254, 263, 275. Yang Kuisong, "An Attempt by the Soviet Union to provide large-scale assistance to the Chinese red army," in *Sulian, Gongchan Guoji yu Zhongguo Geming de Guanxi Xintan* (New studies of the relationship between the Soviet Union, the Comintern, and the Chinese revolution), ed. Huang Xiurong (Beijing: Zhonggong Dangshi Chubanshe, 1995), 305–28, is the most detailed study of the subject.

4. "[CCP] center's telegram to the fourth front army on the current plan and the establishment of the soviet government in Sichuan, Shaanxi, and Gansu, 16 June 1935," *Zhongguo Gongnong Hongjun Disi Fangmianjun Zhanshi Ziliao Xuanbian, Changzheng Shiqi* (Selected materials on the combat history of the fourth front army of the Chinese workers' and peasants' red army, the long march period; hereafter *DFZZ*), 58.

5. "Mao Zedong's report and conclusion at the Ejie meeting, 12 September 1935," *DFZZ,* 151. Mao was not alone in losing hope for a new base in the Shaanxi-Gansu-Ningxia border region. E.g., Zhang Wentian expressed similar opinions to support Mao. See Zhang Peisen et al., *Zhang Wentian zai 1935–1938* (Zhang Wentian from 1935 to 1938) (Beijing: Zhonggong Dangshi Chubanshe, 1997), 29.

6. Zhang Peisen, *Zhang Wentian,* 31–32; Cheng Zhongyuan, *Zhang Wentian Zhuan* (Biography of Zhang Wentian) (Beijing: Dangdai Zhongguo Chubanshe, 1993), 254–57.

7. Military Museum of China, *Mao Zedong Junshi Huodong Jishi* (Record of Mao Zedong's military activities) (Beijing: Jiefangjun Chubanshe, 1994), 179.

8. Since the early years of the republican period, Inner Mongolia had been divided into three "special districts" named Suiyuan, Rehe, and Chahar. In 1928, the KMT government officially turned these districts into provinces.

9. "Central government of the Chinese soviet people's republic's proclamation to the Inner Mongolian people, 10 December 1935," *ZZWX*, 10: 800–2.

10. "[CCP] center's resolution on the question of military strategies, 23 December 1935," *ZZWX*, 10: 589–97.

11. After the People's Republic of China was established in 1949, this document would be treated by the CCP as one that was suitable only to the situation of the 1930s. The re-issuance of the document by the government of Inner Mongolia under Ulanfu in 1964 was actually treated by the CCP center as a crime during the so-called Cultural Revolution. See Tumen and Zhu Dongli, *Kang Sheng yu "Neirendang" Yuan'an* (Kang Sheng and the unjust case of the "Inner Mongolian People's Party") (Beijing: Zhonggong Zhongyang Dangxiao Chubanshe, 1995), 13–14.

12. The English version of the movement's proclamation of September 28, 1933, is in Jagchid Sechin, *The Last Mongol Prince: The Life and Times of Demchugdongrob, 1902–1966* (Bellingham: Western Washington University Press, 1999), 72–74.

13. Demchugdongrub, *Demuchukedonglupu Zishu; Neimenggu Wenshi Ziliao, Di Shisan Ji* (Autobiography of Demchugdongrub; vol. 13 of the Inner Mongolian literary and historical materials) (Huhhot: Neimenggu Wenshi Shudian, 1984), 1–15; Ulanshaob, "Chinese Nationalist Party's policy toward Mongolia, 1928–1949," in *Neimenggu Jindaishi Lunsong* (Collected essays on modern history of Inner Mongolia) (Huhhot: Neimenggu Renmin Chubanshe, 1987), 3: 249–67.

14. Wu Nenqi, *Menguzu Renmin Geming Wuzhuang Douzheng Jishi* (Record of the revolutionary military struggle by the Mongolian people) (Huhhot: Neimenggu Renmin Chubanshe, 1990), 10–14; Baabar, *Twentieth Century Mongolia* (Cambridge: White Horse Press, 1999), 197–200; Compilation Group of Brief History of the Mongolian Nationality, *Mengguzu Jianshi* (Brief history of the Mongolian nationality) (Huhhot: Neimenggu Renmin Chubanshe, 1985), 391–93; Jagchid Sechin, *Last Mongol Prince*, 30.

15. Military Museum of China, *Mao Zedong Junshi Huodong Jishi*, 211–12.

16. Military Museum of China, *Mao Zedong Junshi Huodong Jishi*, 209; Zhou Wenqi and Chu Liangru, *Techu er Fuza de Keti*, 290, 303. In late April 1936, the CCP sent Deng Fa to the Soviet Union via Xinjiang, but he could not reach Moscow until December of the year.

17. Military Museum of China, *Mao Zedong Junshi Huodong Jishi*, 211–13; Cheng Zhongyuan, *Zhang Wentian Zhuan*, 282. This route was first proposed by Zhang Wentian. It was rejected by Mao for the reason that the westward operation could not help enlarge the current base.

18. "Chinese soviet central government's proclamation to the people of the Hui nationality, 25 May 1935," *Minzu Wenti Wenxian Huibian* (Collection of documents on the national question; herafter *MWWH*), 366–67; Dru Gladney, *Muslim Chinese: Ethnic Nationalism in People's Republic* (Cambridge: Council on East Asian Studies, Harvard University, 1996), 27.

19. Documents 16–18, in Alexander Dallin and F. I. Firsov, eds., *Dimitrov and Stalin, 1934–1943: Letters from the Soviet Archives* (New Haven, Conn.: Yale University Press, 2000), 85–105.

20. Zhang Guotao, *Wo de Huiyi* (My memoirs) (Beijing: Xiandai Shiliao Congcan Chubanshe, 1980), 3: 296–97; Military Museum of China, *Mao Zedong Junshi Houdong Jishi*, 233–36; Zhou Wenqi and Chu Liangru, *Techu er Fuza de Keti*, 295–300, 303; Documentary Research Office of the CCP Central Committee, *Mao Zedong Nianpu* (The chronicle of Mao Zedong's life), 3 vols. (Beijing: Zhongyang Wenxian Chubanshe, 1993), 1: 610–14; "[CCP] center to the Comintern on the movement directions of the western route army and the main force of the red army, 13 November 1936," *DFZZ*, 883; "[CCP] center to Xu Xiangqian and Chen Changhao on the western route army's operation orientation, 23 November 1936," *DFZZ*, 899.

21. Military Museum of China, *Mao Zedong Junshi Houdong Jishi*, 213–14, 220–21, 235, 238; Documentary Research Office, *Mao Zedong Nianpu*, 1: 608–9.

22. "[CCP] center's new operation plan, 8 November 1936," *DFZZ*, 874–75; "Lin Yuying, Zhu De, Zhang Guotao to Xu Xiangqian and Chen Changhao on the operation plan of the western route army, 19 November 1936," *DFZZ*, 892–93; "Military-political committee of the western route army to the presidium of the military council on the army's strength and operation orientation, 6 January 1937," *DFZZ*, 922; "Presidium of the military council to Xu Xiangqian and Chen Changhao on the western route army's operation orientation, 7 January 1937," *DFZZ*, 923; "[CCP] center to Zhou Enlai and Bo Gu on assisting the western route army and stopping the offensive by the two Mas, 24 January 1937," *DFZZ*, 935; "[CCP] center to Zhou Enlai on solving the western route army's precarious situation and the conditions for negotiating with Ma Hongkui and Ma Bufang, 27 February 1937," *DFZZ*, 953; "Mao Zedong to Liu Bozheng and Zhang Hao on the suspension and intensified training of the western rescue army, 13 March 1937," *DFZZ*, 966; "Materials on the number of the western route army that reached Xinjiang, December 1937," *DFZZ*, 996; Committee on Party History of the Chinese Communist Party District Committee of Hami, *Xilujun Hun* (The Soul of the Western Route Army) (Urumqi: Xinjiang Renmin Chubanshe, 1995), 53, 66; Huang Xiurong, *Sulian, Gongchan Guoji yu Zhongguo Geming de Guanxi Xintan*, 50.

23. Dallin and Firsov, *Dimitrov and Stalin*, 109–10 n. 14.

24. "[CCP] center's secretariate and the presidium of the military council to Xu Xiangqian and Chen Changhao on the western route army's strategic orientation, 17 February 1937," *DFZZ*, 945; "[CCP] center's secretariat's directive to the western route army, 4 March 1937," *DFZZ*, 960; "Zhang Guotao to the military-political committee of the western route army on firmly supporting the center, overcoming difficulties, and prevailing over the enemy, 4 March 1937," *DFZZ*, 961; "Chen Changhao's report on the western route army's failure, 30 September 1937," *DFZZ*, 976–91; Li Xiannian, "Explanations of a few questions on the history of the western route army, 25 February 1983," *DFZZ*, 997–1004; Zhang Guotao, *Wo de Huiyi*, 3: 351–59. Xu Xiangqian and Chen Changhao were the chief military and political officials of the western route army. After the failure, the CCP center focused the criticism on Zhang Guotao and Chen Changhao. But for a long time in the years to come, in the CCP's official history the western route army and the policy of "breakthrough to the Soviet Union" would be labeled as part of the "Guotao line." As indicated by Li Xiannian's "explanations," participants of the western expedition were able to seek a more balanced historical verdict on the western route army only in the post-Mao years.

25. Committee on Party History, *Xilujun Hun*, 52–68, and Li Xiannian, "Explanations of a few questions in the history of the western route army," *DFZZ*, 997–1004, disagree whether or not the CCP center's changing directives to the western route army in

late December 1936 were based on strategic calculations or due to indecision. But both agree that a key period of about a month for the western route army to return to the east or proceed to west was lost.

26. "Xu Xiangqian and Chen Changhao to the central military council on the ninth army's fighting in Gulang, 19 November 1936," *DFZZ*, 890; "Xu Xiangqian and Chen Changhao to the center and Zhu De and Zhang Guotao on the western route army's losses in recent months and the situation analysis, 21 November 1936," *DFZZ*, 894; "Xu Xiangqian and Chen Changhao to the central military council on the battle conditions in Sishilipu, 23 November 1936," *DFZZ*, 897; "Xu Xiangqian and Chen Changhao to Zhu De, Zhang Guotao, and the center on our and the enemy's conditions, 24 November 1936," *DFZZ*, 899.

27. A "three great prohibitions and four great points of attention" was issued to the troops by the Red Army's general political department. These were "prohibition of stationing in the mosques; prohibition of eating pork; prohibition of doing damage to Muslim scriptures; attention to sanitation and hygiene; respect to the habits and customs of the Hui people; avoidance of careless use of the Hui people's utensils; attention to Hui–Han unity." See "Directive from the general political department of the Chinese workers' and peasants' red army on the work with the Hui people, 24 May 1935," *MWWH*, 362–65.

28. Sun Goubiao, "A successful experiment of the Chinese Communist Party's nationality autonomous policy," *Zhonggong Dangshi Ziliao* 57 (February 1996): 114–22.

29. Gao Yi, *Jiang Jieshi yu Xibei Si Ma* (Jiang Jieshi and the four Mas of the northwest) (Beijing: Jingguan Jiaoyu Chubanshe, 1993), 102–43; Wang Jianping, "Recollection on the four-Ma alliance against Sun Dianying," in *Ningxia San Ma* (Three Mas of Ningxia) (Beijing: Zhongguo Wenshi Chubanshe, 1988), 169–80.

30. Gao Yi, *Jiang Jieshi yu Xibei Si Ma*, 23–40; Lu Zhongliang et al., "Ma Hongkui's provincial government and conscription practice," in *Ningxia San Ma*, 181–95; Ma Tingxiu, "The power struggle between Ma Hongkui and the KMT central government," in *Ningxia San Ma*, 234–39; Feng Meishuan, "Ma Hongkui's secret contest with the *Juntong*," in *Ningxia San Ma*, 242–43; "Ma Bufeng's control of the KMT party affairs," Compilation Committee of the Qinghai Provincial Chronicle, *Qinghai Lishi Jiyao* (Important events in the history of Qinghai) (Xining: Qinghai Renmin Chubanshe, 1987), 410–11.

31. Gao Yi, *Jiang Jieshi yu Xibei Si Ma*, 13–23.

32. Li Rongzhen, "The Chinese Communist Party's policy toward the Hui nationality during the Long March," *Zhonggong Dangshi Ziliao*, 60 (December 1996): 111; "Xu Xiangqian and Chen Changhao to the central military council on the estimate of current situation and the western route army's movement, 7 February 1937," *DFZZ*, 942; "Liu Bocheng and Zhang Hao to heads of divisional political departments on the significance of assistance to the western route army, 6 March 1937," *DFZZ*, 963. When the "battle for Ningxia" was still proceeding, Mao Zedong stressed at a politburo meeting that the CCP's policy was to make alliance with all forces except Ma Hongkui. See Documentary Research Office, *Mao Zedong Nianpu*, 1: 582.

33. Gao Yi, *Jiang Jieshi yu Xibei Si Ma*, 184–85.

34. "Chen Changhao's report on the failure of the western route army, 30 September 1937," *DFZZ*, 984.

35. Jonathan N. Lipman, *Familiar Strangers: A History of Muslims in Northwestern China* (Seattle: University of Washington Press, 1997), 167–211.

36. Kai Feng, "What is the disagreement between the party center and the Guotao line, 27 March 1937," *DFZZ*, 1105–9.

37. "Chen Changhao's report on the failure of the western route army, 30 September 1937," *DFZZ*, 988.

38. Documentary Research Office, *Mao Zedong Nianpu*, 1: 612.

39. Benedict Anderson, *Imagined Communities: Reflections on the Origin and Spread of Nationalism* (London: Verso, 1991), 158, n. 6. John W. Garver, *Chinese–Soviet Relations, 1937–1945: The Diplomacy of Chinese Nationalism* (New York: Oxford University Press, 1988), 237–70, contains a well-argued chapter on the CCP's achieving independence from Moscow during World War II. Michael M. Sheng's *Battling Western Imperialism: Mao, Stalin, and the United States* (Princeton, N.J.: Princeton University Press, 1997) is based on some recently declassified Chinese materials and portrays Mao Zedong as a constant loyal follower of Stalin's. The best documented study of the subject is Yang Kuisong's *Zhonggong yu Mosike de Guanxi 1920–1960* (Relationship between the CCP and Moscow) (Taipei: Dongda Tushu Gufen Youxian Gongsi, 1997), which defines the CCP policy as consistent in ideological terms but pragmatic in its relationship with Moscow.

40. Zhou wrote these words in a letter to Zhang Xueliang in 1936, cited in Yang Kuisong, *Xi'an Shibian Xintan*, 69.

41. "CCP center's resolution on the party's mistakes and shortcomings in the anti-imperialist struggle, 2 December 1931," *ZZWX*, 7: 532; Luo Fu, "Opportunistic wavering within the CCP with regard to the struggle for achieving victory of the Chinese revolution first in one or a few provinces, 4 April 1932," *ZZWX*, 8: 610–35; "Growth of the revolutionary crisis and the party's tasks in the north, 24 June 1932," *ZZWX*, 8: 346–62; "CCP central committee's letter to the Hebei provincial committee, 22 July 1932," *ZZWX*, 8: 329–30.

42. Yang Kuisong, *Xi'an Shibian Xitan*, is a standard study of the subject. It performs a detailed analysis of how, after the Xi'an incident, the CCP leadership changed its originally hard-line approach in dealing with Jiang Jieshi and favored a peaceful solution upon receiving directives from Moscow (pp. 322–36). In later years, the CCP would never again change its own policy decision because of pressures from Moscow.

43. Robert V. Daniels, *A Documentary History of Communism, Volume 2: Communism and the World* (London: I. B. Tauris, 1985), 103–5; Yang Kuisong, *Xi'an Shibian Xintan*, 296–336; Zhang Guotao, *Wo de Huiyi*, 3: 330–40, 368–71.

44. When the CCP center adopted northern Shaanxi as its home base in late 1935, the region was named "Shaan[xi]-Gan[su]-Nin[xia] soviet region." In March 1937, the name was changed into "Shaan-Gan-Ning special region" to suit the peace negotiations with the KMT. In September of the same year, a government for the "Shaan-Gan-Ning border region" was formed according to an agreement with the KMT. See Chen Lian, *Kangri Genjudi Fazhan Shilue* (Brief history of the anti-Japanese bases) (Beijing: Jiefangjun Chunbanshe, 1987), 31.

45. Cheng Zhongyuan, *Zhang Wentian Zhuan*, 324–27, 372, 412–13; Liu Shaoqi, "Letter to the central committee on the work in the white [KMT] regions in the past," 4 March 1937, *ZZWX*, 11: 801–18.

46. Documentary Research Office, *Mao Zedong Nianpu*, 2: 528.

47. "Fundamental Principles for the National United Front," author unclear, 20 November 1936, *MWWH*, 525–27.

48. "Resolution of the Central Committee on Current Political Situation and the Party's Tasks," 25 December 1935, _ZZWX,_ 10: 609–17.

49. Luo Fu, "Our Opinion on the Program for National Unity," 11 May 1937, _MWWH,_ 456–58; letter from the CCP central committee to the Comintern on a "draft program for national unity," 27 June 1937, _MWWH,_ 466–67.

50. Edgar Snow, _Red Star over China_ (New York: Random House, 1938), 110.

51. Zhang Peisen, _Zhang Wentian,_ 314, 317, 331.

52. Yang Song, "On nation, 1 August 1938," _MWWH,_ 763–68; Yang Song, "On nationalist movements and the national question in the era of capitalism, 8 and 20 August 1938," _MWWH,_ 769–80; Yang Song, "On national movements and the national question in the era of imperialism, August and October 1938," _MWWH,_ 781–801.

53. Yang Song, "On national movements and the national question in the era of imperialism, August and October 1938," _MWWH,_ 795–96.

54. Mao Zedong, "On the New Phase," 12–14 October 1938, _ZZWX,_ 11: 557–662.

55. June T. Dreyer, _China's Forty Millions: Minority Nationalities and National Integration in the People's Republic of China_ (Cambridge, Mass.: Harvard University Press, 1976), 261–76, summarizes the two different approaches.

56. Mao Zedong, "Chinese revolution and the Chinese Communist Party, December 1939," _MWWH,_ 625–32.

57. Political department of the Eighth Route Army, "Political Textbook for Anti-Japanese Soldiers, December 1939," _MWWH,_ 807–8; Mao Zedong, "The Question of Independence and Self-Reliance in the United Front," 5 November 1938, _MWWH,_ 607.

58. Liu Shaoqi, "Some fundamental questions in the anti-Japanese guerrilla warfare, 16 October 1937," _MWWH,_ 561–65, and Kai Feng, "What is the disagreement between the party center and the [Zhang] Guotao line? 22 February 1938," _MWWH,_ 760–61, are two wartime documents favoring minority peoples' "independence." But, it should be noted that both were written before Mao's "On the New Phase," which was delivered in October 1938. Then, in July 1945, "The CCP central committee's slogans for the celebration of the eighth anniversary of the war of resistance," _ZZWX,_ 15: 175, included the "rights of self-government and self-determination" in the party's demands for the KMT government to improve its "treatment of the minority nationalities at home." At this time a new round of the CCP–KMT civil war was about to begin.

59. Dong Biwu, "Communism and Three People's Principles," 14 June 1937, _MWWH,_ 538–41; Zhou Enlai, "On China's Fascism–New Authoritarianism," 16 August 1943, _MWWH,_ 723–27; "KMT and Nationalism," editorial of the _Jiefang Ribao_ (Liberation daily), September 18, 1943, _ZZWX,_ 14: 566–76; Mao Zedong, "On Coalition Government," April 24, 1945, _MWWH,_ 742–43; Chen Boda, "On China's Destiny," 21 July 1943, _MWWH,_ 945–49.

60. Actually, as an official policy, equality among China's nationalities was first announced by Yuan Shikai in 1912. See Zhao Yuntian, _Zhongguo Bianjiang Minzu Guanli Jigou Yange Shi_ (History of the changing structures of China's administration of frontiers and nationalities) (Beijing: Zhongguo Shehui Kexue Chubanshe, 1993), 425.

61. _Zhonghua minzu_ is a combination of two ancient Chinese characters, _zhong_ for the "central kingdom" and _hua_ for the ancestral clan of the Han named _Huaxia,_ with a modern conception, _minzu_ for nation.

62. The conceptual evolution of _zhonghua minzu_ in modern Chinese politics has been overlooked by standard works on Chinese nationalism and China's ethnopolitics, such as Walker Connor, _National Question in Marxist-Leninist Theory and Strategy_

(Princeton, N.J.: Princeton University Press, 1984); Dreyer, *China's Forty Millions;* Prasenjit Duara, *Rescuing History from the Nation: Questioning Narratives of Modern China* (Chicago: University of Chicago Press, 1995); John Fitzgerald, *Awakening China: Politics, Culture, and Class in the Nationalist Revolution* (Stanford, Calif.: Stanford University Press, 1996); Edward Friedman, *National Identity and Democratic Prospects in Socialist China* (Armonk, N.Y.: M. E. Sharpe, 1995); Germaine A. Hoston, *The State, Identity, and the National Question in China and Japan* (Princeton, N.J.: Princeton University Press, 1994); Colin Mackerras, *China's Minorities: Integration and Modernization in the Twentieth Century* (Hong Kong: Oxford University Press, 1994); and Jonathan Unger, ed., *Chinese Nationalism* (Armonk, N.Y.: M. E. Sharpe, 1996). In his illuminating study, *Muslim Chinese,* 81–93, Gladney correctly points out an ill-informed practice in the field to use "Han" and "Chinese" interchangeably, but his discussion of the rise of a "Han nationalism" from Sun Yat-sen to Mao Zedong overlooks Chinese politicians' attempt to project modern China as a multinational "Central Hua" (*zhonghua*) nation-state, not a Han nation-state.

63. Connor, *National Question,* 67–92, argues that the CCP's self-determination strategy toward the minorities kept alive even when the party embraced the "Han ethno-nationalism" during the war against Japan. John Breuilly, *Nationalism and the State* (Chicago: University of Chicago Press, 1994), 234–40, discusses the different effects of the KMT's "coordination politics" and the CCP's "mobilization politics" in China's "internal frontiers."

64. This is the theme of Chalmers A. Johnson, *Peasant Nationalism and Communist Power* (Stanford, Calif.: Stanford University Press, 1962). Johnson's work has been supplemented by more recent case studies. E.g., Ralph A. Thaxton Jr., *Salt of the Earth: The Political Origins of Peasant Protest and Communist Revolution in China* (Berkeley: University of California Press, 1997), 198–239, admits that in the war years the CCP used anti-Japanese patriotism and socioeconomic reforms to rally the peasants, but he stresses the necessity of understanding the CCP–peasant alliance in northern China in a much longer time frame and in the historical and social context of that particular region. See also Lucien Bianco, *Peasants Without the Party: Grass-Roots Movements in Twentieth-Century China* (Armonk, N.Y.: M. E. Sharpe, 2001).

65. Breuilly, *Nationalism,* 9–15, discusses nationalism as opposition politics, and Anderson, *Imagined Communities,* 113–16, 159–60, sheds light on a transitional relationship between popular and official nationalisms during the process of a revolution.

Chapter 6—Borderization: Trans-Ethnic Reach

1. Yu Zidao, *Changcheng Fengyunlu* (Stormy chronicle of the Great Wall) (Shanghai: Shanghai Shudian Chubanshe, 1993), 82–112.

2. Wang Huichang, *Zhongguo Wenhua Dili* (Cultural geography of China) (Wuchang: Huazhong Shifan Daxue Chubanshe, 1992), 105–83. This is a pioneering study of the historical shifts of China's cultural and political center over the centuries. The author suggests that during its first three or four millenniums, the center of the Chinese civilization was located in the Yellow River Valley of the Central Plain; then, marked by the establishment of the Southern Song Dynasty in 1127 in the Yangtze River Valley, the center shifted to southern China. Wang names the two periods respectively as the "era with the Central Plain as the cultural pivot" (*zhongyuan wenhua zhouxin*

shidai) and the "era with the south of the Yangtze River as the talents' gathering place" (*jiangnan renwen yuansou shidai*).

3. E.g., Wang Huichang, *Zhongguo Wenhua Dili*, 110, agrees with Liang Qichao's remark that "regimes with northern capitals tended to be grandiose in scope and powerful in momentum, but regimes with southern capitals tended to be poor and dormant in scope and frail in momentum" and points out that in Chinese history northern regimes have often vanquished southern regimes. Yet when discussing the impact of a "Han civilizational circle" in eastern and southeastern Asia, Wang simply asserts that western China is part of the "circle" and needs no special clarification (p. 315). Edward Friedman, *National Identity and Democratic Prospects in Socialist China* (Armonk, N.Y.: M. E. Sharpe, 1995), 25–42, 77–86, discusses a "north–south split" of China in China's current reforms, identifying the "northerners" as isolationist and chauvinistic and "southerners" as open and entrepreneurial.

4. Zhao Yuntian, *Zhongguo Bianjiang Minzu Guanli Jigou Yange Shi* (History of the changing structures of China's administration of frontiers and nationalities) (Beijing: Zhongguo Shehui Kexue Chubanshe, 1993), 4–5.

5. John King Fairbank, *China: A New History* (Cambridge: Belknap Press of Harvard University Press, 1992), 77; Shen Youliang, *Zhongguo Beifang Minzu jiqi Zhengquan Yanjiu* (A study of the ethnic groups in norther China and their states) (Beijing: Zhongyang Minzu Daxue Chubanshe, 1998), 337.

6. "CCP center's directive letter on Inner Mongolia work, 24 August 1936," *Minzu Wenti Wenxian Huibian* (Collection of documents on the national question; hereafter *MWWH*), 416–21.

7. "CCP center's directive on Mongol work that should center on assistance to Suiyuan and resistance against Japan, 3 February 1937," *MWWH*, 448–49; "CCP center's letter to the minority nationalities committee regarding the Inner Mongolia work, 7 February 1937," *MWWH*, 451.

8. (Li) Yimang, "A Few Questions in the Works regarding the Hui People, 3 September 1936," *MWWH*, 518–21; Liu Xiao, "Certain Questions in the Work with the Hui people, November 1936," *MWWH*, 528–32; "Organizational Guideline for the Hui Liberation League, (August–September?) 1936," *MWWH*, 533–534; Wang Jiaxiang, "Oppose Japanese imperialist occupation of Inner Mongolia, 22 July 1936," *MWWH*, 506–9; "Mongolian department of the minority nationalities committee: current situation in Suiyuan Mongolia and our tasks and work, June 1937," *MWWH*, 468.

9. Liu Xiao, "A Letter on the work with the Hui people, 24 September 1936," *MWWH*, 522–23; Liu Xiao, "Certain questions in the work with the Hui people, November 1936," *MWWH*, 531–32; "Mao Zedong's telegram to Xie Juezai on the party's current task and the question of setting up nationalist organizations within the Hui people, 19 August 1937," *MWWH*, 555; "Draft platform of the Hui people's revolutionary party, 1937," *MWWH*, 759.

10. Wang Wudian, "Recollection on the KMT 81 army's war of resistance in western Suiyuan," *Ningxia San Ma* (Three Mas of Ningxia) (Beijing: Zhongguo Wenshi Chubanshe, 1988), 100–7; Han Zhesheng, "The battle of the Yikzhao league under Ma Hongbin's command," *MWWH*, 108–10; Compilation Committee of the Qinghai Provincial Chronicle, *Qinghai Lishi Jiyao* (Important events in the history of Qinghai) (Xining: Qinghai Renmin Chubanshe, 1987), 393–95; Yang Ce, et al., *Shaoshu Minzu yu Kangri Zhanzheng* (Minority nationalities and the war of resistant against Japan) (Beijing: Beijing Chubanshe, 1997), 83–85, 89–100.

11. "CCP center's directive letter on the Mongolian work, 10 July 1937," *MWWH,* 545–47. According to Wang Shusheng and Hao Yufeng, *Wulanfu Nianpu* (Chronicle of Ulanfu's life) (Beijing: Zhonggong Dangshi Chubanshe, 1989), 68, as early as 1933 the Comintern directed Yun Ze to win over Prince De in the anti-Japanese struggle. Obviously the Comintern directive did not reach the CCP center which at the time was still in the south.

12. "CCP center's directive letter on the Mongolian work, 10 July 1937," *MWWH,* 545–47.

13. Owen Lattimore, *Studies in Frontier History: Collected Papers, 1929–58* (London: Oxford University Press, 1962), 12, 427–439.

14. Liu Xiao, "Opinions on the Mongolian work, July 1936," *MWWH,* 511–13.

15. Wang Shusheng and Hao Yufeng, *Wulanfu Nianpu,* 56–60.

16. Wang Shusheng and Hao Yufeng, *Wulanfu Nianpu,* 68.

17. Ulanfu, *Wulanfu Huiyilu* (Ulanfu's memoirs) (Beijing: Zhonggong Dangshi Ziliao Chubanshe, 1989), 166–70; Wang Shusheng and Hao Yufeng, *Wulanfu Nianpu,* 75, 80–83, 100–101; Yu Zidao, *Changcheng Fengyunlu,* 462–68.

18. Demchugdongrob, "Demuchukedonglupu Zishu," *Neimenyn Weashi Ziliao* (Literary and historical materials of Inner Mongolia) 13 (1989): 44–47; Jagchid Sechin, *The Last Mongol Prince: The Life and Times of Demchugdongrob, 1902–1966* (Bellingham: Western Washington University Press, 1999), 123.

19. By contrast, in both Prince De's wartime regime and Japan's Manchurian administration, there were individuals with Comintern connections who would survive the war years and start a new wave of the Inner Mongolia autonomous movement at war's end, e.g., Oljeiochir, Khafengga, and Temurbagana.

20. Liu Xiao, "Report to the General Political Department [of the Red Army] and the Party Central Committee on the Mongol Works," 19 July 1936, *MWWH,* 501–4; "The CCP Central Committee's Directive on the Work in Inner Mongolia," 24 August 1936, *MWWH,* 416–21.

21. Military Museum of China, *Mao Zedong Junshi Huodong Jishi* (Record of Mao Zedong's military activities) (Beijing: Jiefangjun Chubanshe, 1994), 216–17; "The CCP Central Committee's Directive on the Independence and Self-Determination Principle for the Minority Nationalities," 24 [month?] 1937, *MWWH,* 579.

22. Jiang Shuchen, *Fu Zuoyi Zhuanlue* (A brief biography of Fu Zuoyi) (Beijing: Zhongguo Qingnian Chubanshe, 1990), 17–19, 21–38, 59–72, 108–10; Zhou Beifeng, "My Memoirs," *Neimenggu Wenshi Ziliao,* 21 (1986): 56–57, 79–85; "Mao Zedong's letter to Fu Zuoyi, 14 August 1936," *MWWH,* 412–13; "CCP center's letter the minority nationalities committee on the Inner Mongolian work, 7 February 1937," *MWWH,* 450–52.

23. "CCP center's directive letter on the Mongolian work, 10 July 1937," *MWWH,* 547.

24. "Directive on the establishment of a guerrilla base in the Daqingsha Mountain and the party's policies concerned, 24 November 1938," *Zhonggong Zhongyang Wenjian Xuanji* (Selected documents of the CCP Central Committee, ZZWX), 11: 787–89; Zhang Peisen et al., *Zhang Wentian zai 1935–1938* (Zhang Wentian from 1935 to 1938) (Beijing: Zhonggong Dangshi Chubanshe, 1997), 302.

25. "Chart 2: Comparison of the Mongolian, Hui, Manchu, and Han populations in the [Suiyuan] province, [1943]" Committee on the Collection of Party History Materials of the CCP Committee of the Inner Mongolian Autonomous Region and the Archives of

the Inner Mongolian Autonomous Region, _Daqingshan Kang Ri Youji Genjudi Ziliao Xuanbian_ (Selected materials on the anti-Japanese guerrilla base in the Daqingshan Mountain; hereafter _Daqingshan_) (Hohhot: Neimenggu Renmin Chubanshe, 1987), 1: 505; Second War Zone Frontier General Mobilization Committee for the National Revolutionary War, "How the Daqingshan anti-Japanese guerrilla base was created, July 1939," _Daqingshan_, 1: 30.

26. "Suiyuan–Chahar administrative office's statement to the nationalities of Suiyuan and Chahar, 1 October 1941," _Daqingshan_, 1: 268; Li Jingquan, "Guerrilla warfare in Daqingshan in the past year, 25 October 1940," _Daqingshan_, 2: 127.

27. "How the Daqingshan anti-Japanese guerrilla base was created, July 1939," _Daqingshan_, 2: 63–64.

28. "CCP committee of the western Shanxi district's directive on the work in Suiyuan, 5 February 1942," _Daqingshan_, 1: 25.

29. (CCP Northwestern Working Committee), "Suiyuan in the war of resistance, November 1940," _Daqingshan_, 2: 382–83; "Suiyuan-Chahar administrative office's letter to the Mongolian compatriots, October 1942," _Daqingshan_, 1: 301–2.

30. Zhou Qingshu et al., _Neimenggu Lishi Dili_ (Historical geography of Inner Mongolia) (Hohhot: Neimenggu Daxue Chubanshe, 1993), 225–30, 283.

31. "Conclusive report on the Daqingshan detachment's work in the past sixteen months, December 1939," _Daqingshan_, 2: 93; "Guan Xiangying to Yun Qing [He Long], 28 [month?] 1940," _Daqingshan_, 1: 85; "Yao Ji and Zhang Dazhi to He Long, Guan Xiangying, and Gan Siqi, 30 June 1941," _Daqingshan_, 1: 103; "CCP center's Shanxi–Suiyuan branch bureau to the Saibei working committee on the work in Suiyuan, 14 March 1943," _Daqingshan_, 1: 40.

32. "Mao Zedong and Teng Daiyuan to He Long, Xiao Ke, Guan Xiangying, Zhu De and Peng Dehuai, 30 March 1938," _Daqingshan_, 1: 3; "Secretariat of the CCP center's opinion on the Daqingshan work, 9 August 1941," _Daqingshan_, 1: 14; "CCP committee of the western Shanxi district's directive on the work in Suiyuan, 5 February 1942," _Daqingshan_, 1: 27–28; "Zhou Shidi and Gan Siqi to Yao Ji, Zhang Dazhi, and Bai Chengming, 20 August 1942," _Daqingshan_, 1: 94; "Suiyuan-Chahar administrative office's outline conclusion on the establishment of the Suiyuan government and the leadership question from April 1941 to December 1942," _Daqingshan_, 1: 309; "Conclusive report on the Daqingshan detachment's work in the past sixteen months, December 1939," _Daqingshan_, 2: 89.

33. "Accommodation" is June Dryer's term for the CCP's nationality policy in contrast to the KMT's "assimilative" approach. In the war years, the Japanese policy toward the Inner Mongols was certainly viewed by the Chinese as "separatist." But because the policy was receptive of the Inner Mongols' ethnonationalist demands in a limit, the Japanese authority was "accommodating" the Inner Mongols within its imperial design.

34. "CCP center's letter to the minority nationality committee on the Inner Mongolian work, 7 February 1937," _MWWH_, 451, 452; "Action program for the society of resisting Japan and rescuing Mongolia, July 1937," _MWWH_, 550.

35. "He Long, Xiao Ke, and Guan Xiangying to Mao Zedong, Liu Shaoqi, Zhu De, Peng Dehuai, and Ren Bishi, July 1938," _Daqingshan_, 1: 66; "Directive on the establishment of the Daqingshan guerrilla base and the party's related policies, 24 November 1938," _ZZWX_, 11: 788; "CCP center's Shanxi–Suiyuan branch bureau to the Saibei working committee on the work in Suiyuan, 14 March 1943," _Daqingshan_, 1: 44; "Suiyuan–

Chahar [CCP] party committee's decision on the administrative work of the Suiyuan-Chahar region, 24 August 1941," *Daqingshan,* 1: 228.

36. Mao Zedong, "On the new phase, 12 to 14 October 1938," *MWWH,* 595.

37. Zhou Wenqi and Chu Liangru, *Teshu er Fuza de Keti—Gongchan Guoji, Sulian he Zhongguo Gongchandang Guanxi Biannian Shih 1919–1991* (Unique and complex subject: a chronicle of the relationship among the Comintern, the Soviet Union, and the Chinese Communist Party, 1919–1991) (Wuhan: Hubei Renmin Chubanshe, 1993), 363.

38. "Eighth Route Army's Office in Xinjiang," *Zhonggong Dangshi Ziliao Zhuanti Yanjiu Ji: Kangri Zhanzheng Shiqi (Er)* (Collected materials on special topic in the CCP history: the period of the war of resistance against Japan) (Beijing: Zhonggong Dangshi Ziliao Chubanshe, 1989), 2: 106–22. Mao Zedong's brother Mao Zetan was among the CCP members in Xinjiang who were persecuted and killed by Sheng Shicai. But the CCP center did not know what happened to them until the end of the war. Dru Gladney's otherwise informative study, *Muslim Chinese: Ethnic Nationalism in People's Republic* (Cambridge: Council on East Asian Studies, Harvard University, 1996), 88, mistakenly suggests that during the war years Mao Zedong was sensitive to the Muslim issue because his brother was a victim of an "intra-Muslim factionalism." For three interpretations of the "Ili rebellion," see Linda Benson, *The Ili Rebellion: The Moslem Challenge to Chinese Authority in Xinjiang, 1944–1949* (M.E. Sharpe, 1990), Andrew D. Forbes, *Warlords and Muslims in Chinese Central Asia: A Political History of Republican Sinkiang, 1911–1949* (Cambridge: Cambridge University Press, 1986), and David D. Wang, *Under the Soviet Shadow: The Yining Incident* (Hong Kong: Chinese University Press, 1999).

39. Zhang Zhende and Zhao Ximin, *Xibei Geming Shi* (A revolutionary history of the northwest) (Xi'an: Shaanxi Renmin Jiaoyu Chubanshe, 1991), 435.

40. Gansu Committee of the Chinese People's Political Consultative Council, *Gansu Jiefangqian Wushinian Dashiji* (A chronicle of events in Gansu in the fifty years prior to the liberation) (Lanzhou: Gansu Renmin Chubanshe, 1980), 191; Zhang Zhende and Zhao Ximin, *Xibei Geming Shi,* 432–41; Wang Duo, *Wushi Chunqiu: Wo Zuo Minzu Gongzuo de Jingli* (Fifty years' events: my experience in the nationality work) (Huhhot: Neimenggu Renmin Chubanshe, 1992), 127.

41. According to Zhang Zhende and Zhao Xiyuan, *Xibei Geming Shi,* 434, 436, 438–39, the KMT's eighth war zone under Zhu Shaoliang used the 35th (Mao Hongbin), 191st (Wu Yunzhou), 97th (Han Xihou), and reserve 7th (Yan Ming) divisions to suppress the first rebellion; the second suppression involved the 97th and reserve 7th divisions and the 57th and 81st armies; the third involved the 97th and 191st divisions and the 42nd army.

42. Zhang Zhende and Zhao Ximin, *Xibei Geming Shi,* 431, 439–40.

43. An official narrative is presented in Yang Ce et al., *Shaoshu Minzu yu Kangri Zhanzheng,* 97. The most famous Hui on the CCP's side during the war year was Ma Benzhai, leader of a military band in Hebei. When Ma died of illness in 1944, in an eulogy the CCP's Northwestern Bureau praised him as a model follower of "the correct path for the Hui nationality and the Chinese Nation to achieve liberation." Yang Huaizhong, *Huizushi Lungao* (Essays on the history of the Hui nationality) (Yinchuan: Ningxia Renmin Chubanshe, 1991), 452–53, discusses how until recently the three uprisings have been avoided by historians in China because of the difficulties to fit these into the CCP's standards for "correct" revolutionary movements.

44. "The Chinese Soviet Central Government's Proclamation to the People of the Hui Nation, 25 May 1936," *MWWH*, 366–67.

45. "The question of the Hui nationality, 15 April 1941," *MWWH*, 897, 904; "Outline on the Hui question by the CCP center's northwestern working committee, April 1940," *MWWH*, 648–56; Luo Xiao, "The Hui question during the war of resistance and national construction, 12 February 1940," *MWWH*, 810–15; Luo Mai, "The long suppressed and struggling Hui nationality, 30 April, 15 May 1940," *MWWH*, 829–39; Luo Mai, "A study of the Hui question, 16 June 1940," *MWWH*, 841–56. Among these, only the first document mentions the Hai-Gu rebellion.

46. "The question of the Hui nationality," 14 April 1941, *MWWH*, 898–904. This is a CCP pamphlet published during the war years.

47. Wang Duo, *Wushi Chunqiu*, 62–63, 81–82; "Suiyuan in the war of resistance, November 1940," *Daqingshan*, 2: 386–87.

48. Owen Lattimore, "Mongolia and the Peace Settlement, 8 June 1943," Council on Foreign Relations, *Studies of American Interests in the War and Peace: Territorial Series*, No. T–B 63, p. 7.

49. Zhang Peisen, *Zhang Wentian*, 303.

50. Huang Shijian and Zhang Xicheng, "On the 'Yekejuu League incident,'" *Neimenggu Jindaishi Luncong* 1 (1982): 269–71; Ochirkhuyagtu, "Recollections on the Yekejuu League's 'March 26th incident,'" *Neimenggu Wenshi Ziliao* 2 (1979): 1–3.

51. Ochirkhuyagtu, "Recollections," 3–9.

52. Huang Shijian and Zhang Sicheng, "On the 'Yekejuu League incident,'" 273–76; Wu Nenqi, "Before and after the establishment of the Mongol independent brigade of Inner Mongolia," *Zhonggong Dangshi Ziliao* 11 (1984): 308–25; Ochirkhuyagtu, "Recollections," 9.

53. Bai Rubing, "A brief discussion of my work in Sui[yuan] and [Inner] Mongolia," *Zhonggong Dangshi Ziliao* 9 (1984): 131–32; Duan Baohe and Sun Jie, "The Party's United Front Work among the Princes and Upper Classes of Inner Mongolia between 1935 and 1945," *Neimenggu Tongzhan Lilun Yanjiu* (Inner Mongolian study of united front theories) 2 (1989): 26–28; Zhao Huishan, "United Front Work among the Nationality Upper Classes of Yekejuu League," *Neimenggu Tongzhan Lilun Yanjiu* 4 (1987): 21–25; "CCP Central Committee's Directive Letter on the Mongol Work, 10 July 1937," *MWWH*, 545-547; "Decisions on the Work in Sui[yuan] and [Inner] Mongolia, 22 November 1938," *MWWH*, 612–17; "Mao Zedong, Luo Fu, and Xiao Jingguang's directive on the Border Region's sending the Red Army to Inner Mongolia to resist Japan, 16 November 1937," *MWWH*, 576; "CCP center's decision on the work in the enemy-occupied Suiyuan, 5 April 1940," *ZZWX*, 12: 352–57.

54. "Gao Gang's letter to He Jinnian on the question of Yekejuu league, 11 May 1943," *MWWH*, 714; "CCP center's northwestern bureau's directive to the Sanbian district committee on the Yekejuu league incident, 1943," *MWWH*, 716; Ochirkhuyagtu, "Recollections," 10. "Diehards" (*wangupai*) was a term used by the CCP in the war years to refer to those KMT officials who seemed more interested in fighting the CCP than resisting the Japanese.

55. "The Jinnian report on the question of Yekejuu league, 7 May 1943," *MWWH*, 712–13.

56. "CCP center's northwestern bureau's directive to the Sanbian district committee on the Yekejuu league incident, 1943," *MWWH*, 715–17. At the time the CCP's information about the situation in Yekejuu was not accurate. E.g., some CCP documents assumed

that Prince Sha and the head of Yekejuu League were two different persons. Bai Yincang was a collaborator with the KMT and was killed by Prince Sha's guards during the incident, but CCP information reported that he was killed by the KMT. There is no evidence that either Chen Changjie or the Japanese plotted the Yekejuu incident as suspected by the CCP.

57. Ren Bingjun, "The 'March Twenty-Sixth' Incident in the Yekejuu League," *Neimenggu Wenshi Ziliao* 2 (1979): 15–24; Hu Fengtai, "Reminiscence about the Battle of the Uushin Banner during the Yekejuu League incident," *Neimenggu Wenshi Ziliao* 2 (1979): 38–51; "Gao Gang's letter to He Jinnian on the question of the Yekejuu League, 11 May 1943," *MWWH*, 714.

58. Dong Qiwu, *Rongma Chunqiu* (My military career) (Beijing: Zhongguo Wenshi Chubanshe, 1986), 245. The CCP's "Suiyuan–Chahar administrative office" issued ordinances in 1941 to encourage land cultivation in the region but stipulated that the Mongolian land must not be opened up without the Mongols' agreement. See the "Suiyan-Chahar administrative office's ordinance on the regulations for opening up wasteland, 14 September 1941," and the "Suiyuan-Chahar administrative office's public notice on administrative programs, 1 October 1941," in *Daqingshan*, 1: 249–50, 265.

59. "CCP center's northwestern bureau's directive to the Sanbian district committee on the Yekejuu league incident, 1943," *MWWH*, 717.

60. Wang Duo, *Wushi Chunqiu*, 95, 99–102.

61. Wang Duo, *Wushi Chunqiu*, 125–53.

62. Ya Hanzhang, "A Brilliant Historian of the Hui Nationality," in *Bai Shouyi Minzu Zongjiao Lunji* (Essays on nation and religion by Bai Shouyi), ed. Bai Shouyi (Beijing: Beijing Shifan Daxue Chubanshe, 1992), 696–703. According to Liu Chun, "Recollections on my involvement in the nationality work during the period of resistance against Japan," *Neimenggu Dangshi Ziliao* 1 (1988): 235–37, he drafted both of the "outlines." He mentions Shen Xiaxi, a Hui from Shanghai, and Kong Fei, a Mongol, as participants in the studies but does not specify their contributions.

63. There are three versions about Yun Ze's initiation to communism. The standard party literature in China, such as Wang Shusheng and Hao Yufeng, *Wulanfu Nianpu*, 24, and Ulanfu, *Wulanfu Huiyilu*, 50–54, identifies Li Dazhao, founder of the CCP and head of the CCP's regional committee for northern China, as the one who ushered Yun Ze into communism. The event took place in the fall of 1923, when Li Dazhao personally conversed with Yun Ze and several other Mongolian students at the Mongolian-Tibetan Academy in Beijing. Jagchid Sechin, in his *The Last Mongol Prince*, 26, indicates that a well-known Mongolian writer named Buyannemeku acted as a Comintern agent among the young Mongolian students of the Mongolian-Tibetan Academy. Yun Ze was one of those enlisted. Christopher Atwood called my attention to his study *Young Mongols and Vigilantes in Inner Mongolia's Interregnum Decades, 1911–1931* (Boston: Brill Academic Publishers, 2002) and pointed out a CCP member named Han Linfu, not Li Dazhao, as the one responsible for the CCP's initial work among the Inner Mongols. Atwood generously summarized for me his arguments relevant to the discussion here: "(1) Han Linfu (who after 1929 left the party) was the mainspring of all CCP work among the Mongols. (2) He worked with a distinctive view of Inner Mongolia that saw the Mongols as having become all sedentarized as peasants and hence as only secondarily ethnic in character and primarily a Chinese peasant population. (3) The appeal of Han Linfu's organizations was solely to the Hohhot Tumeds and the southern Rehe Mongols where settlement pattern was intermixed with the Chinese. 4) Even so, the CCP-

oriented Young Mongols also formed a pan-Mongolian 'Youth Party' that explictly advocated pan-Mongolian unity and secession from China (a petition to this effect was signed by such Inner Mongolian CCP martyrs as Rong Yaoxian and Duo Songnian)." According to Zhang Guotao's *Wo de Huiyi* (1: 324) and a recent official publication in China, Party History Research Office of the CCP Committee of the Beijing Municipality, *Zhongguo Gongchandang Beijing Lishi* (History of the CCP in Beijing) (Beijing: Beijing Chubanshe), 96, 99, 101, Han Linfu was a CCP member and an alternate member of the Executive Committee of the KMT Central Committee between 1924 and 1927. In 1924, he was in charge of the Inner Mongolia work of the KMT Beijing Executive Department, and in March 1925, he went to Inner Mongolia along with three other CCP members, Yu Shude, Li Yuzhi, and Jiyatai, to set up CCP-KMT organizations. Although Atwood's point on the early Inner Mongolian CCP members' pan-Mongolian tendency is very important, it does not necessarily contradict the standard CCP history in Yun Ze's case.

64. Wang Shusheng and Hao Yufeng, *Wulanfu Nianpu,* 23–24, 33, 36–49, 100–1, 119, 123, 126–27, 129, 130.

65. "Guideline for the Representative Assembly and Administrative Organization of the Shaan-Gan-Ning Border Region," 12 May 1937, *MWWH,* 462–63.

66. "Shaan-Gan-Ning Border Region government's directive on the personnel of the Nationality Affairs Committee, 9 April 1945," *MWWH,* 738; Wang Duo, *Wushi Chunqiu,* 59–60. Before taking up his position at the Nationality Affairs Committee, Zhao was the secretary of the CCP's working committee in the Yekejuu League.

67. Dreyer, 71; Hao Shiyuan, *Zhongguo de Minzu yu Minzu Wenti: Lun Zhongguo Gongchandang Jiejue Minzu Wenti de Lilun yu Shijiang* (China's nationalities and nationality question: on the CCP's theories and practices for solving the nationality question) (Nanchang: Jiangxi Renmin Chubanshe, 1996), 86; Jiang Ping, ed., *Zhongguo Minzu Wenti de Lilun yu Shijian* (The theories and practices regarding China's nationality question) (Beijing: Zhonggong Zhongyang Dangxiao Chubanshe, 1994), 169.

68. Zhang Erju, *Zhongguo Minzu Quyu Zizhi Shigang* (Outline history of China's [minority] nationalities' regional autonomy) (Beijing: Minzu Chubanshe, 1995), 4–5, 7–41. Although a useful survey of the subject, Zhang's study is mistaken in suggesting that the CCP definitely adopted "regional autonomy" as the solution of China's nationality question in a October 1945 directive on its Inner Mongolian policy. After Japan's defeat, the KMT government used "local autonomy" as a device to evade some frontier nationalities' demand for "high-degree self-government" in their own territories. For a while, the CCP sought a political solution of its conflict with the KMT and did not want to challenge the "constitutional structure" of the Chinese republic. Only by the spring of 1947, when the CCP and the KMT had already been in a full-scale civil war, the CCP decided to organize an Inner Mongolian autonomous government for the entire Inner Mongolian region.

69. "Report and proposals submitted to the second meeting of the Border Region Political Council by the Shaan-Gan-Ning Border Region government's Nationality Affairs Committee, November 1941," *MWWH,* 939.

70. "Draft provisional organic act of the Shaan-Gan-Ning Border Region government's Nationality Affairs Committee, 25 October 1941," *MWWH,* 934.

71. "Civil Administrative Office of the Shaan-Gan-Ning Border Region government's reply on the question of establishment of Hui autonomous regions in the Ding and Yanchi counties, 21 May 1942," *MWWH,* 698–99; "Resolution passed by the second meeting

of the Political Council of the Shaan-Gan-Ning Border Region government, 10 April 1942," *MWWH*, 943.

72. Documentary Research Office of the CCP Central Committee, *Mao Zedong Nianpu* (Chronicle of Mao Zedong's life) (Beijing: Zhongyang Wenxian Chubanshe, 1993. 3 vols.), 1: 467; Zhang Peisen, *Zhang Wentian*, 157; Bai Rubing, "A brief discussion of my work," 117–20. These organizations included "Sanbian special committee" (summer–December 1936, and fall 1937–April 1938), "minority nationality working committee" (December 1936–winter 1937), "Mongolian working committee" (April–May 1938), "Suiyuan-Mongolian working committee" (May–November 1938), and "northwestern working committee" (early 1939).

73. Mao Zedong, "On the New Phase," 12–14 October 1938, *ZZWX*, 11: 557–662; Wang Duo, *Wushi Chunqiu*, 52–53; Li Weihan, *Huiyi yu Yanjiu* (Reminiscence and study) (Beijing: Zhonggong Dangshi Chubanshe, 1986), 2: 451–52; *MWWH*, 648 n. 1; Cheng Zhongyuan, *Zhang Wentian Zhuan* (Biography of Zhang Wentian) (Beijing: Dangdai Zhongguo Chubanshe, 1993), 426–27. At the time, Zhang Wentian was the CCP's "secretary general" but in reality assisted Mao Zedong by taking charge of the party's propaganda and organizational work. The other members of the committee were Deng Fa, Gao Gang, Gao Zili, Jia Tuofu, Li Weihan, Li Fuchun, Wang Ruofei, Xiao Jingguang, and Xie Juezai. Li Weihan and Jia Tuofu were in charge of the committee's daily work. In May 1941, the committee merged with the Border Region's party committee and became the CCP central committee's northwestern bureau. The bureau was headed by Gao Gang and the members were Chen Zhengren, Jia Tuofu, Li Zhuoran, Lin Boqu, Wang Shitai, Xiao Jingguang, and Zhang Bangying.

74. Cheng Zhongyuan, *Zhang Wentian Zhuan*, 412–13, 415–16; Yang Kuisong, *Zhonggong yu Mosike de Guanxi, 1920–1960* (Relationship between the CCP and Moscow) (Taipei: Dongda Tushu Gufen Youxian Gongsi, 1997), 430–32.

75. Liu Chun was a student of the Shanghai Mongolian and Tibetan College for about two years before he joined the CCP in northern Shaanxi in 1936. Another member with similar background was Wang Duo, a student from the frontier administration department of the Northeastern University. The other initial members of the office were Guo Jing, Kong Fei (Mongol), Ma Wenliang (Hui), Shen Xiaxi (Hui), Qin Yi, Ya Hanzhang, Zhou Renshan, and Zhu Xiafu. Later, some Tibetan and Yi cadres would also be added to the office. See Liu Chun, "Recollections on my involvement," 228–30, 232, 236; Wang Duo, *Wushi Chunqiu*, 53–54.

76. Liu Chun, "Recollections on my involvement," 230–32; Wang Duo, *Wushi Chunqiu*, 54–55, 58–95.

77. Li Weihan, *Huiyi yu Yanjiu*, 2: 454–55; Liu Chun, "Recollections on my involvement," 237.

78. "CCP center's northwestern working committee: outline on the Hui nationality question, April 1940," *MWWH*, 650; "CCP center's northwestern working committee: outline on the Mongolian nationality question during the war of resistance, July 1940," *MWWH*, 662; Li Weihan, *Huiyi yu Yanjiu*, 2: 455. In the early 1920s, when still following the Bolshevik discourse of the "national question," the CCP literature used "self-important and narrowly construed [*zida de xiayi de*] nationalism" to criticize all kinds of "incorrect" attitudes toward the subject. Then, in the early 1930s, "pan-Mongolism" was used to name Prince De's separatist tendency. Mao Zedong was the first CCP leader who fixed "parochial nationalism" to the minority nationalities. See Qu Qiubai, "October revolution and the weak nations, 7 November 1924," *MWWH*, 63–64; "Letter from

the CCP center's representative in the north to the Inner Mongolian party committee, 7 July 1934," *MWWH*, 232, 233; "Chinese soviet central government's proclamation to the Inner Mongolian people, 20 December 1935," *MWWH*, 322.

79. "CCP center's northwestern working committee: outline on the Hui nationality question, April 1940," *MWWH*, 648–56; "CCP center's northwestern working committee: outline on the Mongolian nationality question during the war of resistance, July 1940," *MWWH*, 657–67. Unless otherwise noted, the following discussion is based on the same sources.

80. According to the "outline" on the Hui nationality, the "Great Hanism" against the Hui started under the Manchu rulers of the Qing Dynasty!

81. Chang Jiang, *Zhongguo de Xibei Jiao* (China's northwestern corner) (Tianjin: Da Gong Bao Chubanbu, 1938), 155, 304; *Huizu Jianshi* (A brief history of the Hui nationality) (Yinchuan: Ningxia Renmin Chubanshe, 1978), 24, 58; Wang Riwei, "An Examination of the Evolution of Names for the Uigur Nationality," in *Huizu, Huijiao, Huimin Lunji* (Essays on the Hui nationality, Hui religion, and Hui people), ed. Bai Shouyi and Jin Jietang, (Hong Kong: Zhongshan Tushu Gongsi, 1974). This is a reprint of essays published in the 1930s), 31–49; Li Qian, ed., *Huibu Gongdu* (Documents on the Hui section) (Shanghai: Zhongguo Yinshuachang, [1925]).

82. Chiang Kai-shek, *China's Destiny* (New York: Roy Publishers, 1947), 39.

83. "Work orientation in the National People's Army, 3 November 1926," *MWWH*, 45; "The CCP center's letter to Liu Bojian on the Work within the Northwestern Army, 9 November 1926," *MWWH*, 46; "The Sixth National Congress of the CCP's Resolution on the National Question, 9 July 1928," *MWWH*, 87; "The Second Plenum of the Sixth National Congress of the CCP's Conclusion on the Organizational Question, 25 June 1929," *MWWH*, 109; "Resolution on the Minority Nationalities within China, November 1931," *MWWH*, 169; "The Political Department of the Chinese Workers and Peasants Red Army's Directive on the Work with the Hui People, 24 May 1936," *MWWH*, 362–65. Luo Xiao, "The Hui Question in the War of Resistance and National Construction, 20 February 1940," *MWWH*, 812, indicates that in 1928 the Comintern called upon the CCP to pay attention to the "national character" of a Hui rebellion in Gansu.

84. "Proclamation of the Chinese Soviet Central Government to the People of the Hui Nationality, 25 May 1936," *MWWH*, 366–67.

85. "CCP Center's Resolution on the Political Situation and Tasks after the Meeting between the First and the Fourth Front Armies, 5 August 1935," *MWWH*, 307.

86. Luo Mai (Li Weihan), "A Study of the Hui Question, 16 June 1940," *MWWH*, 850–52. Li was in charge of the secretariat of the Northwestern Working Committee and this writing was published in the CCP journal *Jiefang* (Liberation). Not informed by the documents discussed here, Gladney, *Muslim Chinese*, 88–89, suggests mistakenly that the CCP did not decide on the Hui's nationality status until 1949. Luo Mai's article indeed indicates disagreements on the matter within the party, but the CCP's official policy was clear enough.

87. Actually, as indicated in Liu Chun, "How to unite the Mongolian nationality in the resistance against Japan for survival, 20 March 1940," *MWWH*, 819–28, there was an opinion within the CCP that the Han cultivation of the Mongol land, a sinicization process, should be suspended or even reversed wherever possible. In the war years, Fan Changjiang was a reporter for *Da Gong Bao* (Grand public daily) and his book, *Zhongguo de Xibei Jiao*, (Tainjin: Dabong Bao Guan, 1958), 53, 269, 284, discussed the prob-

lem of opium smoking and cultivation in the northwest. Although both the Hui and Han cultivated opium, the former did not smoke it while more than half of the "superior" Han population did.

88. According to Ulanfu, in the postwar years the CCP made a decision to uphold the "banner of Mongol nationalism" only as a reaction to Inner Mongols' strong demands for autonomy. See Wang Shusheng, "Great deeds in history and valuable legacy to the coming generations," *Wulanfu Jinian Wenji* (Essays to memorialize Ulanfu) (Hohhot: Neimenggu Renmin Chubanshe, 1989), 1: 375–76.

89. Owen Lattimore, *Studies in Frontier History: Collected Papers, 1929–58* (London: Oxford University Press, 1962), 135–36.

Chapter 7—Epilogue: From the "Chinese Nation" to China of Nations?

1. Stevan Harrell, "Introduction: Civilizing Projects and the Reaction to Them," in *Cultural Encounters on China's Ethnic Frontiers,* ed. Stevan Harrell (Seattle: University of Washington Press, 1995), 17–27.

2. Rogers Brubaker, *Nationalism Reframed: Nationhood and the National Question in the New Europe* (Cambridge: Cambridge University Press, 1996), 85–86, defines "nationalizing" nationalism as a post-independence stance by a "core nation" that claims ownership of the polity and seeks means to promote its cultural, economic, linguistic, and demographic attributes and its political hegemony in its "own" state as compensations to its pre-independence sufferings. China never lost its independence, but its "semicolonial" status fostered the "victim mentality" of its "core nation," the Han.

3. Richard Pipes, *The Formation of the Soviet Union: Communism and Nationalism, 1917–1923* (Cambridge, Mass.: Harvard University Press, 1954), 49.

4. This control did not include Outer Mongolia. According to a 1945 agreement between the KMT and the Soviet governments, Outer Mongolia was allowed to choose its independence from China. The CCP's military prowess was only one of the reasons for the CCP's success in the borderlands. I have discussed these reasons in Xiaoyuan Liu, *China's Central Asian Identity in Recent History: Across the Boundary between Domestic and Foreign Affairs,* Asia Program Occasional Paper 78 (Washington, D.C.: Woodrow Wilson International Center for Scholars, 1998), and Xiaoyuan Liu, "The Kuomintang and the 'Mongolian Question' in the Chinese Civil War, 1945–1949," *Inner Asia* 1 (1999): 169–94.

5. Jiang Ping, ed., *Zhongguo Minzu Wenti de Lilun yu Shijian* (The theories and practices regarding China's nationality question) (Beijing: Zhonggong Zhongyang Dangxiao Chubanshe, 1994), 113–14.

6. Zhou Enlai, "On a few questions concerning the People's Political Consultative Council, 7 September 1949," *Minzu Wenti Wenxian Huibian* (Collection of documents on the national question; hereafter *MWWH*), 1267.

7. *Dangdai Zhongguo Minzu Gongzuo Dashiji, 1949–1988* (Chronicle of important events in contemporary China's nationality work, 1949–1988) (Beijing: Minzu Chubanshe, 1989), 3–4.

8. Walker Connor, *National Question in Marxist-Leninist Theory and Strategy* (Princeton, N.J.: Princeton University Press, 1984), 38.

9. Shu Guang Zhang, *Deterrence and Strategic Culture: Chinese–American Confrontations, 1945–1958* (Ithaca, N.Y.: Cornell University Press, 1992), argues that because of their different "strategic cultures," the PRC and the United States perhaps perceived the other side wrongly as a threat. Connor, *National Question*, 38, 83–87, contends that after 1949 the CCP's going back on its promise of national self-determination to the minority nationalities was just a typical "post-power" exercise of the Leninist strategy.

10. After the Cultural Revolution, during the political trend of reversing "unjust, fabricated, and wrong cases," the CCP admitted a "mistake of excessiveness" in identifying "local nationalists" but then rehabilitated all those who had been persecuted under the label. The case against the Inner Mongolian People's Revolutionary Party was declared unjust and fabricated, and the "ultra-leftists" represented by Mao's wife Jiang Qing were blamed for the wrongdoing. See the relevant documents in State Nationalities Affairs Commission and Documentary Research Office of the CCP Central Committee, *Xinshiqi Minzu Gongzuo Wenxian Xuanbian* (Selected documents on the nationality work during the new era) (Beijing: Zhongyang Wenxian Chubanshe, 1990; hereafter *XMGW*), 21–22, 150–53.

11. Ulanfu, "The Glorious Path of the Nationalities' Regional Autonomy, 14 July 1981," *XMGW*, 139.

12. Yang Jingren, "The Task of the Nationality Work during the Period of Socialist Modernization Construction, 22 May 1979," *XMGW*, 9.

13. "CCP Center's Notice on the Distribution of the 'Minutes of the Symposium on the Tibet Work,' 7 April 1980," *XMGW*, 33–47; Wang Lixiong, *Tianzang: Xizang de Mingyun* (Sky Burial: The Fate of Tibet) (Brampton, Ontario: Mirror Books, 1998), parts 3 and 4, 267–449, offers the most informative and incisive account of the conditions in Tibet since the 1980s.

14. Li Peng, "Improve the Nationality Work and Strive Diligently for All the Nationalities' Co-Prosperity, 15 February 1990," *XMGW*, 440–41.

15. "Notice of the CCP Central Committee on the Circulation of the 'Minutes of the Symposium on Tibetan Work', 7 April 1980," *XMGW*, 34.

16. Yang Jingren, "The Task of the Nationality Work during the Period of Socialist Modernization Construction, 22 May 1979," *XMGW*, 5–13; "Report by the United Front Department of the CCP Central Committee and the State Nationalities Affairs Commission on Several Important Questions in the Nationality Work, 23 January 1987," *XMGW*, 305–21; Li Peng, "Improve the Nationality Work and Strive Diligently for All the Nationalities' Co-Prosperity, 15 February 1990," *XMGW*, 440.

17. Historica Sinica, *Zhonghua Minguoshi Minzu Zhi* (Nationalities gazette of the history of the Republic of China) (Taipei: Guoshiguan, 1995), 33.

18. "Generic ethnonym" is a term from Dru Gladney, *Muslim Chinese: Ethnic Nationalism in People's Republic* (Cambridge, Mass.: Council on East Asian Studies, Harvard University, 1996), 87. Gladney questions the legitimacy of Sun Yat-sen's using *zhonghua minzu* as an ethnic identity for the Han but overlooks the fact that after Sun the term was changed by the KMT and the CCP into a political identity for all ethnic groups of China.

19. Jiang Jieshi to Wang Chonghui, 17 February 1943, 003/2419, Zuigao guofang weiyuanhui dang'an, kuomintang zhongyang weiyuanhui dangshihui (Records of the supreme council of national defense, historical commission of the Kuomintang central committee, Taipei); three other documents from the same source are Wu Guozhen to

Wang Chonghui, 4 March 1943, Wang Chonghui to Jiang Jieshi, 18 March, 1943, and Wang Chonghui to Wu Guozhen, March 1943.

20. Fei Xiaotong et al., *Zhonghua Minzu Duoyuan Yiti Geju* (The structure of the Chinese nation's plural unitary body) (Beijing: Zhongyang Minzu Xueyuan Chubanshe, 1989), 1–36.

21. *Renmin Ribao* (People's daily), 12 April 2001.

22. Ray Huang, *China: A Macro History* (Armonk, N.Y.: M.E. Sharpe, 1990), 265.

23. Brubaker, *Nationalism Reframed*, 2–4, 26–29, 41–43. It should be pointed out that Brubaker's argument about the importance of the institutionalized nationalities' "rights" and the "multinationality" in the USSR does not deny the Russian domination of the Soviet system. For the issue of "Soviet Russian nationalism," see the insightful essays in Robert Conquest, ed., *The Last Empire: Nationality and the Soviet Future* (Stanford, Calif.: Hoover Institution Press, 1986).

24. Information Office of the State Council of the People's Republic of China, "National Minorities Policy and Its Practice in China," September 1999 (Beijing), www.china.org.cn/english/whitepapers/minoritiespolicy/.

25. Brubaker, *Nationalism Reframed*, 63.

Bibliography

Scholarly Works and Documentary Collections in English

Adelman, Jeremy, and Stephen Aron. "From Borderlands to Borders: Empires, Nation-States, and the Peoples in Between in North American History." *American Historical Review* 104(3) (1999): 814–40.

Adshead, S. A. M. *China in World History.* New York: St. Martin's Press, 1988.

Amelung, Iwo, and Joachim Kurtz. "Researching Modern Chinese Technical Terminologies: Methodological Consideration and Practical Problems." Paper presented at an international workshop at the University of Göttingen, Göttingen, October 24–25, 1997; www.gwdg.de/-oas/wsc/ttreport.htm.

Anderson, Benedict. *Imagined Communities: Reflections on the Origin and Spread of Nationalism.* London: Verso, 1991.

Anderson, John. *The International Politics of Central Asia.* Manchester: Manchester University Press, 1997.

Anderson, Malcolm. *Frontiers: Territory and State Formation in the Modern World.* Oxford: Polity Press, 1996.

Arkush, David. "Orthodoxy and Heterodoxy in Twentieth-Century Chinese Proverbs." In *Orthodoxy in Late Imperial China,* ed. K. C. Liu. Berkeley: University of California Press, 1990.

Atwood, Christopher P. "A Buriat Agent in Inner Mongolia: A. I. Oshirov (c. 1901–1931)." In *Opuscula Altania,* ed. Edward H. Kaplan and Donald W. Whisenhunt. Bellingham: Western Washington University Press, 1994.

———. *Young Mongols and Vigilantes in Inner Mongolia's Interregnum Decades, 1911–1931.* Boston: Brill Academic Publishers, 2002.

Baabar. *Twentieth Century Mongolia.* Cambridge: White Horse Press, 1999.

Banuazizi, Ali, and Myron Weiner, eds. *The New Geopolitics of Central Asia and Its Borderlands.* London: I. B. Tauris, 1994.

Barfield, Thomas J. *The Perilous Frontier: Nomadic Empires and China.* Cambridge: Basil Blackwell, 1989.

Barnett, A. Doak. *China's Far West: Four Decades of Change.* Boulder, Colo.: Westview Press, 1993.

Benson, Linda. *The Ili Rebellion: The Moslem Challenge to Chinese Authority in Xinjiang, 1944–1949*. Armonk, N.Y.: M. E. Sharpe, 1990.

Bianco, Lucien. *Peasants without the Party: Grass-Roots Movements in Twentieth-Century China*. Armonk, N.Y.: M. E. Sharpe, 2001.

Breuilly, John. *Nationalism and the State*. Chicago: University of Chicago Press, 1993.

Brubaker, Rogers. *Nationalism Reframed: Nationhood and the National Question in the New Europe*. Cambridge: Cambridge University Press, 1996.

Chow Tse-tsung. *The May Fourth Movement: Intellectual Revolution in Modern China*. Stanford, Calif.: Stanford University Press, 1967.

Cohen, Warren, I. *East Asia at the Center: Four Thousand Years of Engagement with the World*. New York: Columbia University Press, 2000.

Connor, Walker. *The National Question in Marxist-Leninist Theory and Strategy*. Princeton, N.J.: Princeton University Press, 1984.

Conquest, Robert, ed. *The Last Empire: Nationality and the Soviet Future*. Stanford, Calif.: Hoover Institution Press, 1986.

Crossley, Pamela Kyle. *Orphan Warriors: Three Manchu Generations and the End of the Qing World*. Princeton, N.J.: Princeton University Press, 1990.

———. *A Translucent Mirror: History and Identity in Qing Imperial Ideology*. Berkeley: University of California Press, 1999.

Dallin, Alexander, and F. I. Firsov, eds. *Dimitrov and Stalin, 1934–1943: Letters from the Soviet Archives*. New Haven, Conn.: Yale University Press, 2000.

Daniels, Robert V. *A Documentary History of Communism, Volume 2: Communism and the World* London: I. B. Tauris, 1985.

Davis, John F. *The Chinese: A General Description of the Empire of China and Its Inhabitants*. New York: Harper and Brothers, 1836.

Degras, Jane, ed. *Soviet Documents on Foreign Relations*. New York: Octagon Books, 1978.

d'Encausse, Hélène Carrère. *The Great Challenge: Nationalities and the Bolshevik State, 1917–1930*. New York: Holmes & Meier Publishers, 1992.

d'Encausse, Hélène Carrère, and Stuart R. Schram, eds. *Marxism and Asia*. London: Allen Lane, 1969.

Di Cosmo, Nicola. *Ancient China and Its Enemies: The Rise of Nomadic Power in East Asian History*. Cambridge: Cambridge University Press, 2002.

Dikötter, Frank. *The Discourse of Race in Modern China*. Stanford, Calif.: Stanford University Press, 1992.

Dirlik, Arif. *The Origins of Chinese Communism*. Oxford: Oxford University Press, 1989.

Diuk, Nadia, and Adrian Karatnycky. *The Hidden Nations: The People Challenge the Soviet Union*. New York: William Morrow, 1990.

Dreyer, June T. *China's Forty Millions: Minority Nationalities and National Integration in the People's Republic of China*. Cambridge, Mass.: Harvard University Press, 1976.

Duara, Prasenjit. *Rescuing History from the Nation: Questioning Narratives of Modern China*. Chicago: University of Chicago Press, 1995.

Eley, Geoff, and Ronald G. Suny, eds. *Becoming National*. Oxford: Oxford University Press, 1996.

Ellenman, Bruce A. *Diplomacy and Deception: The Secret History of Sino-Soviet Diplomatic Relations, 1917–1927*. Armonk, N.Y.: M. E. Sharpe, 1997.

Fairbank, John King. *China: A New History*. Cambridge: Belknap Press of Harvard University Press, 1992.

Fiskesjo, Magnus. "On the 'Raw' and 'Cooked' Barbarians of Imperial China." *Inner Asia* 1(2) (1999): 139–68.

Fitzgerald, John. *Awakening China: Politics, Culture, and Class in the Nationalist Revolution.* Stanford, Calif.: Stanford University Press, 1996.

Forbes, Andrew D. W. *Warlords and Muslims in Chinese Central Asia: A Political History of Republican Sinkiang, 1911–1949.* Cambridge: Cambridge University Press, 1986.

Forbes, H. D. *Ethnic Conflict: Commerce, Culture, and the Contact Hypothesis.* New Haven, Conn.: Yale University Press, 1997.

Friedman, Edward. *National Identity and Democratic Prospects in Socialist China.* Armonk, N.Y.: M. E. Sharpe, 1995.

Garver, John W. *Chinese–Soviet Relations, 1937–1945: The Diplomacy of Chinese Nationalism.* New York: Oxford University Press, 1988.

Gellner, Ernest. *Nations and Nationalism.* Ithaca, N.Y.: Cornell University Press, 1983.

Gladney, Dru C. *Muslim Chinese: Ethnic Nationalism in the People's Republic.* Cambridge, Mass.: Council on East Asian Studies, Harvard University, 1996.

Goldstein, Melvyn C. *The Snow Lion and the Dragon: China, Tibet, and the Dalai Lama.* Berkeley: University of California Press, 1997.

Grousset, Rene. *The Empire of the Steppes: A History of Central Asia.* New Brunswick, N.J.: Rutgers University Press, 1994.

Gurr, Ted Robert. *Minorities at Risk: A Global View of Ethnopolitical Conflicts.* Washington, D.C.: United States Institute of Peace Press, 1993.

Hansen, Valerie. *The Open Empire: A History of China to 1600.* New York: W. W. Norton, 2000.

Harrell, Stevan, ed. *Cultural Encounters on China's Ethnic Frontiers.* Seattle: University of Washington Press, 1995.

Hobsbawm, E. J. *Nations and Nationalism since 1780.* Cambridge: Cambridge University Press, 1991.

Hostetler, Laura. *Qing Colonial Enterprise: Ethnography and Cartography in Early Modern China.* Chicago: University of Chicago Press, 2001.

Hoston, Germaine A. *The State, Identity, and the National Question in China and Japan.* Princeton, N.J.: Princeton University Press, 1994.

Huang, Ray. *China: A Macro History.* Armonk. N.Y.: M. E. Sharpe, 1990.

Jagchid Sechin. *The Last Mongol Prince: The Life and Times of Demchugdongrob.* Bellingham: Western Washington University Press, 1999.

Jenner, W. J. F. *The Tyranny of History: The Roots of China's Crisis.* New York: Penguin Press, 1992.

Johnson, Chalmers A. *Peasant Nationalism and Communist Power.* Stanford, Calif.: Stanford University Press, 1962.

Kirby, William. *Germany and Republican China.* Stanford, Calif.: Stanford University Press, 1984.

Kotkin, Stephen, and Bruce A. Elleman, eds. *Mongolia in the Twentieth Century: Landlocked Cosmopolitan.* Armonk, N.Y.: M. E. Sharpe, 1999.

Laitinen, Kauko. *Chinese Nationalism in the Late Qing Dynasty: Zhang Binglin as an Anti-Manchu Propagandist.* London: Curzon Press, 1990.

Lattimore, Owen. *Manchuria: Cradle of Conflict.* New York: Macmillan, 1932.

———. *Inner Asian Frontiers of China.* London: Oxford University Press, 1940.

———. "Mongolia and the Peace Settlement, 8 June 1943." *Studies of American Interests in the War and Peace: Territorial Series* (Council on Foreign Relations) T–B 63 (1943).

————. *Studies in Frontier History: Collected Papers, 1929–58.* London: Oxford University Press, 1962.

Lih, Lars T., et al., eds. *Stalin's letters to Molotov.* New Haven, Conn.: Yale University Press, 1995.

Lipman, Jonathan N. *Familiar Strangers: A History of Muslims in Northwestern China.* Seattle: University of Washington Press, 1997.

Liu Xiaoyuan. *A Partnership for Disorder: China, the United States, and Their Policies for the Postwar Disposition of the Japanese Empire, 1941–1945.* New York: Cambridge University Press, 1996.

————. *China's Central Asian Identity in Recent History: Across the Boundary between Domestic and Foreign Affairs.* Occasional Paper 78, Asia Program. Washington, D.C.: Woodrow Wilson International Center for Scholars, 1998.

————. "The Kuomintang and the 'Mongolian Question' in the Chinese Civil War, 1945–1949." *Inner Asia* 1 (1999): 169–94.

Luk, Michael Y. L. *The Origins of Chinese Bolshevism: An Ideology in the Making, 1920–1928.* Hong Kong: Oxford University Press, 1990.

Macherras, Colin. *China's Minorities: Integration and Modernization in the Twentieth Century.* Hong Kong: Oxford University Press, 1994.

Paine, S. C. M. *Imperial Rivals: China, Russia, and Their Disputed Frontier.* Armonk, N.Y.: M. E. Sharpe, 1996.

Pantsov, Alexander. *The Bosheviks and the Chinese Revolution, 1919–1927.* Honolulu: University of Hawaii Press, 2000.

Pipes, Richard. *The Formation of the Soviet Union: Communism and Nationalism, 1917–1923.* Cambridge: Harvard University Press, 1954.

Poems of Mao Tse-tung. Translated and annotated by Wong Man. Hong Kong: Eastern Horizon Press, 1966.

Price, Jane L. *Cadres, Commanders, and Commissars: The Training of the Chinese Communist Leadership, 1920–45.* Boulder, Colo.: Westview Press, 1976.

Pye, Lucian W. *Warlord Politics: Conflict and Coalition in the Modernization of Republican China.* New York: Praeger Publishers, 1971.

Richard, L. *Comprehensive Geography of the Chinese Empire and Dependencies.* Shanghai: T'usewei Press, 1908.

Rossabi, Morris, ed. *China among Equals: The Middle Kingdom and Its Neighbors, 10th–14th Centuries.* Berkeley: University of California Press, 1983.

Rudelson, Justin Jon. *Oasis Identity: Uyghur Nationalism along China's Silk Road.* New York: Columbia University Press, 1997.

Schram, Stuart. *Mao Tse-tung.* Baltimore: Pelican Books, 1974.

Schwartz, Benjamin I. "The Maoist Image of World Order." In *Image and Reality in World Politics,* ed. John C. Farrell and Asa P. Smith. New York: Columbia University Press, 1967.

Selden, Mark. *The Yenan Way in Revolutionary China.* Cambridge: Harvard University Press, 1971.

Sheng, Michael M. *Battling Western Imperialism: Mao, Stalin, and the United States.* Princeton, N.J.: Princeton University Press, 1997.

Smal-Stocki, Roman. *The Nationality Problem of the Soviet Union and Russian Communist Imperialism.* Milwaukee: Bruce Publishing Company, 1952.

Smith, Anthony D. *The Ethnic Origins of Nations.* Oxford: Basil Blackwell, 1999.

Smith, Richard J. *Chinese Maps: Images of All under Heaven.* Hong Kong: Oxford University Press, 1996.

Snow, Edgar. *Red Star over China.* New York: Random House, 1938.

Swisher, Earl. *China's Management of American Barbarians: A Study of Sino-American Relations, 1841–1861.* New Haven, Conn.: Far Eastern Publications, 1951.

Tang, Peter S. H. *Russian and Soviet Policy in Manchuria and Mongolia, 1911–1931.* Durham, N.C.: Duke University Press, 1959.

Thaxton, Ralph A. *Salt of the Earth: The Political Origins of Peasant Protest and Communist Revolution in China.* Berkeley: University of California Press, 1997.

Thongchai, Winichakul. *Siam Mapped: A History of the Geo-Body of a Nation.* Honolulu: University of Hawaii Press, 1994.

Unger, Jonathan, ed. *Chinese Nationalism.* Armonk, N.Y.: M. E. Sharpe, 1996.

Vogel, Ezra F., ed. *Living with China: U.S.–China Relations in the Twentieth Century.* New York: W. W. Norton, 1997.

Waldron, Arthur. *The Great Wall of China: From History to Myth.* Cambridge: Cambridge University Press, 1990.

Waley-Cohen, Joanna. *The Sextans of Beijing: Global Currents in Chinese History.* New York: W. W. Norton, 1999.

Wang, David D. *Under the Soviet Shadow: The Yining Incident.* Hong Kong: Chinese University Press, 1999.

Whiting, Allen. *Soviet Policy in China, 1917–1924.* Stanford, Calif.: Stanford University Press, 1968.

Wong, R. Bin. *China Transformed: Historical Change and the Limits of European Experience.* Ithaca, N.Y.: Cornell University Press, 1997.

Wright, Mary Clabaugh. *The Last Stand of Chinese Conservatism: The Tung-chih Restoration, 1862–1874.* Stanford, Calif.: Stanford University Press, 1957.

Yang, Benjamin. *From Revolution to Politics: Chinese Communists on the Long March.* Boulder, Colo.: Westview Press, 1990.

Yeh Wen-hsin. *Provincial Passages: Culture, Space, and the Origins of Chinese Communism.* Berkeley: University of California Press, 1996.

Zhang Shu Guang. *Deterrence and Strategic Culture: Chinese–American Confrontations, 1945–1958.* Ithaca, N.Y.: Cornell University Press, 1992.

Scholarly Works and Documentary Collections in Chinese

Arkush, David. *Zhongguo Minzhong Sixiang Shilun* (*Northern Chinese Folk Materials and Popular Mentality*). Beijing: Zhongyang Minzu Daxue Chubanshe, 1995.

Bai Rubing. "Tan tan wo zai Suimeng gongzuo de qingkuang" (A brief discussion of my work in Sui[yuan] and [Inner] Mongolia). *Zhonggong Dangshi Ziliao* (Materials on Chinese communist history) 9 (1984): 117–38.

Bai Zhensheng et al. *Xinjiang Xiandai Zhengzhi Shehui Shilue, 1912–1949* (Brief political and social history of modern Xinjiang, 1912–1949). Beijing: Zhongguo Shehui Kexue Chubanshe, 1992.

Cai Hesen. "Lun Chen Duxiu zhuyi" (On Chen Duxiuism). In *Bao Luo Ting zai Zhongguo de Youguan Ziliao* (Materials on Borodin in China). Beijing: Zhongguo Shehui Kexue Chubanshe, 1983.

Cao Wanru, ed. *Zhongguo Gudai Ditu Ji* (Ancient atlas of China). 3 vols. Beijing: Wenwu Chubanshe, 1990–97.

Central Archives. *Zhonggong Zhongyang Wenjian Xuanji* (Selected documents of the Chinese Communist Party Central Committee). 18 vols. Beijing: Zhonggong Zhongyang Dangxiao Chubanshe, 1989.

Chang Jiang. *Zhongguo de Xibei Jiao* (China's northwestern corner). Tianjin: Da Gong Bao Chubanbu, 1938.

Chen Lian. *Kang Ri Genjudi Fazhan Shilue* (Brief history of the anti-Japanese bases). Beijing: Jiefangjun Chunbanshe, 1987.

Chen Yongfa. *Zhongguo Gongchan Geming Qishi Nian* (Seventy years of the Chinese communist revolution). Taipei: Lianjing, 1998.

Cheng Zhongyuan. *Zhang Wentian Zhuan* (Biography of Zhang Wentian). Beijing: Dangdai Zhongguo Chubanshe, 1993.

Committee on the Collection of Party History Materials of the CCP Committee of the Inner Mongolian Autonomous Region and the Archives of the Inner Mongolian Autonomous Region. *Daqingshan Kang Ri Youji Genjudi Ziliao Xuanbian* (Selected materials on the anti-Japanese guerrilla base in the Daqingshan Mountain). Hohhot: Neimenggu Renmin Chubanshe, 1987.

Committee on Party History of the Chinese Communist Party District Committee of Hami. *Xilujun Hun* (The Soul of the Western Route Army). Urumqi: Xinjiang Renmin Chubanshe, 1995.

Compiling Committee of the Historical Materials Series on the People's Liberation Army. *Hongjun Changzheng Huiyi Shiliao* (Reminiscences of the Red Army's Long March). Beijing: Jiefangjun Chubanshe, 1992.

Compilation Committee of the Qinghai Provincial Chronicle. *Qinghai Lishi Jiyao* (Important events in the history of Qinghai). Xining: Qinghai Renmin Chubanshe, 1987.

Demchugdongrob. "Demuchukedonglupu Zishu" (Autobiography of Demchugdongrob). *Neimenggu Wenshi Ziliao* (Literary and historical materials of Inner Mongolia) 13 (1984): 1–211.

Documentary Research Office of the CCP Central Committee. *Zhou Enlai Nianpu* (The Chronicle of Zhou Enlai's life). Beijing: Zhongyang Wenxian Chubanshe, 1989.

———. *Xinshiqi Minzu Gongzuo Wenxian Xuanbian* (Selected documents on the nationality work during the new era). Beijing: Zhongyang Wenxian Chubanshe, 1990.

———. *Mao Zedong Nianpu* (The chronicle of Mao Zedong's life). 3 vols. Beijing: Zhongyang Wenxian Chubanshe, 1993.

Dong Qiwu. *Rongma Chunqiu* (My military career). Beijing: Zhongguo Wenshi Chubanshe, 1986.

Duan Baohe and Sun Jie. "1935–1945 nianjian dang zai Neimenggu wanggong shangceng zhong de tongzhan gongzuo" (The party's united front work among the princes and upper classes of Inner Mongolia between 1935 and 1945). *Neimenggu Tongzhan Lilun Yanjiu* (Inner Mongolian study of united front theories) 2 (1989): 26–28.

Editorial Board of Contemporary China's Nationality Work. *Dangdai Zhongguo Minzu Gongzuo Dashiji, 1949–1988* (Chronicle of important events in contemporary China's nationality work). Beijing: Minzu Chubanshe, 1989.

Fan Xiuchuan, ed. *Zhongguo Bianjiang Guji Tijie* (Annotated bibliography of ancient works on China's frontiers). Urumqi: Xinjiang Renmin Chubanshe, 1995.

Fei Xiaotong et al. *Zhonghua Minzu Duoyuan Yiti Geju* (The structure of the Chinese nation's plural unitary body). Beijing: Zhongyang Minzu Xueyuan Chubanshe, 1989.

Gansu Committee of the Chinese People's Political Consultative Council. *Gansu Jiefang-qian Wushinian Dashiji* (A chronicle of events in Gansu in the fifty years prior to the liberation). Lanzhou: Gansu Ren min Chubanshe, 1980.

Gao Yi. *Jiang Jieshi yu Xibei Si Ma* (Jiang Jieshi and the four Mas of the northwest). Beijing: Jingguan Jiaoyu Chubanshe, 1993.

Ge Jianxiong. *Tongyi yu Fenlie: Zhongguo Lishi de Qishi* (Unification and division: revelation of Chinese history). Beijing: Sanlian Shudian, 1994.

Ge Jianxiong et al. *Jianming Zhongguo Yimin Shi* (A brief history of migration in China). Fuzhou: Fujian Renmin Chubanshe, 1993.

Gu Weijun. *Gu Weijun Huiyilu* (Memoir of Gu Weijun). 13 vols. Beijing: Zhonghua Shuju, 1983–92.

Hao Shiyuan. *Zhongguo de Minzu yu Minzu Wenti: Lun Zhongguo Gongchandang Jiejue Minzu Wenti de Lilun yu Shijiang* (China's nationalities and nationality question: on the CCP's theories and practices for solving the nationality question). Nanchang: Jiangxi Renmin Chubanshe, 1996.

Hao Weimin. "Di yi er ci guonei geming zhanzheng shiqi de neimenggu rennin gemingdang" (Inner Mongolian people's revolutionary party during the first and second domestic revolutionary wars). In *Zhongguo Menggushi Xuehui Chengli Dahui Jikan* (Proceedings of the inaugural conference of the Chinese society of Mongolian historical studies). Hohhot: Zhongguo Menggushi Xuehui, 1979.

Historica Sinica. *Zhonghua Minguoshi Minzu Zhi* (Nationalities gazette of the history of the Republic of China). Taipei: Guoshiguan, 1995.

Historica Sinica. *Zhonghua Minguo Shi Dili Zhi (Chugao)* (Geographic gazetteer of the history of the Republic of China; preliminary edition). Taipei: Guoshiguan, 1980.

Huang Shijian and Zhang Xicheng. "Guanyu Yimeng shibian" (On the Yekejuu league incident). *Neimenggu Jindaishi Luncong* (Collected essays on modern Inner Mongolian history) 1 (1982): 106–23.

Huang Xiurong, ed. *Sulian, Gongchan Guoji yu Zhongguo Geming de Guanxi Xintan* (New studies of the relationship between the Soviet Union, the Comintern, and the Chinese revolution). Beijing: Zhonggong Dangshi Chubanshe, 1995.

Hu Fengtai. "Yimeng shibian Wushenqi zhanyi huiyi" (Reminiscence about the battle of Uushin banner during the Yekejuu league incident). *Neimenggu Wenshi Ziliao* 2 (1979): 38–51.

Huizu, Huijiao, Huimin Lunji (Essays on the Hui nationality, Hui religion, and Hui people). Hong Kong: Zhongshan Tushu Gongsi, 1974.

Huizu Jianshi (A brief history of the Hui nationality). Yinchuan: Ningxia Renmin Chubanshe, 1978.

Institute of Historical Studies of the Xinjiang Academy of Social Science. *Xinjiang Jianshi* (A brief history of Xinjiang). Urumqi: Xinjiang Renmin Chubanshe, 1987.

Jiang Ping, ed. *Zhongguo Minzu Wenti de Lilun yu Shijian* (The theories and practices regarding China's nationality question). Beijing: Zhonggong Zhongyang Dangxiao Chubanshe, 1994.

Jiang Shuchen. *Fu Zuoyi Zhuanlue* (A brief biography of Fu Zuoyi). Beijing: Zhongguo Qingnian Chubanshe, 1990.

Jiangxi Provincial Archives. *Zhongyang Keming Genjudi Shiliao Xuanbian* (Selected historical materials on the central revolutionary base). Nanchang: Jiangxi Remin Chubanshe, 1982.

Kong Xiandong and Gu Peng. "Changzheng zhong de hongxing bao" (Red star daily during the Long March). *Zhonggong Dangshi Ziliao* 60 (December 1996).

Li Qian, ed. *Huibu Gongdu* (Documents on the Hui section). Shanghai: Zhongguo Yin-shuachang, 1925.

Li Rongzhen. "Changzheng shiqi zhongguo gongchandang dui huizu de zhengce" (The Chinese Communist Party's policy toward the Hui nationality during the Long March). *Zhonggong Dangshi Ziliao* 60 (December 1996).

Li Rui. *Zaonian Mao Zedong* (Young Mao Zedong). Shenyang: Liaoning Renmin Chu-banshe, 1993.

Li Weihan. *Huiyi yu Yanjiu* (Reminiscence and study). Beijing: Zhonggong Dangshi Chubanshe, 1986.

Li Yushu. *Waimenggu Chezhi Wenti* (The question of Outer Mongolia's cancellation of independence). Taipei: Zhongyang Yanjiuyuan Jindaishi Yanjiusuo, 1976.

Liangong (Bu), Gongchan Guoji yu Zhongguo Guomin Keming Yuandong, 1920–1925 (Soviet Communist Party [Bolshevik], the Comintern, and the Chinese nationalist revolutionary movement, 1920–1925). Originally published in Russian. Moscow, 1994. Translated and compiled by the First Division of the Party History Research Office of the Chinese Communist Party Central Committee. Vols. 1–6. Beijing: Beijing Tushuguan Chubanshe, 1997. Vols. 7–12. Beijing: Zhongyang Wenxian Chu-banshe, 2002.

Liu Baoming. *Minzu Wenti yu Guoqing Jiaoyu Duben* (Study materials on the national-ity question and the state of the country). Beijing: Zhongyang Minzu Xueyuan Chubanshe, 1992.

Liu Chun. "Kangri zhanzheng shiqi canjia minzu gongzuo de huiyi" (Recollections on my involvement in the nationality work during the period of resistance against Japan). *Neimenggu Dangshi Ziliao* 1 (1988): 228–46.

Liu Jinren. "Yi Suiyuan dageming shiqi de geming douzheng" (Reminiscence on the revolutionary struggle in Suiyuan during the period of the great revolution). *Nei-menggu Dangshi Ziliao* (Inner Mongolian materials on the party history) 2 (1989): 174–91.

Liu Zaifu and Lin Gang. *Chuantong yu Zhongguoren* (Tradition and the Chinese). Hefei: Anhui Wenyi Chubanshe, 1999.

Luo Guangwu. *Xin Zhongguo Minzu Gongzuo Dashi Gailan, 1949–1999* (A survey of the important events in the nationality work of the new China, 1949–1999). Beijing: Huawen Chubanshe, 2001.

Luo Hong and Sun Zhongyao. "Wo dang bangzhu Feng Yuxiang bing cucheng Wuyuan shishi shimo" (Our party's assistance to Feng Yuxiang and facilitation of the military effort from Wuyuan). *Neimenggu Dangshi Ziliao* 1 (1988): 247–66.

Luo Rongqu, ed. *Cong Xihua dao Xiandaihua: Wusi Yilai Youguan Zhongguo de Wen-hua Quxiang he Fazhan Daolu Lunzheng Wenxuan* (From Westernization to mod-ernization: selected post-May fourth essays on China's cultural tendencies and road of development). Beijing: Beijing Dazue Chubanshe, 1990.

Mao Zedong. *Mao Zedong Shuxin Xuanji* (Selected correspondence of Mao Zedong). Beijing: Renmin Chubanshe, 1983.

———. *Mao Zedong Wenji* (Manuscripts of Mao Zedong). 5 vols. Beijing: Renmin Chu-banshe, 1993–96.

———. *Mao Zedong Zaoqi Wengao* (Early writings of Mao Zedong). Changsha: Hunan Chubanshe, 1995.

Mao Zhenfa and Zeng Yan. *Bianfang Lun* (On frontier defense). Beijing: Junshi Kexue Chubanshe, 1996.

Ma Ruheng and Ma Dazheng. *Qingdai de Bianjiang Zhengce* (Frontier policies of the Qing Dynasty). Beijing: Zhongguo Shehui Kexue Chubanshe, 1994.

Mei Jian, ed. *Yan'an Mishi* (Inside history of Yan'an). Beijing: Hongqi Chubanshe, 1996.

Military Museum of China. *Mao Zedong Junshi Huodong Jishi* (Record of Mao Zedong's military activities). Beijing: Jiefangjun Chubanshe, 1994.

Ochirhuyaktu. "Yimeng 'san er liu' shibian de huiyi" (Recollections on the "March 26th incident" in Yekejuu league). *Neimenggu Wenshi Ziliao* 2 (1979): 1–14.

Office of Party History Sources, the CCP Committee of Huhhot Municipality. "Guanyu dageming shiqi Suiyuan nongmin yundong qingkuang de baogao" (Report on the investigation of the conditions of the Suiyuan peasant movement during the great revolution period). *Neimonggu Dangshi Ziliao* (Materials on the party history of Inner Mongolia) 2 (1989): 256–69.

Party History Office of the Inner Mongolian CCP Committee. *Neimenggu Dang de Lishi he Dang de Gongzuo* (History and works of the party in Inner Mongolia). Huhhot: Neimenggu Renming Chubanshe, 1994.

Party History Research Office of the CCP Committee of the Beijing Municipality. *Zhongguo Gongchandang Beijing Lishi* (History of the CCP in Beijing). Beijing: Beijing Chubanshe, 2001.

Qu Qiubai. *Qu Qiubai Wenji* (Essays by Qu Qiubai). Beijing: Remin Chubanshe, 1989.

Ren Bingjun. "Yikezhao meng 'san er liu' shibian" (The "March 26th" incident in Yekejuu league). *Neimenggu Wenshi Ziliao* 2 (1979): 15–24.

Ren Yinong et al. *Minzu Zongjiao Zhishi Shouce* (Handbook of nationalities and religions). Beijing: Zhonggong Zhongyang Dangxiao Chubanshe, 1994.

Second Historical Archives of China. *Jiang Jieshi Nianpu Chugao* (Preliminary draft of the chronicle of Jiang Jieshi's life). Beijing: Dang'an Chubanshe, 1992.

Second Historical Archives of China and the Chinese Institute of Tibetan Studies. *Huang Musong, Wu Zhongxin, Zhao Shouyu, Dai Chuanxian Fengshi Banli Zangshi Baogaoshu* (Reports by Huang Musong, Wu Zhongxin, Zhao Shouyu, and Dai Chuanxian on their missions to Tibet). Beijing: Zhongguo Zangxue Chubanshe, 1993.

Shen Changyou. *Mao Zedong yu Gongchan Guoji* (Mao Zedong and the Comintern). Beijing: Dangjian Duwu Chubanshe, 1994.

Shen Youliang. *Zhongguo Beifang Minzu jiqi Zhengquan Yanjiu* (A study of Chinese northern nationalities and their regimes). Beijing: Zhongyang Minzu Daxue Chubanshe, 1998.

State Nationality Affairs Committee. *Mengguzu Jianshi* (Brief history of the Mongolian nationality). Hohhot: Neimenggu Renmin Chubanshe, 1985.

State Nationality Affairs Committee and Documentary Research Office of the CCP Central Committee. *Xinshiqi Minzu Gongzuo Wenxian Xuanbian* (Selected documents on the nationality work in the new era). Beijing: Zhongyang Wenxian Chubanshe, 1990.

Sun Goubiao. "Zhongguo gongchandang minzu zizhi zhengce de chenggong changshi" (A successful experiment of the Chinese Communist Party's nationality autonomous policy). *Zhonggong Dangshi Ziliao* 57 (1996): 114–22.

Ulanfu. *Wulanfu Huiyilu* (Ulanfu's memoirs). Beijing: Zhonggong Dangshi Ziliao Chubanshe, 1989.

Ulanshaob. "Zhongguo guomindang de dui meng zhengce" (The Kuomintang's policy toward Mongolia, 1928–1949). In *Neimenggu Jindaishi Lunsong* (Collected essays on modern history of Inner Mongolia). 3 vols. Hohhot: Neimenggu Renmin Chubanshe, 1987.

United Front Department of the Central Committee of the Chinese Communist Party. *Minzu Wenti Wenxian Huibian* (Collection of documents on the national question). Beijing: Zhonggong Zhongyang Dangxiao Chubanshe, 1991 (internal circulation).

Wang Duo. *Wushi Chunqiu: Wo Zuo Minzu Gongzuo de Jingli* (Fifty years' events: my experience in the nationality work). Hohhot: Neimenggu Renmin Chubanshe, 1992.

Wang Huichang. *Zhongguo Wenhua Dili* (Cultural geography of China). Wuchang: Huazhong Shifan Daxue Chubanshe, 1992.

Wang Jianmin. *Zhongguo Minzuxue Shi* (History of ethnic studies in China). Kunming: Yunnan Jiaoyu Chubanshe, 1997.

Wang Jianping. "Youguan si Ma lianmeng duikang Sun Dianying and huiyi" (Recollection on the four-Ma alliance against Sun Dianying). In *Ningxia San Ma* (Three Mas of Ningxia). Beijing: Zhongguo Wenshi Chubanshe, 1988.

Wang Lixiong. *Tianzang: Xizang de Mingyun* (Sky Burial: The Fate of Tibet). Brampton, Ontario: Mirror Books, 1998.

Wang Riwei. "Dui Weiwu'er zu mingcheng yanbian de kaocha" (An Examination of the Evolution of Names for the Uigur Nationality). In *Huizu, Huijiao, Huimin Lunji* (Essays on the Hui nationality, Hui religion, and Hui people), ed. Bai Shouyi and Jin Jietang. Hong Kong: Zhongshan Tushu Gongsi, 1974.

Wang Shusheng. "Fenggong chui qingshi jinnang liu huoren" (Great deeds in history and valuable legacy to the coming generations). In *Wulanfu Jinian Wenji* (Essays to memorialize Ulanfu), vol. 1. Hohhot: Neimenggu Renmin Chubanshe, 1989.

Wang Shusheng and Hao Yufeng. *Wulanfu Nianpu* (Chronicle of Ulanfu's life). Beijing: Zhonggong Dangshi Ziliao Chubanshe, 1989.

Wong Dujian et al., eds. *Zhongguo Minzu Guanxishi Yanjiu* (Studies of China's nationality relations). Beijing: Zhongguo Shehui Kexue Chubanshe, 1984.

Wulanfu Jinian Wenji (Essays to memorize Ulanfu), vol. 1. Huhhot: Neimenggu Renmin Chubanshe, 1989.

Wu Nenqi. "Neimeng Menggu dulishi jianli qianhou" (Before and after the establishment of the Mongol independent brigade of Inner Mongolia). *Zhonggong Dangshi Ziliao* 11 (1984): 308–25.

———. *Mengguzu Renmin Geming Wuzhuang Douzheng Jishi* (Record of the armed revolutionary struggle by the Mongolian people). Hohhot: Neimeng Renmin Chubanshe, 1990.

Ya Hanzhang. "Huizu de jiechu shixuejia" (A brilliant historian of the Hui nationality). In *Bai Shouyi Minzu Zongjiao Lunji* (Essays on nationalities and religions by Bai Shouyi), ed. Bai Shouyi. Beijing: Beijing Shifan Daxue Chubanshe, 1992.

Yang Ce et al. *Shaoshu Minzu yu Kang Ri Zhanzheng* (Minority nationalities and the war of resistant against Japan). Beijing: Beijing Chubanshe, 1997.

Yang Huaizhong. *Huizushi Lungao* (Essays on the history of the Hui nationality). Yinchuan: Ningxia Renmin Chubanshe, 1991.

Yang Kuisong. *Xi'an Shibian Xintan: Zhang Xueliang yu Zhonggong Guanxi zhi Yanjiu* (A new examination of the Xi'an incident: a study of the relationship between Zhang Xueliang and the CCP). Taipei: Dongda Tushu Gongsi, 1995.

———. *Zhonggong yu Mosike de Guanxi, 1920–1960* (Relationship between the CCP and Moscow, 1920–1960). Taipei: Dongda Tushu Gufen Youxian Gongsi, 1997.

———. *Mao Zedong he Mosike de En En Yuan Yuan* (Benefactions and Disaffections between Mao Zedong and Moscow). Nanchang: Jiangxi Renmin Chubanshe, 1999.

Ye Xinyu. "Yihai jiemeng yu dang de minzu zhengce" (Alliance at the Yi Lake and the party's nationality policy). *Zhonggong Dangshi Ziliao* 58 (1996): 189–96.

Yu Xilai. "Xinxing shijie daguo de chengzhang zhilu: guangrong yu mengxiang—20 shiji zhongguo lishi zongchengji de huigu" (The growing course of a new world power: glory and dreams—China's historical achievements during the 20th century in retrospect). *Zhanlue yu Guanli* (Strategy and management) 6 (December 1999).

Yu Zidao. *Changcheng Fengyun Lu* (Stormy chronicle of the Great Wall). Shanghai: Shanghai Shudian Chubanshe, 1993.

Zhang Erju. *Zhongguo Minzu Quyu Zizhi Shigang* (Outline history of China's nationality regional autonomy). Beijing: Minzu Chubanshe, 1995.

Zhang Guotao. *Wo de Huiyi* (My memoirs). Beijing: Xiandai Shiliao Biankan Chubanshe, 1980.

Zhang Peisen et al. *Zhang Wentian zai 1935–1938* (Zhang Wentian from 1935 to 1938). Beijing: Zhonggong Dangshi Chubanshe, 1997.

Zhang Zhende and Zhao Ximin. *Xibei Geming Shi* (A revolutionary history of the northwest). Xi'an: Shaanxi Renmin Jiaoyu Chubanshe, 1991.

Zhao Huishan. "Zai Yimeng minzu shangceng zhong de tongzhan gongzuo" (United front work among the nationality upper classes of Yekejuu league). *Neimenggu Tongzhan Lilun Yanjiu* 4 (1987): 21–25.

Zhao Yuntian. *Zhongguo Bianjiang Minzu Guanli Jigou Yange Shi* (History of the changing structure of Chinese administration of the frontier nationalities). Beijing: Zhongguo Shehui Kexue Chubanshe, 1993.

Zhongguo Gongnong Hongjun Disi Fangfianjun Zhanshi Ziliao Xuanbian, Changzheng Shiqi (Selected materials on the combat history of the fourth front army of the Chinese workers' and peasants' red army, the long march period). Beijing: Jiefangjun Chubanshe, 1992.

Zhongguo Zonghe Dituji (Atlas of China). Beijing: Zhongguo Ditu Chubanshe, 1990.

Zhong Su Guojia Guanxi Shi Ziliao Huibian, 1917–1924 (Collected documents on the history of the Chinese–Soviet state relationship, 1917–1924). Beijing: Zhongguo Shehui Kexue Shubanshe, 1993.

Zhongwai Lishi Wenti Ba Ren Tan (Eight scholars on questions in Chinese and foreign histories). Compiled by the Research Center on Social Sciences Development in Universities, the State Committee on Education. Beijing: Zhonggong Zhongyang Dangxiao Chubanshe, 1998.

Zhou Beifeng. "Wo de huiyi" (My memoirs). *Neimonggu Wenshi Ziliao* 21 (1986): 1–139.

Zhou Enlai. *Zhou Enlai Xuanji* (Selected works of Zhou Enlai). Beijing: Renmin Chubanshe, 1984.

———. *Zhou Enlai Junshi Wenxuan* (Selected military works of Zhou Enlai). Beijing: Renmin Chubanshe, 1997.

Zhou Qingshu et al. *Neimenggu Lishi Dili* (Historical geography of Inner Mongolia). Huhhot: Neimenggu Daxue Chubanshe, 1993.

Zhou Wenqi and Chu Liangru, *Techu er Fuza de Keti—Gongchan Guoji, Sulian, he Zhongguo Gongchadang Biannianshi, 1919–1991* (Unique and complicated subject: a chronological history of the relationship between the Comintern, the Soviet Union, and the CCP). Wuhan: Hubei Renmin Chubanshe, 1993.

Index

231